Major Ideologies: An Interpretative Survey of Democracy, Socialism, and Nationalism

Major Ideologies: An Interpretative Survey of Democracy, Socialism, and Nationalism

ALEXANDER J. GROTH
University of California, Davis

75-519

JOHN WILEY & SONS, INC.
New York · London · Sydney · Toronto

To Marilyn

Preface

Three ideological mainstreams of the modern world—democracy, socialism, and nationalism—are the theme of this work. Their development and interrelationships are traced historically, with particular emphasis on the institutional and policy expressions associated with each.

Special emphasis is given here to the concept of sociopolitical mobilization as underlying the rise of democracy in Europe. Socialism and nationalism are discussed both as ideological responses to this mobilization and also as "correctives" (in different ways) to the qualities of democracy: its voluntarism, secularism, and individualism.

This survey not only provides the beginning student with background information about each ideology but also discusses the ways in which these ideologies relate to one another: where they meet and where they diverge, and the nature of the problems to which they address themselves.

ALEXANDER J. GROTH

Contents

1. Ideology: What Does It Tell Us About Politics?   1
2. The Genesis of Modern Ideologies   19
3. Liberal Democracy   37
4. Socialism   61
5. Nationalism   85
6. Communism Under Lenin and Stalin   109
7. The Impact of the Second World War   129
8. Postwar Communism   144
9. Democracy, Socialism, and the New Left   172
10. Nationalism, Democracy, and Socialism in the Third World   197
11. Conclusion   216
    Index   233

Major Ideologies: An Interpretative Survey of Democracy, Socialism, and Nationalism

Ideology: What Does It Tell Us About Politics?

POLITICAL IDEOLOGIES

We shall begin the study of the major ideologies with some basic concepts. What precisely is an "ideology"? What relevance does it have for understanding "politics"? Is "ideology" a mere relic of history, something that explains the past more adequately than it explains the present?

The term "ideology" has, historically, received somewhat different definitions, ranging from simply a "politico-social program," in a 1948 edition of *Webster's New International Dictionary* to a more complex "organization of opinions, attitudes and values—a way of thinking about man and society."[1]

An ideology may be—but need not necessarily be—coherent, systematic, and rational. If it is fairly persistent and pervasive, in the sense that a particular point of view or orientation occurs whenever an individual, group, or organization engages in action or discussion on any given subject, the bias takes on the shape of "ideology." The ideology may be simple and fragmentary or broad and complex.[2] It may be

[1] T. W. Adorno et al., in *The Authoritarian Personality* (New York: Harper, 1950), p. 2.

[2] For a view of "ideology" as a social group's rationalized, "skewed" total picture of its world, see Karl Mannheim, *Ideology and Utopia: An Introduction to the Sociology of Knowledge, trans.* by L. Wirth and E. Shils (New York: Hartcourt, Brace, 1936).

1

"ideology" with respect to politics, economics, religion, morality, education, money, or other subjects. With respect to politics, an ideology usually has specific implications for the following important processes, as recently set out by one prominent political scientist.[3] Who should rule? How should rulers be selected? By what principles should they (government) operate? What reforms, if any, should society undertake? What institutions should be altered or maintained? In addition, as some writers point out, an ideology usually implies an argumentative defense of some values and opposition to others; it implicitly "tells" people what to think and how to act; hence, it may be described as "normative." It also generally implies a particular view of reality: of what man, society, and even the physical world are like in their nature, behavior, and relationship to one another.

It is in this broad sense that we shall examine the modern ideologies, and it is in this sense that the importance and relevance of ideology for the politics of today, yesterday and, no doubt, tomorrow, can be really appreciated. Whether radical or conservative, innovative or rigidly traditionalist, political ideologies are, above all, belief systems with which social institutions and processes may be manipulated toward what David Easton calls "authoritative allocation of values."

If we define our subject matter too *narrowly*, confining the term "ideology" to explicitly organized, neatly arranged axioms of a specific orientation, we shut out much of the real world of politics. If politics is seen as a process in which men reconcile, sometimes violently, value conflicts, and make decisions as to who gets what, how, and why, it is obvious that biases—competing ways of looking at and evaluating the world—are at the very center of politics. The clash of widely divergent and pervasive biases among men is unaffected by the ingenuity of scholarly definitions.[4] Conflict, strife, and war go on—in the apparent absence

Mannheim's treatment of the subject made explicit the equivalent implied use of the term by Karl Marx. In a recent study, James P. Young emphasizes the normative, direction-seeking perspective of ideology: ". . . there is a very important distinction to be made between ideology defined as a system of ideas concerning the existing social order, and at the same time concerning actions to be taken regarding it . . . . A healthy political system must have some set of values, some long-range goals which can function as a guide to both short-run and long-run policy formulation. The system must operate with some conception of the public interest, some general idea of welfare; it is this which ideologies seek to provide." *The Politics of Affluence: Ideology in the United States Since World War II* (San Francisco: Chandler, 1968) p. 205.

[3] Robert Lane, *Political Ideology* (New York: Free Press, 1962), pp. 13–16.

[4] See Daniel Bell, *The End of Ideology: On the Exhaustion of Political Ideas in the Fifties*, rev. ed. (New York: Free Press, 1962), particularly pp. 393–407, and the excellent riposte by Joseph La Palombara, "Decline of Ideology: A Dissent and An

of "ideological differences." The militants, the activists, and the "concerned citizens" may or may not be glad to hear that they are not "dogmatic ideologues," but they continue voicing demands and making claims that are *often*, if not always, predictable from deeply felt, long-standing, shared biases. The propensity of human biases to *cluster*, over a period of time and with respect to a variety of situations, is an empirical test of the existence of ideologies.

If ideologies do involve belief-clusters, then their existence should enable us to employ useful labels. Thus, in the United States, the term "Wallace-democrat," for example, might connote a whole range of attitudes on such related issues as school desegregation, federal enforcement of civil rights laws, equal housing and employment opportunities for blacks and whites, and so forth. "Conservative" might be an instant clue to attitudes on government spending, taxes, federal-state relations, social welfare, and private property.

But, it will be immediately objected, all labels are deceiving because people who identify with them do not really *all* believe the same things. Moreover, terms such as "liberal," "conservative," or "socialist" do not actually involve the same beliefs today as they did, say, a hundred years ago; it can also be said that they mean different things in different places. When Russia's Leonid Brezhnev talks about "socialism," for example, does he mean the same thing by it as Britain's Harold Wilson or Sweden's Olof Palme?

In this kind of critique, we are really asked to consider the context for each political action or actor in order to appreciate its meaning. We are told to ponder the particular circumstances in which specific persons have come to espouse something or other, and to beware of sweeping, misleading generalizations.

There is obvious merit in this positivist critique, but it can be easily overdone. Political labels derived from ideological orientations need not describe *all* members of a particular group to be useful. It may be sufficient that they help us distinguish *predominant* attitudes in one human collectivity as opposed to another. Moreover, they need not remain fixed and static for all time and in all places, in order to preserve some recognizable identity vis-à-vis other attitudes or beliefs.

The discovery of "common denominators" among outwardly different

Interpretation," *American Political Science Review*, Vol. LX, No. 1, March 1966, pp. 5–16. La Palombara argues that what is observable is not a decline but change in the nature of particular ideologies, their expressions, and the commitment to them by people under different circumstances. The problem hinges on definitions; some observers insist that "ideologies" must somehow be "dogmatic, utopian, rational or flamboyant." Pp. 7, 8.

things is an aid to understanding the world. The idea that no two things —even the same word contemplated by two different persons—are really "the same," is indeed a usefully sobering one. Carried to its extreme, however, it inhibits understanding. All generalizations about nature, plants, animals, or men require a focus on their common properties.

A fruitful discussion of ideology always requires some attention, however, to the social and historical context in which various terms are used. One can find references, for example, to conflicts between "conservatives" and "liberals" in Soviet or East European politics, and also the same references in American politics. In the first instance, "conservative" usually means Stalinist or neo-Stalinist; in the second, it might well refer to a supporter of Senator Barry Goldwater. The term "radical" like "conservative," could refer to a man's temperament or religion as much as to his politics. And even if we knew that it referred to politics, we would only know that it connotes some extreme tendency, without knowing its direction, objects, or intensity.

Depending on the perspective used, American conservatism and liberalism could be seen as but two branches of the ideology of liberal democracy; their Soviet counterparts are representative of socialism.

Finally, there is good reason to believe that if a particular, here-and-now situation can illuminate for us some general concept, the reverse is true also. We can learn about ideas by studying the people who hold them; but clearly another way of understanding the people is through their ideas. If certain belief systems do indeed have common features and/or certain common circumstances of origin, we can use this general knowledge to understand other, new situations. Thus the study of European nationalism may help us appreciate non-European nationalisms, even though there may be many differences in the phenomena compared.

Knowledge of ideologies would be a veritable master key to politics if we knew (1) what biases or predispositions particular people had (what their "ideologies" were), (2) which of these they would invoke in any given situation, assuming that some of their biases clashed with others, and (3) that they could indeed act as they wished. We could then predict people's behavior, and specifically we could predict political action under all sorts of circumstances.

The study of ideologies does, in fact, take us *some way* toward this objective; and therein lies its practical significance. If we discover that X strongly believes Y, this has implications for X's behavior under various circumstances. But, alas, the complexity of the real world makes even the most faithful delineation of someone's ideological profile only one indication of what he might do.

We recognize that people are often attached to conflicting principles.

Thus, a man may be very parsimonious with his money and therefore, other things being equal, we could be reasonably sure that he would not contribute to many charities or, at any rate, give little compared with other people of similar means. Yet, he may also be intensely religious and the contributions he might make under the auspices of a church or under the influence of a cleric might well be "out of character," or contrary to his usual predisposition for spending on non-religious objects, activities, and so forth. In this case, the man's generosity will depend on how he identifies requests put to him.

In some situations, the individual may not be free (or may not feel free) to indulge his real preference or bias. He may be under direct threat of reprisal if he does, or he may think that the price of indulging one preference will likely result in the loss of another even more immediately valuable to him. A man may be attached to certain libertarian values, individualism, freedom, equality, and the like, but may feel constrained to support autocratic politicians, foreign or domestic, in order to ward off "the spread of communism," prevent a depression, protect his land holdings, secure a job, or simply keep the peace—at a price.

Here it may be appropriate to add that the biases of most people are partly rational and conscious but also partly irrational and subconscious. The consistency of views which some analysts seek in popular preferences often are simply not there. Even those writers who think of themselves as "political philosophers" and attempt to evolve, consciously, elaborate schemes of political ideology frequently fall short of the ideal of logical rigor and consistency. Even for these philosophers, the rigor of a system can be established only by the most elaborate artifices of subsequent commentators, and often with very unconvincing results.[5]

Symmetry and coherence of ideological orientation have probably always been lowest on the level of the private individual. There we find people reacting to different values with the least obligation of working out a coherent pattern for their preferences. The man-in-the-street is under no obligation, like the political philosopher, to make his argu-

5 On the inconsistencies of John Locke's political ideas, see, e.g., Bertrand Russell, *A History of Western Philosophy* (New York: Simon and Schuster, 1959): "(Locke) is always sensible, and always willing to sacrifice logic rather than become paradoxical. He enunciates general principles which, as the reader can hardly fail to perceive, are capable of leading to strange consequences; but whenever the strange consequences seem about to appear, Locke blandly refrains from drawing them," P. 606; cf. pp. 636–637. For two different interpretations and adaptations of Edmund Burke to problems of American society see Russell Kirk, *The Conservative Mind* (Chicago: Regnery, 1960) and *A Program for Conservatives* (Chicago: Regnery, 1954); and Peter Viereck, *Conservatism Revisited*, rev. ed. (New York: Macmillan, 1962).

ments conform with those he may have advocated earlier to an audience of critical scholars. He need not worry about the public impact of his opinion on the actions of others as political party managers might, because he is not a manager of political work; his views are never publicized. He can easily afford to be as inconsistent as he wishes. There are no practical incentives for him to say, "Now, if I really believe X, then I cannot possibly accept Y as being right."

Given this discount, we still find people in general clustering important values under various traditional labels of political ideology. According to a 1966 study in France, certain traditional, classical 19th–20th century ingredients of the division between "Left" and "Right" survived among a sample of the French electorate as follows:

Among those who identified themselves as "extreme rightists" 82 percent disagreed with the statement that "aid to church schools should be suppressed." Only 12 percent agreed and 6 percent expressed no opinion. Among the "extreme leftists" 63 percent agreed, and only 33 percent disagreed. On the question of whether "government should be made less authoritarian," 73 percent of the extreme Left agreed, but only 26 percent of the extreme Right did; 62 percent disagreed. Asked whether large, privately owned companies should be nationalized, 58 percent of the Left agreed but 47 percent of the Right disagreed.[6]

Although these are all fairly substantial figures, consistency of political opinions is, in some ways, filtered out even more coherently and consistently at the level of the organization than at the level of the rank and file. This does not mean that parties, their leaders and officials, do not sometimes take contradictory stands, or change them from time to time. It does mean that they tend to affirm some themes and reject others with a consistency greater than can be found in any large sampling of popular, private opinion.

To illustrate, Republican party platforms for a century have included commendable references to private enterprise; since the 1940's they have warned against the dangers of communist aggression and subversion; they have blamed the Cold War on the Communists and urged a policy of restraining the Soviet Union. There is every indication that in all this the platforms have echoed the sentiments of solid majorities of persons identifying themselves as "Republicans" over the years. But these platforms did not reflect at all the dissent among those relatively

---

[6] Cited by Martin Harrison, *French Politics* (Lexington, Mass: D. C. Heath, 1969), p. 143. We may note that inasmuch as these questions were all long-time themes of "left-wing" and "right-wing" propaganda, the responses, pro and con, indicated to what extent those who identified with particular ideological "labels" also believed the officially disseminated programs associated with them.

few Republicans who thought that the U. S. policy toward Russia ought to be "friendly" as Henry Wallace urged in 1948 rather than wary as Truman and Dewey did.

Party and group leadership must always consider the problem of "what will be the effect of our stand on X with respect to Y, Z, and Q?" "How will the attitudes and actions of our various possible supporters and opponents be affected if we do or say such-and-such?" Occasionally, the need for rationally calculated prudence may mean an ideological coherence at the top—in official statements and actions of a party or trade union—which is all but the reverse of the belief among the rank and file on one or some issues. An illustration of this is the matter of economic versus political liberalism among worker organizations in Europe and the United States. By all available survey data, workers and persons from the more economically deprived strata have tended to express highly authoritarian and intolerant attitudes toward aliens and dissenters. But as Seymour Martin Lipset has pointed out, . . . "workers judged by the politics of their parties, were often the backbone of the fight for greater political democracy, religious freedom, minority rights and international peace, while the parties backed up by the conservative middle and upper classes in much of Europe tended to favor more extremist political forms, to resist the extension of suffrage, to back the established church, and to support jingoist foreign policies."[7]

The paradox of this ideological refinement is to be found, as Lipset points out, in two factors. First, the political attributes of democracy, such as freedom of organization and speech, were found to be highly useful for the attainment of the economic objectives of labor: "a better standard of living, social security, shorter hours . . ."[8] Second, given the common, shared aspirations between group leadership and the rank and file, the latter had supported many policies deemed useful and necessary by the former, even if it did not always really "love and understand" them.

In a similar vein, the leadership of various socialist and liberal parties in east-central Europe had managed—in Germany, Poland, and Russia—to keep all overt anti-Semitic appeals out of these parties' public discourse because it deemed them harmful and self-defeating. In view of widespread popular prejudices this was no mean feat.[9]

[7] See *Political Man* (Garden City, N.Y.: Doubleday, 1960), p. 99.

[8] Ibid., pp. 126–127.

[9] On how certain notions, in this case anti-Semitism and animosity toward other ethnic groups, become "accepted coin of the realm" see A. J. Groth, "Parliament and Ethnic Conflict in Pre-War Poland," *Slavic Review*, Vol. XXVII, No. 4, December 1968, pp. 564–580.

Indisputably, organizations such as the American Medical Association, the NAM, the CIO-AFL, or the Democratic or Republican parties *aggregate* the claims put forward by their members. This process usually involves reconciling contradictory positions and adopting stands somewhere between the most extreme claims of particular supporters. The process of aggregation not only achieves a watering down but also eliminates the mosaic of diversity from the consensual package of the party or group's official stance, and thus gives the group a discernible, coherent image or profile usually over a considerable period of time. For years the Republican party stood for "sound money" at home and "isolationism" abroad even if these positions did not characterize all who voted the Republican ticket in the 1890's, 1920's, or 1930's. Analogous differences have existed between programs and rank-and-file beliefs in the Democratic party as well.

Although American politics has been generally regarded as remarkably pragmatic, ideological orientations have been important here, too. A 1960 study by three American political scientists concluded that:

"Despite the brokerage tendency of the American parties, their active members are obviously separated by large and important differences. The differences, moreover, conform with the popular image in which the Democratic party is seen as the more "progressive" or "radical," the Republican as the more "moderate" or "conservative" of the two. In addition, the disagreements are remarkably consistent, a function not of chance but of systematic points of view, whereby the responses to any one of the issues could reasonably have been predicted from knowledge of the responses to the other issues."[10]

The researchers found the following attitudinal differences on related issues among a sample of the American electorate: 18.6 percent of Democrats favored increased government regulation of business but only 7.4 percent of Republicans did; 39.0 percent of Democrats favored increased farm price supports, while only 23.0 percent of Republicans did; 74.9 percent of Democrats favored increased federal aid to education and 64.8 percent of Republicans agreed; 32.0 percent of Democrats favored increased corporate taxes and 23.3 percent of Republicans did; 24.6 percent of Democrats wanted to increase taxes on business in general, while only 15.9 percent among the Republicans agreed; 59.0 percent of Democrats wanted to increase the minimum wage and 43.5 percent among Republicans agreed. 69.4 percent of Democrats wanted

---

[10] See Herbert McClosky, Paul J. Hoffman, Rosemary O'Hara, "Issue Conflict and Consensus Among Party Leaders and Followers," in J. R. Owens and P. J. Staudenraus (eds.), *The American Party System* (New York: Macmillan, 1968), p. 361.

to increase social security benefits and 57.0 percent of Republicans did, too; 39.3 percent of Democrats wanted increased regulation of public utilities but only 26.0 percent of Republicans agreed. On the other hand, only 46.6 percent among Democrats were in favor of higher controls of trade unions but 57.8 percent among Republicans.

Interestingly, on each of these issues attitudinal differences between Republican leaders and Democratic leaders were much wider than those among the rank and file. Among the leaders, for example, 20.2 percent of Democrats wanted increased government regulation of business but only 0.6 percent of Republicans shared this view; increased farm price supports had the backing of 43.4 percent of Democratic leaders, while only 6.7 percent of the Republicans agreed; 66.2 percent of Democrats favored increased-federal aid to education and only 22.3 percent among Republican leaders agreed; 32.3 percent of Democrats favored increased corporate taxes but only 4.0 percent among Republicans approved of this. Only 12.6 percent of Democratic leaders wanted generally higher taxes on business, but among Republicans a mere 1 percent agreed. An increased minimum wage was favored by 50.0 percent of Democrats and 15.5 percent of Republicans. Increased social security benefits were regarded as desirable by 60.0 percent of Democrats and 22.5 percent of Republicans. Increased regulation of public utilities was supported by 59.0 percent among Democrats and 17.9 percent among Republicans. Finally, 59.3 percent of Democratic leaders favored increased control of trade union activities but among Republicans the figure was 86.4 percent.[11]

Thus, the authors of this particular study summarized the ideological division as follows:

"One side of this cleavage is marked by a strong belief in the power of collective action to promote social justice, equality, humanitarianism, and economic planning, while preserving freedom; the other is distinguished by faith in the wisdom of the natural competitive process and in the supreme virtue of individualism, "character," self-reliance, frugality and independence from government. To this cleavage is added another frequent source of political division, namely, a difference in attitude toward change between "radicals" and "moderates," between those who prefer to move quickly or slowly, to reform or to conserve. . . . However crudely, the American parties do tend to embody these com-

[11] Ibid, pp. 355–359. The authors questioned 3193 delegates (1788 Democrats and 1232 Republicans) to their respective national conventions of 1956 for a sample of leadership opinion. A Gallup Poll of 1484 voters across the country was used for a sample of the rank and file.

peting points of view and to serve as reference groups for those who hold them."[12]

The higher propensity of organizations to espouse coherent and persistent ideological themes is also characteristic of whole states or regimes. In the case of communism and fascism, these have been the official doctrines of states. Mussolini's Italy, Hitler's Germany, and a host of Marxist-Leninist states since Lenin's Russia have claimed to be guided by the tenets of their respective ideologies. Observers have compared communist doctrine to a "holy writ" in the reverence accorded it by Soviet, Chinese, and East European politicians and propagandists. Indeed, the sanctions applied among the communist states for the "sin of heresy" find parallels in the punishment of dissenters by the medieval church. No proposition can be openly advanced against it. In the case of democratic regimes, the underlying ideology is never made into a compulsory creed for all the citizens. Nor is it, like Marxism-Leninism, advertised as infallible, and as *the* truth. It is, however, to be found embedded in various constitutional documents, and its indirect influence is very considerable even if it is not compulsory or held to be an "official" truth.

An analogy between individuals and organized groups—even nation-states—is warranted in one important sense. Organizations cannot *always* control the environment in which they operate any more than individuals can. They respond in complex ways to a complex world, and the knowledge of a single ideological position of a state or party may not always be enough to predict its behavior.

In the communist states, Marxism-Leninism is invoked to explain and to justify each turn of policy, every declaration by the leaders, every state project, and every plan. When leaders quarrel, they establish the legitimacy of their positions in terms of the tenets of the creed, as did, successively, Stalin and Trotsky, Malenkov and Khrushchev, Brezhnev and Mao Tse-tung. It is always important for them to establish a strong case of loyally and correctly interpreting the doctrines of Marxism-Leninism. Thus the written opinions of Karl Marx, Frederick Engels, and Vladimir Ilich Lenin are of great practical consequence to any

---

[12] Ibid, pp. 368–369. It is worth noting, too, that ideological perceptions and responses in the United States have been found to differ from election to election. Fewer voters were apparently making ideological choices between Stevenson and Eisenhower in 1956 than between Goldwater and Johnson in 1964. The conduct of Goldwater's campaign and his image with the voters all tended to heighten ideological, conservative-liberal responses by voters. See John Osgood Field and Ronald E. Anderson, "Ideology in the Public's Conceptualization of the 1964 Election," *Public Opinion Quarterly*, Vol. 33, No. 3, Fall 1969, pp. 380–398.

official dialogue conducted in Moscow, Peking, Tirana or East Berlin. If a policy appears to clash with what Marx and Lenin advocated, a case has to be made that a departure is *necessary* to achieve the "essential objectives" of the doctrine under new circumstances. And, in fact, both Marx and Lenin can be quoted on the need for just this kind of "adaptation to new realities." If, on the other hand, a policy or an action appears to fit well with the pronouncements of communism's great sages, it is regarded as evidence in its favor; it buttresses its prestige and increases the chances of its acceptability by members of the ruling Party. In any case, within the framework of communist rule, there is no room for indifference to justification-by-ideology—however farfetched. No Party leader can publicly afford to say, "So, what?" if reproached about an inconsistency between his views and those of Marx or Lenin.

Thus, to know something about the ideology of communism is to know by what book of rules conflicts are umpired in the several communist-governed political systems. But what does ideology tell us about the substantive directions of policy? This is a much more complex question. We can *prove* that in some political systems public discussion of virtually everything involves heavy recourse to ideological themes. We can resort to simple content analysis of newspapers, books, radio broadcasts, official documents, and the like. But how can we prove that ideology, or even some reasonable number of components of an ideology, have a causative influence on what people think and how they act? Is it all a matter of mere "window dressing"?

A number of reasonable inferences may be made from some striking *correlations* between "ideology" and "action." If we begin with the fact that in some political systems certain political beliefs are given a monopoly position in the education of the youth and in all public media of information, entertainment, and propaganda, and if we compound this knowledge by the fact that this monopoly has effectively existed in some of these systems for decades, and if we consider that even informal, clandestine dissemination of opposite views and beliefs has been deterred by the harshest punishment, then it is indeed difficult *not* to expect some ideological impacts on thought and action in such systems.[13] Actually, we have some survey evidence, gathered from defectors from the Soviet Union in the 1950's, which shows that even those people who, given a

---

[13] In the literature of this subject, see, for example, Herbert H. Hyman, *Political Socialization* (Glencoe, Ill.: Free Press, 1959); Lester W. Milbrath, *Political Participation* (Chicago: Rand McNally, 1965), and Kenneth Prewitt and Richard E. Dawson, *Political Socialization* (Boston: Little, Brown, 1969).

chance, abandoned the Soviet regime, absorbed many official tenets into their own thinking. Thus, even persons who saw themselves as "rejecting the system" came to believe many of its claims.[14]

But what about the policies of the leaders? Are they motivated by ideology or by opportunism, thirst for power, external pressures, or even mere happenstance? It is useful to note that choices such as the ones posed above are sometimes seen in an unnecessarily exclusive way. Motives are frequently mixed, and there is no reason why goals of, say, personal aggrandizement should not be combined with ideologically established values in a political hierarchy as much as they might be, say, in a religious one. The leader's incentive to act may be personal but the nature of the actions may be prescribed and limited by his social environment. A bishop could not succeed to the papacy by excelling in blood purges; Stalin could not have succeeded as Secretary General of the CPSU by excellence in prayers.

To what extent does ideology, then, shape the total environment of political action?

In answering this question, we must fall back on the substantial but not ultimately conclusive evidence of *correlation* between articulated beliefs on the one hand and actions on the other.

In his biography of Adolf Hitler, British historian Alan Bullock wrote that Hitler always kept his word—except when he gave it.[15] The totalitarian record of Nazi Germany was indeed a remarkable realization, not of the promises that Hitler had made to foreign diplomats, but of the ideals of *Mein Kampf*. First published eight years before Hitler became Chancellor of Germany in 1933, it foretold several of Nazism's most characteristic policies. In *Mein Kampf*, Hitler espoused his commitment to a policy of ruthless expansionism for Germany, to repudiation of the 1919 peace settlement at Versailles as "unjust"; he even made clear *how* and *where* he intended to destroy the Versailles *status quo* and to establish the German Reich as a world power. France was to be rendered harmless and Britain forced to give up her European role;

[14] Thus, Alex Inkeles and Raymond A. Bauer, in their study, *The Soviet Citizen* (Cambridge: Harvard University, 1959), showed that among hundreds of persons who had escaped from the USSR, in all social classes, there were high levels of acceptance of various Soviet institutions, including economic and police regimentation; even among those who professed abject hatred toward their rulers. "Approximately two-thirds of each social group favored . . . state planning and ownership of the economy . . . . Only 14 percent favored an essentially capitalist system" (p. 242). Only about a third believed people should be allowed to say things against the government" (p. 247).

[15] See Alan Bullock, *Hitler: A Study in Tyranny* (New York: Harper, 1952) pp. 293, 305–307.

Germany in collaboration with Italy, was to establish great power hegemony over the European continent and, above all, extend her possessions and influence to the east and southeast. All Germans were to be united in one state. *Drang-nach-osten* was explicitly the hallmark of Hitler's policy. The Soviet Union was to be destroyed, and the Ukraine, in fact, and all the lands to the east and southeast of Germany's borders were to supply food, raw materials, and (slave) labor for their German rulers.

These objectives were grounded on an explicitly racist ideology that held up the Germans as a "master race" who "deserved" by their superiority and their strength to rule over others. While Germans were supermen, Slavs were described as subhuman, a race fit only for service to its masters.

One can even find the *sequence* of Hitler's foreign policy in *Mein Kampf*: neutralization of the power of the West, Britain, and France, precedes the onslaught on the Soviet Union. The method for realizing Nazi objectives—through violence and war—was also implicit in several themes of *Mein Kampf*. Hitler's explicit rejection of pacificism and internationalism as cowardly and Jewish orientations, his glorification of the strong and contempt for the weak, his enthusiasm for the army as the foremost training ground of the German society all pointed clearly even to the methods that Hitler was likely to choose in pursuit of his aims. All that was lacking in *Mein Kampf* was a timetable!

We may note, parenthetically, that what Hitler had to say in *Mein Kampf* was not taken very seriously by many people in Germany before 1933 and by many people abroad including diplomats and statesmen of neighboring powers until at least 1939. Some thought that, as the old saying goes, Hitler's "bite was bound to prove less awesome than his bark." They hoped that he might either change his views, or be forced by others around him and by external circumstances to modify them. Yet, Hitler went on to fulfill his vision that he had delineated in 1925 both with respect to foreign policy and to his domestic programs. To be sure, he did not spell out the extermination of the Jews in any public pronouncement. But what he did have to say about Jews in his "book of principles" could not have entailed *less* than the wholesale expulsion and persecution of Jews. And it was clearly consistent with and supportive of the program of extermination embodied in the Final Solution.

Western choices for "interpreting the Nazis" may be illustrated with two quotations by Hitler. The first was offered by the Nazi Feuhrer for the benefit of world diplomats and public opinion in a speech to the German Reichstag. The second was from his statement of ideological principles in *Mein Kampf*. Thus, in March 1935, Hitler declared:

"At no moment of my struggle on behalf of the German people have I ever forgotten the duty incumbent on me and on us all firmly to uphold European culture and European civilization. . . .

"Why should it not be possible to put an end to this useless strife (between France and Germany) which has lasted for centuries and which has never been and never will be finally decided by either of the two nations concerned? Why not replace it by the rule of reason? The German people have no interest in seeing the French people suffer. . . ."[16]

In 1927, however, Hitler had said:

"We must be absolutely clear on the fact that France is the permanent and inexorable enemy of the German; the key to her foreign policy will always be her desire to possess the Rhine frontier, and to secure that river for herself by keeping Germany broken up and in ruins.[17] If the German nation is to stop the rot which threatens Europe . . . it must ascertain who its most dangerous opponents are so as to strike at them with all its concentrated force."[18]

For a variety of reasons that included an understandable fear of war itself, lack of public support in behalf of risky "get-tough-with-Germany" policies, and clever reassurances from Berlin, most Western statesmen believed that peaceful accommodation with Hitler was indeed possible.

When the British Prime Minister, Neville Chamberlain, went to Munich in October 1938 to negotiate the cession of Sudetenland by Czechoslovakia to the Nazis, he not only had ample access to all the threats and boasts that Hitler had made over the years but he also had behind him the experience of the Nazi march into the Rhineland in 1935 and the far more shocking take-over of Austria in 1938.

But Chamberlain clung to the last vestige of hope. Why should Hitler be "unreasonable," if others were not? War might devastate Germany just as much as other countries. Surely, the responsibilities of high office, now that Hitler was Germany's Chancellor, would make him reconsider the radical views that he expressed as an obscure office seeker struggling to win a following.

Thus Chamberlain came to hope and believe that in spite of Nazism's aggressive, world-domination oriented ideology, he could do business with Hitler. In the wake of his Munich journey, Chamberlain explained his position in these obviously quite reasonable terms:

[16] Ibid, p. 314.

[17] See E. T. S. Dugdale (trans. and ed.), *My Battle* (Boston: Houghton Mifflin, 1933), p. 266.

[18] Ibid, p. 270.

"History teaches us that no form of government ever remains the same. The change may come by slow degrees or it may come suddenly like an explosion. But change in one form or another is inevitable and it would seem to follow, therefore, that we should be careful not to shut ourselves off from contact with any country on account of a system which in the course of time may well undergo such modifications as to render it very different from what it is today."[19]

And, having met the Nazi Fuehrer, Chamberlain subsequently wrote in a private letter to his sister:

". . . in spite of the hardness and ruthlessness I thought I saw in his face, I got the impression that here was a man who could be relied upon when he had given his word."[20]

Even with all the benefit of hindsight—knowing *both* what the Nazis preached and what they did—we can do no more than point out the correlations. To most people they may seem causative in nature. The Nazis did what they wanted and said they would do. But, logically, there can be no such absolute certainty about these correlations. Thus, the British historian, A. J. P. Taylor, in his *Origins of the Second World War* (London: Hamilton, 1961) has just sufficient room for the argument that not Hitler but Western statesmen should be blamed for the outbreak of the war. After all, we cannot be *sure* that Hitler would not have acted *differently*, if others had behaved differently toward him. Is it not *possible* that Hitler did change his mind about various things after obtaining power, and the sequence of events after September 1, 1939 owes more to a confluence of particular circumstances than to his conscious evil designs? Such *possibilities,* however implausible and unlikely, cannot be logically ruled out. And they are endemic in any appraisal of ideologies and their influences in general.

Since the end of World War II a perennial theme of discussion has been the role of ideology in Soviet foreign policy, and in the foreign policies of other communist-ruled states, notably China.

Much of the current perception of political conflict, both international and domestic, tends to be ideological.[21] The view that the Cold War is a struggle between the ideals of "communism" and "capitalism," or

19 Neville Chamberlain, *In Search of Peace* (New York: G. P. Putnam's Sons, 1939), p. 243.

20 Quoted by Keith Feiling, *The Life of Neville Chamberlain* (London: Macmillan, 1947), p. 367.

21 See K. J. Holsti, "National Role Conceptions in the Study of Foreign Policy," *International Studies Quarterly*, Vol. 14, No. 3, September 1970, pp. 233–309.

"communism" and "democracy," has been and still is so prevalent that it has had a profound impact on world events however exaggerated or distorted this notion may actually be.[22]

The current war in Indochina aptly illustrates this. In one sense, some Vietnamese have been fighting other Vietnamese (and eventually Americans) ostensibly for control of the state of South Vietnam. But much of the world has not identified the issue in such limited terms. To many Americans, conditioned by years of Cold War confrontations, this geographically remote conflict has always been a classic case of "communist aggression against the free world." American intervention in Southeast Asia has been frequently justified on the assumptions of the late John Foster Dulles' "domino theory": if Vietnam "falls," other states in the area will soon follow; the Communists' appetite for conquest will be simply whetted by a victory. In another variant of ideological perceptions of the war, it has been argued that American failure to stop "communism" in Southeast Asia will be interpreted throughout the world as unwillingness or inability to stop "communism" anywhere. Thus, America's guarantees to the NATO powers against Russia are seen as jeopardized by a possible failure to oppose the Viet Cong. In this view, both the Viet Cong and the Soviets are considered as one and the same: communist aggressors. For reasons analogously related to their ideological perceptions of the "peoples' just struggle against U.S. imperialism," Red China and the USSR have not only involved themselves in the conflict but also invested it with a significance of worldwide proportions.

Among other current examples of conflicts that are heavily ideological in nature is the Arab-Israeli struggle. The ancient land of Palestine has become the focus of a passionate nationalist attachment to Jews not only in Israel itself but also to millions of Jews living elsewhere around the world, who see it as a second homeland and a spiritual shrine of the whole Jewish people. On the other hand, it has become a symbol and a rallying cry for a powerful Arab nationalism, too. The complex of values associated with "Palestine," or "Israel," influences the beliefs and behavior of many Algerian Arabs and European or American Jews, far removed

---

[22] The following quotations are illustrative: ". . . There are some people—and I regret to say some governments—who have not yet accepted the fact that but for Russian intransigence the world would now be enjoying the pursuits of peace." Harry S. Truman, *New York Times*, April 28, 1957, quoted in Kenneth Waltz, *Man, the State and War* (New York: Columbia University Press, 1965), p. 157. "Wherever you go, whomever you talk to, the important world problems all have a common denominator: Communism. The world's troubles would become relatively inconsequential if it were not for the everlasting conniving and trouble making of the Reds." William Randolph Hearst, Jr., Editor-in-Chief, The Hearst Newspapers, *San Francisco Sunday Examiner and Chronicle*, December 22, 1968.

from the actual scene of the conflict, and having no direct, material interest in it.

To sum up, "ideology" may offer us important clues to (a) attitudes of individuals—what they are likely to accept or reject, support or oppose; (b) institutional devices likely to be employed by a group, party, or state; (c) the nature of goals and policies pursued by such entities; and (d) the character of the social, economic, and cultural "payoffs" under the dispensation of a particular ideology.

Certainly, all of these exciting possibilities must be properly qualified. For one thing, we cannot expect "ideology" to be a clue to individual attitude or behavior if it is not *internalized*. We must have some evidence that the people whose behavior we wish to predict really believe X, Y, or Z. It would be wrong to say "Mr. Smith lives in a democratic state, therefore we can assume that he subscribes to certain ideological tenets identified with democracy." He may or may not, and the same disclaimer would certainly apply to Mr. Ivanov of the USSR.

If we can be sure that our subjects really adhere to a particular political bias, we must still temper our predictive expectations with the reminder that people's thinking is rarely unidimensional. They may well believe different things about different but interrelated subjects or differently about the same things in different circumstances. Mr. X may be a "liberal" in religion but "conservative" in politics. Confronted with a particular issue that he interprets as being "more a matter of religion than of politics" his attitude and behavior may well surprise some of his conservative friends.

Finally, for a great many reasons beliefs and biases are only one of the "inputs" of human action. There are always numerous other restraints on the behavior of individuals and whole political systems such that certain basic preferences and objectives become modified, muted and, on occasion, thwarted. Even rulers of states—and they sometimes more than other people—cannot always *do* or *express* what they really *feel* or *want*. Thus, ideology is only one clue among many.

Nevertheless, we can illustrate, through correlation, some of the predictive possibilities of ideology. If we knew that a group adhered to the ideology of communism, the odds on its hostility to the social and political institutions of the United States circa 1970 would be overwhelming. Its attitude toward the USSR and Red China, on the other hand, would not be predictable from known adherence to beliefs characterizable merely as *a* variety of "communism." The odds on any group so described pursuing a dictatorial form of government under the leadership of one party would be extremely high. No dominant Communist party from Cuba to North Korea has as yet offered us a deviance. The chances of outright land confiscation for medium and large farm owners under the rule of such a group would be overwhelming. The chances of land collectivization, while lower, would still be quite high. Thus far, Yugoslavia and Poland would not fit this pattern. The odds on high investment in the devolpment of popular culture and mass education would be overwhelming. (See Chapter 8.)

Our list of ideologies is not exhaustive, though it is representative of the political mainstream of the twentieth century. And the three great ideological traditions are by no means wholly *exclusive* of one another. They frequently overlap, adapt, and borrow both language and ideas from one another. It is useful to remind ourselves when studying ideologies that belief systems are produced by and disseminated among people whose interests and predispositions change. Thus nuances and, above all, the uses of political ideologies (no matter how constant the formulas are) always undergo alterations.

Now we shall trace the rise and characteristic features of three dominant ideological systems of modern times: democracy, socialism, and nationalism. The approach here is developmental. How and why have these ideologies come into existence? How are they interrelated? In describing them, we may keep in mind the following considerations useful for analytical and comparative purposes.

1. What is the ideology's characteristic general view of man and society? What are its assumptions about how and why people behave as they do, not necessarily in any one specific political/social system but universally? What capacity do men have for different modes of behavior? What factors are crucial, primary, or even particularly significant in inducing them to change?

2. What is the ideology's blueprint for change? Given a particular view of what man and society are like, what goals and directions does the ideology envalue or suggest?

3. What are the characteristic means of social control and manipulation that the ideology advocates?

4. What variations exist within and among particular political value systems, such that the exponents of two ostensibly different ideologies might be sometimes found to have much in common, while the exponents of one ideology might be actually further apart in their ideas?

5. What are some of the characteristic practical problems in the application of various ideologies?

CHAPTER 2

The Genesis of Modern Ideologies

A formidable set of difficulties relates to the precise origin of, and the credit for, the development of various characteristic political concepts. What beliefs or tenets are to be regarded as "essential" to an ideology and which ones as merely accidental, occasional, or even extraneous? How would we identify, if at all, the "same ideology" at different periods of history and in different places? How are we to deal with the problem of *overlapping* among belief-systems which—considerably different at some points—may be in substantial agreement at others?

If we seek to credit a particular writer or philosopher with, say, being a contributor to the "concept of democracy," we face some interesting problems. Suppose we can agree that something he wrote or said is part of this concept. Did he originate or merely borrow his ideas? Did he mean by his words, in his time, what we think of them today? Moreover, are we really entitled to consider him a "democratic thinker" because of these particular contributions? The conscious intentions and the total outlook of many political philosophers, writers, and pamphleteers are easily disputed.

None of these problems admits of a clear-cut, total solution, and there are many different yet fruitful methods of analyzing political ideas depending on the context in which they are used.

Here we deal with three major political-ideological traditions: democracy, socialism, and nationalism. These traditions by no means exhaust the universe of political belief-systems, and they are substantially overlapping in both origin and content. Broadly defined, however, and given adequate attention to different representatives of each species, these traditions subsume most of the secular political belief-systems extant since the nineteenth century.

A study of political ideas per se, as abstract concepts, would inevitably take us back into antiquity, since it is difficult to name *any* political notions that do not find some intellectual forerunners in Plato and Aristotle and generally among the thinkers of classical Greece. Our concern, however, is not with political ideas *primarily* as philosophers' notions, but as widely diffused intellectual value-systems, overtly and systematically propagandized to millions of people.

Thus the ideas of certain great thinkers and writers described here are presented so as to reflect significant, historically influential attitudes or biases within larger sections of public opinion. In some cases, political philosophers may have merely articulated notions already current in the societies of their time. In other instances, they could be described as forerunners of certain popular ideals. So far as the study of ideologies is concerned, the importance of all speculative schemes of politics, original or otherwise, is wholly social. They are useful insofar as they illuminate the aspirations and preferences of significant strata of society over the course of time. They are important because, and only if, they are linked to more prevalent (even if sometimes mute and diffuse) political value-systems.

Viewed, in this perspective, the beginnings of our political ideologies may be realistically traced to Europe during the so-called Age of Reason, from approximately the middle of the seventeenth century to the beginning of the nineteenth. For it was during this period of time, symbolically expressed by the British Glorious Revolution of 1689, the American Revolution of 1775, and the French Revolution of 1789, that ideas became tools, or weapons, for the mobilization of the masses. Ideas began to be used for popular persuasion, and popular persuasion gradually became not only increasingly important but even indispensable to the process of government. It required the rise of the masses to give force to the formulation and dissemination of systematic, secular ideological orientations and, in turn, the penetration of such orientations assured the continuing importance of the masses in the process of governance.

A cluster of social, economic, cultural, and political developments in Europe led to establishment of all three of our ideological traditions: democracy, socialism, and nationalism, each with its various branches. The ideas of the philosophers and the scholars were pressed into the service of rival political interests. Each faction inevitably claimed and emphasized the propositions most useful to itself from the most prestigious and best-known available sources.

The ideologies of democracy, socialism, and nationalism grew out of a great ferment in the lives of European peoples, a ferment which for want of a better term may be called "social mobilization."

In the definition of Karl W. Deutsch:

"Social mobilization . . . denotes . . . a number of more specific processes of change, such as changes of residence, of occupation, of social setting, of face-to-face associates, of institutions, roles, and ways of acting, of experiences and expectations, and finally of personal memories, habits and needs, including the need for new patterns of group affiliation and new images of personal identity. Singly, and even more in their cumulative impact, these changes tend to influence and sometimes to transform political behavior."[1]

According to Deutsch, the concept implies that "these processes tend to go together in certain historical situations and stages of economic development (and) that these situations are identifiable and recurrent, in their essentials, from one country to another."[2]

The process of accelerating social mobilization in Europe from the late Middle Ages onwards contributed heavily to the establishment of new ideological political movements. In the broadest sense, these movements offered themselves as the intellectual, moral, and organizational brokers of change and reintegration. They sought to redefine human values, institutions, and roles in a world that was caught up in a veritable turmoil of change. Social mobilization promoted increased demands on government for services and regulations. It widened the scope of politics, the areas of conflict and, above all, the membership of the "politically relevant strata." It gave a new dimension and a new urgency to the problems of political communication and organization.[3]

The process of mobilization resulted from a number of causes, all interacting over a long period of time and reaching a visibly striking junction in the century of the Great Revolutions (1689–1789).

Not merely in medieval times but during most of man's social existence, the whole process of government had been highly elitist. Formal participation in decision-making, actual scrutiny and control of the decision-makers, informed attention to and intense concern with the process of what David Easton has called "authoritative allocation of values"—all these were characteristic of only a small minority in virtually every European society, including even the very prototype of democratic polity,

---

[1] "Social Mobilization and Political Development," *The American Political Science Review*, Vol. LV, No. 3, September 1961, p. 493.

[2] Ibid.

[3] See Ibid., pp. 499–501.

ancient Athens. Government was distinctly the prerogative of the few.[4] Prior to the eighteenth century politics was something in which the "common man" took part fitfully, if at all, amidst an occasional riot or rebellion.[5]

This was especially true of largely rural societies in which the population was widely dispersed and communication and interaction were extremely difficult. The impact of the masses upon government was minimized by overwhelming illiteracy and ignorance. The great majority of people in all societies could neither read nor write. In addition most people did not possess the mobility for acquainting themselves with the conditions of life, economy, culture, religion, administration, or even geography of distant regions—and sometimes even of those but a few miles away from their village or township.[6] Although patterns of life were occasionally subject to cataclysmic disruptions as a result of wars, banditry, plague, and/or famine, in many ways they tended to remain stable and set for centuries. Traditions represented the rule rather than the exception. Families often did not change places of residence for generations. Occupational patterns were far more stable than they have been since the period of the commercial and industrial revolutions of modern times; the sons of peasant farmers were likely to remain in the occupations of their fathers from one generation to another. Over hundreds of years, the degree of technological innovation to which a man might be

[4] See Walter R. Agard, *What Democracy Meant to the Greeks* (Madison: University of Wisconsin Press, 1960) pp. 69–70; citizenship requirements in Athens in the fourth century B.C. excluded all but males of 18 years of age born of Athenian citizen parents. Resident aliens, slaves, women and children accounted for about 90 percent of the population. A Roman census of 47 A.D. put the number of "citizens" *and* their families at 5,984,000, out of between 70 and 90 million persons then estimated to have lived in the Empire. But under the Empire, citizenship no longer connoted suffrage. Lee Michael Grant, *The World of Rome* (London: Weidenfeld and Nicolson, 1960), p. 76. Compare John Crook, *Law and Life of Rome* (Ithaca: Cornell University Press, 1967).

[5] See Chalmers Johnson, *Revolutionary Change* (Boston: Little, Brown, 1966), pp. 136–317, on peasant uprisings as means of participation in politics. Compare Gabriel A. Almond and G. Bingham Powell, *Comparative Politics* (Boston: Little, Brown, 1966), pp. 75–76 and 81–82, on "anomic" interest articulation of this sort.

[6] On persistent patterns of rural life in and since the Middle Ages see, e.g., Helen D. Irvine, *The Making of Rural Europe* (New York: Dutton, 1923); H. S. Bennett, *Life on the English Manor 1150–1400* (Cambridge: University Press, 1956). Compare E. A. Kosminsky, *Studies in the Agrarian History of England in the Thirteenth Century* (New York: Kelley and Millman, 1956); he reports that urban population in England rose by less than 7 percent in nearly 300 years—from 5 to about 12 percent of the total English population between 1086 and 1377 (p. 322). See also G. E. Fussell, *The English Rural Labourer* (London: Batchworth, 1949), particularly pp. 142–44. Marc Bloch, *French Rural History* (Berkeley: University of California Press, 1966), pp. 160–170 and 213–218, on rates of social and technological change.

subjected in his work—say, that of a ploughman or a blacksmith—was all but nil. Many social relationships and cultural stimuli tended to be similarly persistent and very narrowly defined. To a medieval peasant, the lord of the manor was someone who had held a social, economic, and political position of such long duration that he could well regard his own status vis-à-vis the lord's as immutable—as natural as rain, snow, or sunshine. The sources from which a man might draw all his knowledge of the world outside his own household were also likely to be stable and narrowly circumscribed.

In many ways, not only for medieval but also for ancient societies, religion was an absorbing concern that subsumed political life within it. The functions of government were nearly everywhere closely linked with the values and institutions of religion. Even among regimes that were *not* theocracies ruled by priests, the legitimacy of political authority—of kings, emperors, and magistrates—was grounded in religious sanctions. Priest and ruler, if not one and the same, were generally regarded as two emanations or faces of a single divine authority. Religious rites and symbols everywhere underlay the political ones. The particular nature of religion depended on place and period, to be sure, but its association with secular political authority was highly persistent and prevalent.

And in ancient as well as medieval times those who tampered with or questioned the sacred character of an established religious authority were seldom tolerated. They were persecuted and despised not only because priests and rulers did not abide dissent, but even more because religion was an intensely powerful force in the life of most ordinary people. It had few cultural rivals for centuries. The authority of science and technology, as well as the opportunity—for most people, at least—to hear views different from their priest's through modern agitation, entertainment, or travel still lay in the future.[7]

Gradually, the conditions that made for widespread human passivity in political life weakened and dissolved. Among the factors that precipitated the changes were undoubtedly the expansion of trade in the period of the Crusades; the cultural, scientific and economic advances and the secularization of life during the period of the Renaissance; the discoveries of such men as Columbus, Vasco de Gama, Magellan, and Balboa, and the closely related so-called Commercial Revolution of the sixteenth century with its enclosures and emergent money economy; the conflicts of the

---

[7] On influence of religion in the daily lives of people during the late Middle Ages, cf. H. S. Bennett, op. cit., pp. 27–37 and 319–336. See also Nimian Smart, *The Religious Experience of Mankind* (New York: Scribner's, 1969), pp. 314–374 and 424–441; and "Religion and Modernity" in John Cogley's *Religion in a Secular Age* (New York: Praeger, 1968), pp. 71–112, particularly.

Reformation which exposed the authority of religion to unprecedented, bruising frontal attacks throughout most of western and central Europe; and the incipient Industrial Revolution of the eighteenth century with its Pandora's box of inventions and economic and social adaptations.

Thus, in the history of medieval Europe, the Crusades (1096–1099, 1147–1149, 1189–1192, 1202–1204, 1212, 1218–1221, 1228–1229, 1248–1268, 1270–1272), ostensibly dedicated to the recapture of the Holy Land from "infidels," stimulated: an increased volume of trade with the Middle East and the development of banking and a money economy to support it; the rise of prosperous towns and cities; in many areas, a decline in the power of the feudal nobility killed off in the fighting; a substantial freeing of serfs, in part to enable them to fight in the Crusades but with many of them flocking to the towns; and, to complete the cycle, improvements in the means of travel and navigation for the support of this increased movement of people and goods across land and sea.

In turn, all these physical, cultural, and economic events had their social and political repercussions. The numbers and importance of the merchant class increased. Landed nobility and feudalism declined. The merchants strove to bring an increased measure of law and order into politics so as to protect their growing trade activities. To accomplish this, they supported efforts to centralize and augment the power of kings against that of the unruly nobility. Their efforts, though not everywhere successful, led to the rise of strong monarchies. In turn, the consolidation of royal power with unified laws, bureaucracies, and armed forces led to an upsurge in the sense of national identity and unity.

The growing accumulation of urban wealth spurred a revival and increase in learning, which produced new discoveries in science and technology, as well as a great upsurge in art, letters, and humanistic scholarship. People became more intellectually conscious and critical of their environment; all the foundations of the social, political, economic and, above all, religious life of Europe underwent critical reassessment.

In England, the Tudors consolidated a strong monarchical government in the aftermath of the Wars of the Roses (1455–1485). In France, a similar development was brought about partly in the wake of the Hundred Years' War (1337–1453) and the Wars of Religion of the sixteenth century. In Spain, Ferdinand and Isabella achieved similar results at the end of the fifteenth century and the work of national consolidation was notably continued by Charles V and Philip II in the 1500's.

Under the auspices of Europe's national monarchies, intensive geographic exploration and overseas expansion added to the growing ferment of European life. The 1492 voyage of Columbus on behalf of the Spaniards was followed in 1497 by the Portuguese, Vasco de Gama, who sailed around the Cape of Good Hope to India, and Cabral's voyage to both Brazil and India in 1500; in the early 1500's, the Spaniards, Ponce de Leon, Balboa, Cortez, and Pizarro explored and conquered lands in the Americas; Magellan's expedition of 1519–1522 became the first successful circumnavigation of the globe. Numerous English explorers, including John and Sebastian Cabot, Willoughby, Chancellor Frobisher, and others made voyages in the North Atlantic, as did the Frenchman, Jacques Cartier. In the words of historian Robert Ergang:

"The result of these explorations was that by the end of the sixteenth century the Europeans had learned the general outlines of the greater part of the world. Also they had opened a new world of commerce and had found vast wealth in the form of precious metals. Both the new commerce and the new supply of precious metals gave a great impetus to the rise of capitalism . . . ."[8]

The growth of secular political power in Europe on the one-hand, and the decline of both feudal nobility and Papacy on the other, proceeded apace since the fourteenth century. What began as movements of schism and reform in the 1300's, notably with the critical work of Marsiglio of Padua (1270–1342), the so-called Great Schism of 1378–1417 (in which an Italian Pope ruled in Rome and a French one in Avignon) and the Conciliar Movement of the 1400's, ended in the permanent rupture of the Universal Church in the Reformation of the sixteenth century.

The slaughter and the devastation of the wars of Reformation in which Catholics and Protestants vied to out-kill each other ultimately unleashed powerful trends toward secularism in Europe. People grew weary and wary of religious conflict. Many felt that the time had come when belief in abstract spiritual ideals and symbols must not be allowed to cause wanton destruction of the material here-and-now: lives and property.[9] Some came to regard all religions as equally absurd and prone to deadly fanaticism. Even more often, people wanted to narrow down the scope of religion's influence in everyday life by "banishing it inward," that is, making it a matter of each individual's private conscience rather than a

---

[8] See *Europe from the Renaissance to Waterloo* (Boston: D.C. Heath, 1954), p. 120.

[9] Both Thomas Hobbes, in the seventeenth century, and Jean Bodin, in the sixteenth, sought to make the sovereign power of princes strong in response to the chaos, strife, and turmoil of religious conflicts. To forestall men who set religious conflict above the competence of earthly sovereigns, they both advanced the ideal of powerful kingships. See R. M. Murray, *The Political Consequences of the Reformation* (New York: Russell and Russell, 1960), pp. 165–166. On the primacy of securing civic peace and order, cf. M. M. Goldsmith, *Hobbes's Science of Politics* (New York: Columbia University Press, 1966), p. xv, and F. S. McNeilly, *The Anatomy of Leviathan* (London: Macmillan, 1968) p. 254.

state-imposed universal obligation. This tendency to secularism often showed itself in the readiness to "look the other way" in cases of religious dissent. Thus, even though only one religion might be supported and favored by the State, the disabilities or persecution meted out to citizens who did not subscribe to it would be moderated or administered without much fervor. To the extent that royal power and the established elitist political order was either based on or aided by religious beliefs, the decline in popular zeal, attachment, and even interest in religion, eroded the structure of power that it supported.

Similarly, developments in science, technology, and economy under-mined the old systems of power, both secular and spiritual. New dis-coveries about the behavior of matter, shape of the earth, nature of the universe, the hitherto unexplained mysteries of biology, chemistry, and physics made many people sceptical of traditional church teachings. They appeared to be refuted by ever new discoveries; and these also generated a new faith—in the promise of science and technology to improve man's life and to give him new knowledge of untold and unlimited dimensions. For many, faith in God and religion was taking second place to an enthusiasm for reason and science. Man's mind, his powers of observation, analysis, and invention could seemingly conquer all obstacles and pene-trate all mysteries.

The pillar of elitist government in most of medieval Europe—the landed nobility—was seriously weakened by accumulating technological and economic changes. In the fourteenth century the discovery of gun-powder and its adaptation to armaments changed the nature of warfare. The skills of swordsmen and lancers, in which the feudal aristocrats excelled, became obsolete. Masses of rifle-toting infantrymen could hence-forth decide the outcome of war; castles and moats could not resist artil-lery bombardment. New trade routes, the rapid expansion of commerce and manufactures put an end to barter, autarky, and economic isolation in Europe. The significance of land declined while liquid assets and moneyed wealth moved to the cities, away from rural lands to the urban merchants, financiers, and manufacturers.

Coincidentally, science and learning continued to revolutionize men's lives. Although medieval scholars had preserved the intellectual achieve-ments of earlier civilizations and sometimes added to them, a great quanti-tative expansion of education did not begin to take place until the twelfth century (the so-called later Middle Ages). Gradually, learning passed from religious to secular auspices. The significance of quasi-scientific pursuit such as magic, alchemy, and astrology declined. In the middle of the fifteenth century a single invention, or rather an adaptation of several already known processes—printing—produced a new impetus in the development of science and technology. In the 1450's, Johann Gutenberg produced a printed version of the Latin Bible. Thenceforth, a veritable flood of scientific, popular, and political literature cascaded in Europe.

By 1550, Nicholas Copernicus had published his heliocentric theory of the universe. In the seventeenth century, men like Kepler, Galileo, and Newton, carried theoretical and empirical studies of the physical world to new heights. The publication by Sir Isaac Newton of his *Principia* (*The Mathematical Principles of Natural Knowledge*) in 1687 not only had a great influence on man's scientific knowledge but also on social and political thought, for beyond calculus and the universal law of gravitation was the salient idea of a world ordered by rational principles. It suggested to those with humanistic and social interests that the world which man inhabited was not ruled by miracle, chance, or magic, but that it possessed an underlying regularity of certain basic processes and causes; man could discover these, apprehend them as "rules," and presumably use them to his advantage. Science as the learning of the opinions of ancient writers gradually gave way to empirical observation and testing in physics, astronomy, chemistry, biology, and medicine. It gave rise to analogous efforts in politics, where men began to search for rational principles of social organization apart from mere authority and tradition, whether secular or religious.

Thus, in the sixteenth and seventeenth centuries, a voluminous political literature addressed itself to the nature of political obligation, the basic character and origin of the state, to the questions of power and of right and wrong, all conceived in a new way.

Most of this writing, whether or not explicitly identified with the so-called School of Natural Law, tended to be "naturalistic," and included thinkers as diverse as Niccolo Machiavelli, Jean Bodin, Hugo Grotius, Thomas Hobbes, John Locke, and Baron de Montesquieu.

Certainly all of these thinkers had different normative ideas as to what the political order *ought* to be like. But they all attempted to construct their political-philosophical systems on the basis of what they believed "is" rather than what "ought" to be. Although they differed in their views about the place of God and religion in man's world, their idea-systems were all basically secular. That is, they all assumed a regularity of cause-effect relationships in the political world which—whether they were divinely created or not—were analogous to the Newtonian laws of the physical world. In the last analysis, they were as applicable and understandable for an atheist as for a believer. They ultimately depended on the evidence of human reason or experience, or both, rather than on mystery, Divine revelation, or the scholastic authority of the sages.

The confluence of technology, science, literature, and philosophic speculation led to an age of intellectual greatness in Europe in the eighteenth-century period of the so-called Enlightenment. There again, "cause" and "effect" became intertwined. To be sure, the great thinkers and writers of this age pursued their activities in response to a new, unheard of scale of popular demand. More people could now read books than ever before. Newspapers and magazines were increasingly popular. Hundreds of scientific and cultural societies, circles, and associations were being established. An ever-increasing, affluent middle class eagerly purchased all sorts of reading matter, from popular dictionaries to abstract scholarly journals. But the men who catered to this demand for the printed word did not simply react. They shaped the ideas, ideals, and expectations of their publics. Among those who thus most famously revolutionized the belief-systems of their readers were the *philosophes* of the Great French Encyclopedia published in 17 volumes between 1751 and 1772 in Paris by Denis Diderot.[10] In various forms these men expressed the ideas of the great revolutions of their age. They received inspiration from the English Revolutions of 1642 and 1689, and they provided the intellectual ammunition for the American Revolution of 1775 and the forthcoming Great French Revolution of 1789. They disseminated sundry subversive ideas about individual liberty, freedom of conscience, deism and atheism, constitutionalism, republicanism, limited government, laissez-faire, enlightened despotism and, most characteristically of the age, a striking faith in human progress through science, technology, and learning.[11] There was hardly a subject of human concern in the eighteenth century in which the Encyclopedists did not profoundly challenge the accumulated traditions of church, state, and society of their time.

In addition to the intellectual mobilization of the time, uprooting from old ways and the adoption of new ones was furthered by the dramatic progress of the Industrial Revolution. Here, too, the process was very

[10] See John G. Hibben, *The Philosophy of the Enlightenment* (New York: Scribner's, 1910); Ernst Cassirer, *The Philosophy of the Enlightenment* (Princeton: Princeton University Press, 1951); Isaiah Berlin, *The Age of Enlightenment* (Boston: Houghton Mifflin, 1956); Harold Nicolson, *The Age of Reason, 1700–1789* (London: Constable, 1960); Louis L. Snyder, *The Age of Reason* (New York: Van Nostrand, 1955).

[11] The quintessence of eighteenth-century optimistic rationalism is expressed by Marquis de Condorcet (1743–1794). He envisioned the abolition of inequality among nations; great progress toward egalitarianism within; and the increasing "perfection of mankind" including eradication of poverty, emancipation of women, abundant welfare and education to all, fully democratic and tolerant rule, and world government preceded by development of a universal language. See his *Sketch for a Historical Picture of the Human Mind*, trans. by J. Barraclough, introd. by S. Hampshire (London: Weidenfeld and Nicholson, 1955), particularly pp. 172–202.

much a cultivation of already established tendencies, the product of past changes and inventions.

In the eighteenth century the great commercial wealth that had accumulated since the Middle Ages now harnessed the power of machines to vastly augment the production and exchange of goods and services. Beginning with England, which was favored by abundant capital as well as the resources of coal and iron, the Industrial Revolution swept the world within a century. It came first to the textile industry where the combination of steam-powered machinery and large-scale production caused an enormous increase in the output and profit of the clothes-making establishments. The successive eighteenth-century inventions of men like Kay, Hargreaves, Crompton, Cartwright, and Eli Whitney all furthered this process. Between 1730 and 1815, British import of raw cotton rose from 1.5 to 100 million pounds. The productiveness of labor was vastly increased, and the use of steam-powered machinery on a large scale spread to other branches of the economy. By the early 1820's the factory system was already well established in England. The spinning wheel and the hand loom gave way to machines. Horses, oxen, and water mills were replaced by steam engines. The revolution in manufactures had widespread impact. Technologically, for example, it was closely linked with a revolution in transportation and communications. In England, a network of canals, roads, and railways soon changed the face of the countryside. According to Robert Ergang, between 1760 and 1774, the British Parliament passed 524 acts dealing with road construction and 89 acts dealing with canals between 1790 and 1794.[12]

The consequent changes in agriculture and, more generally, in the society-at-large were enormous and profoundly traumatic. In the wake of these developments came massive urbanization; great population increases; accumulation of even greater wealth; diffusion of still newer learning and skills; rise of new social classes: workers, white and blue collar employees, bureaucrats; and the growth of powerful criticism of social conditions, hitherto accepted dogmas, and traditional authorities.

When James I ascended the throne of England in 1603, the doctrine of the Divine Right of Kings, which he espoused, was still far from a preposterous royal usurpation, even in Great Britain. Its difficulty was that the processes of social change, begun well before James' accession, were making the doctrine increasingly untenable. The revolution directed against his successor, Charles I, culminating in the victory of Oliver Cromwell

---

[12] See Robert Ergang, *Europe, from the Renaissance to Waterloo* (Boston: D.C. Heath, 1954), p. 563.

and the execution of the king in 1649, reflected profound social as well as political change. The middle class, which sought royal protection in the late middle ages and the Renaissance, now chafed under it. It had now grown vigorous and self-confident and was unwilling to continue playing the role of a mere object or even that of a subordinate in political decisions affecting its welfare.

In Britain the restoration of Charles II in 1660 was but a short-lived pause in the process of this revolution. It was ultimately consummated in 1689 with the flight of James II, the accession of William and Mary of Orange, the passage of the Bill of Rights of 1689, and the so-called Settlement Act of 1701, vesting power of conveying the crown itself in Parliament.

Britain pioneered the course of the new age both economically and politically. Middle class revolutions against royal absolutism were soon occurring elsewhere, and the consequences of pervasive social change were being translated into spectacular political upheavals. The ideas and slogans of democracy were major manifestations of new social trends, and so were the ideals of socialism and nationalism. Each represented a response to particular changes and new problems in the European societies.

The ideology of democracy signaled the growing importance of the individual, his capacities and his aspirations, as opposed to traditional, collective, status-bound authorities, secular and religious. It also reflected the increasing mass dimension of politics in its emphasis upon the notion of popular sovereignty. Put in different terms, democracy or democratic liberalism was the emergent orientation toward what we could call today majority rule and the protection of individual rights by the state. It was an ideology which, increasingly since Britain's Glorious Revolution, sought to justify political power in essentially secular terms, as derived from and subject to the people. Concern for legal and political freedom, and legal and political equality among citizens, became the distinguishing features of this orientation.

In the seventeenth and eighteenth centuries, freedom—from restraint and oppression—became a rallying cry for new strata of enterprising men. Their concern was with the apparent opportunities and abundance implicit in trade, industry, technology, and science. These were seen as restricted by the rigid, arbitrary, and traditional religious and secular powers, first by anarchical noblemen and second by capricious, hereditary monarchs. The concerns of these men were practical and secular, even if their optimism was occasionally visionary.[13]

13 See H. N. Brailsford, *The Levellers and the English Revolution* (Stanford: Stanford University Press, 1961), pp. 523–539, on the claims of the democratically minded British "Levellers" of the 1640's: universal male suffrage (except for pau-

While the importance of these new middle class elements in royal bureaucracies steadily increased in England, France, and other countries in the sixteenth and seventeenth centuries, the remaining traditional perquisites of the landed nobility came to be resented more than ever. To the prosperous and energetic bourgeois, the noble seemed a useless relic of a bygone era. His remaining political and legal privileges seemed to his middle class competitors sheer and intolerable usurpation.

Thus the old political order was assailed by new social forces with essentially secular slogans of "popular sovereignty," "liberty," and "equality." It seemed unreasonable to the rising, capable, hard-working bourgeois that public offices should be given to men simply because of noble birth rather than merit; or that significant power should remain in the hands of people who were apparently neither talented, productive, nor useful but merely "well-born." It seemed unreasonable that legal privileges on behalf of such men should constitute obstacles to "progress"—to the free purchase and sale of land; to the unencumbered passage of goods from one part of a country to another; to the open employment of labor from agriculture to industry and to commerce. Popular sovereignty, liberty, and equality became the rallying cries of middle class revolutionists. They gave a sense of direction and self-justification to the revolutionary elements. They also tended to bring together all those popular forces which, having gained some measure of social-political awareness, perceived a mutual interest in the support of these newly articulated values. They helped to unify in one revolutionary direction diverse social, economic, religious, and political interests whose common denominator was that they were all "outs" trying to replace the "ins." More than that, they needed to discredit the values of a system that they found discriminatory and untenable. They also needed to establish an alternative, appropriate value-system upon which an alternative decision-making mechanism, or political structure, could be based.[14]

Thus the slogans that characterized the French Revolution of 1789—

pers . . .); equality before the law; religious tolerance; abolition of monopolies and of consumption taxes; freedom of the press and publicly provided primary schools and hospital health care, were among their modern-sounding demands. A forerunner of contemporary communism was Gerrard Winstanley's radical "Digger" following; see L. H. Bere's, *The Digger Movement in the Days of the Commonwealth* (London: Holland and Mertin, 1961), and George H. Sabine, *The Works of Gerrard Winstanley* (New York: Russell and Russell, 1965).

[14] As D. W. Brogan writes in his *Price of Revolution* (London: Hamilton, 1952), the strength of nationalism lies in "its provision of a political home . . . a sense of kinship, not merely membership. A nation is a family not an institution" (p. 110). "In all the great revolutions ideologies have served to cement, or better yet, galvanize, all sorts of heterogeneous social elements." Compare p. 3.

Liberty, Equality, Fraternity—were in a sense coalitional devices through which all sorts of aggrieved "have-nots," some prosperous, some poor, some urban, some rural, could all politically combine.

But behind broad slogans and wide coalitions there were inevitably significant cleavages. These are reflected in the different meanings and emphases in the political thought of the Age of Reason, and hence given to the "core themes" of democratic ideology. What precisely was the meaning of "popular sovereignty"? Did it mean government directly by the people or government by the people's representatives? If the latter, then how and by what sort of representation? Was it merely a slogan or a practical idea? How important was the notion of popular sovereignty itself compared with some of the other characteristic democratic themes —equality and liberty for the individual? Indeed, was popular sovereignty *reconcilable* with individual right to equality and freedom or was it possibly a new form of tyranny and privilege exercised by a majority? Who were the "people" or "citizens" in whom ultimate power should properly reside? Everyone? All adult males? All taxpayers? Property holders as well as paupers? Similarly, the ideals of individual liberty and equality meant different things to different people. How far and in what directions should these principles be extended? Was legal and political equality for all men, without any qualifications, a desirable and a practical objective? Was legal and political equality enough, or was it perhaps but a prologue to a more important economic and social equality as well? Was liberty desirable only insofar as men could distinguish between "freedom" and "license"—a condition of true liberty under law, guaranteeing the safety and security of all on the one hand, and an unbridled anarchy of "catch-as-catch-can" on the other? To these questions, different answers have been provided in the course of history. The democratic tradition has had diverse spokesmen and interpreters, and wide differences among its several branches.

The concerns with freedom, equality, and popular sovereignty received some radical, sweeping interpretations and some very guarded and conservative ones. Thus, a "democrat" for whom a very narrowly defined concept of individual liberty was much more important than the power-to-the people principle might be barely distinguishable from a conservative proponent of enlightened despotism. A radical democrat for whom equality could know no bounds might be practically indistinguishable from a socialist. This problem of ideological overlaps brings us to a consideration of the other traditions.

Alongside an emergent democratic ideology in the eighteenth century developed other ideological responses (and subsequently also shapers) of social change, notably socialism and nationalism.

The material and cultural changes in Europe accumulating since the

Crusades undoubtedly brought new opportunities and opened fresh vistas to a rising bourgeoisie. They promoted attitudes of optimism and self-confidence, particularly among the men of commerce and science, and understandably led to political ideas that emphasized secular over religious values, individual achievement over traditional status, freedom over passive deference, legal equality and wider diffusion of power away from the hands of seemingly obsolescent monarchs, aristocrats, and priests. But if the impact of the changes with respect to parts of European society may be thus assessed, it was by no means universally applicable to all strata.

The commercial and industrial revolutions that culminated in the flowering of capitalism first in England and then in other European countries had their seamy side. The opportunities of businessmen were frequently the woes of the workers.

Poor farmers were being displaced from the lands which they and their families had tilled for generations, crowded into ramshackle, slumlike rural areas, and compressed into large industrial armies anonymously turning out products for unseen capitalist employers. The lot of these people—no longer able to earn a livelihood in the countryside against the competition of the larger, richer, more efficient "capitalist" farmers—was frequently one of abysmal poverty, social degradation, and uprooting from familiar surroundings to a life spent in dingy, dreary sweatshops, mines, and the slum dwellings of factory towns. The opportunities for leisure, for education, health care, and cultural development often associated with urban life were largely denied to these new proletarians, as Karl Marx called them. Their conditions of work and their meager incomes made the age of Industrial Revolution a nightmare for millions of workingmen.[15] And it was no less so for the urban and rural unemployed. For these people, unable in "bad times "to fall back on the land as even a medieval serf could, there was little alternative between factory employment and starvation. Yet the very freedom of the private businessman to hire and fire whomever he wanted, as and when he wanted, turned countless people into society's unwanted orphans. Driven from the land and denied employment, they were left with no recourse against entrepreneurs whose essentially personal concerns sometimes led them to refuse workers jobs or pay them as little as competition for labor would allow. The fortunes of some of the more successful bourgeois stood in sharp and disturbing contrast to the poverty and despair of workers.

In this social context, the various adaptations of socialist doctrine began

[15] On the industrial and agricultural revolutions, see Arnold Toynbee, *Lectures on the Industrial Revolution of the Eighteenth Century in England* (London: Longmans, Green, 1908); Charles Beard, *The Industrial Revolution* (New York: Greenwood Press, 1969); and J. L. and Barbara Hammond, *The Rise of Modern Industry* (London: Methuen, 1966).

to take root and grow in influence among the masses of people. The special focus of socialist ideology was upon the value of *equality* in material, economic sense rather than merely, if at all, upon political-legal equality, and upon the general importance of material-economic conditions as prerequisites for human, social happiness, freedom, and fulfillment. Certainly, as with democracy, socialism was never one clearly defined doctrine but rather an orientation, a discernible tendency, or perhaps a tradition with numerous branches. Some socialists were men who rejected the changes induced by modern technology and economy and advocated, in various forms, a return to autarky and primitivism as the only feasible means for securing stable equality and satisfactory material conditions of existence to men. Others preached accommodation to change and progress toward still different ("higher") stages of development. To these men, the miseries of their day were seen as a necessary price to be paid for a future happiness. They believed that industrial technology would bring about an abundance that would be eventually justly distributed. Some believed that socialism is, and ought to be, a logical extension of democracy, proceeding from formal-legal to economic and social equality for all men. Still others rejected the political tradition of democracy as barren of the promise of true social justice—inherently incapable of achieving true, material equality. They regarded all political forms and systems of the exploiters, whether royal, noble or, above all, bourgeois, as equally enslaving and hypocritical in any talk about "freedom," "equality," and the like.

Just as in the democratic tradition there has always been a variance in the interpretations of the precise nature and limits of basic concepts, so also among "socialists" the meaning of equality and its relationship to individual freedom and to the exercise of political power has varied. Indeed, socialism has been characterized by significant degrees of alienation, acceptance, and rejection of contemporary society. In some versions of the creed, the social world was seen as split up into inexorably antagonistic exploiter and exploited classes; in others, class distinctions were believed to involve much less hopeless antagonisms, and in some they played hardly any role at all. Thus, men of similar orientation—toward making society economically more equitable for each and every member of it—have run the gamut of hope and despair, withdrawal and collaboration, reform through persuasion and revolution through violence.

If the implicit tendency of the democratic tradition was to unshackle the individual and, somehow, to make him collectively the source of political power, socialism represented still another response to the new conditions of European life. It sought to impose a policy direction on society, which to some people appeared as simply one step further on the road to democracy or "more" democracy—that is, toward a "true" liberty, a "true" fraternity and, above all, a "true" equality; to others, however, socialist ideas of economic equality, with overtones of collective enforcement, seemed incompatible with individual freedom; still others viewed social-ism as an attempt to reintegrate society atomized into a chaos of indi-vidual bits and pieces by the very doctrines of liberal democracy and the operations of a free-for-all, capitalist economy.

If, however, socialism was an attempt to reintegrate society, it was an attempt from the "Left." The cooperative world with which it sought to replace the competitive world of capitalism and liberalism was to be brought about by a redistribution of wealth between the "haves" and the "have-nots." It required the accomplishment, in one way or another, of substantial social and economic changes. Soon it was joined by a reinte-grative attempt from the "Right"—that is, from those who wanted to control social and economic upheaval rather than spread it. These ele-ments deplored the alleged chaos and the capricious, destructive self-seeking of capitalism and liberalism. They resented the seeming triumph of materialism and egoism over spiritualism and tradition. They viewed the efforts of socialists to bridle the "capitalist anarchy of self-seeking" as misdirected, pernicious, and untenable. The socialist remedy was seen as unsatisfactory and often even worse than democracy.

From the nationalist point of view, socialism divided society into war-ring camps of "haves" against "have-nots," thus attacking a larger unity that ought to exist among men: the unity of nation. The nationalists sought to integrate society above the "predatory" level of class, group, or individual self-interests onto an allegedly higher plane of one common, national interest. At the beginning of the nineteenth century, nationalism was, in large measure, closely identified with democracy. The vision of the nation was also a vision of the People-in-Arms. It evoked the images of the common people of France rallying *en masse,* to the defense of the Revolution of 1789 against foreign tyrant-aggressors. It was a vision of Everyone as a member of the Nation, and the nation, as the greatest and most sacred of man's social identifications, the proper repository of highest human allegiance.

In both its progressive and its reactionary forms, nationalism was linked to democracy, and was a response to the conditions of social mobilization in Europe just as much as socialism and democracy. All of these doctrines addressed themselves to the emergence of a new politics, the arrival of the common man, as it were, weaned and secularized away from the stabilizing (even if, as some would argue, ossifying) traditions of religion, economy, and society. All addressed themselves to the central question of man's new place in the scheme of governance. Democracy and socialism both accentuated the challenge to tradition and status quo by a variety of means; both made man, his earthly welfare, the measure of all things. Nationalism, however, moved in another direction. It accepted the new popular character of politics but increasingly it tended to appropriate its images and its style in order to reestablish traditions and hierarchies, not to abolish them. Above all, even in its most democratic varieties, nationalism, unlike democracy and socialism, was largely transcendental. It made certain symbols and ideals that were external to man the focus of highest loyalties. The happiness of the fatherland and its interest were invariably regarded as worthy of ultimate human sacrifice. The collective national interest, rather than individual happiness (even in a proximate sense), was the supreme value of nationalism, regardless of how open its view was of who constituted the "nation." Thus, the relatively progressive and democratically oriented nationalists stood together with their more reactionary brethren in terms of common transcendental goals. For conservative nationalists, who became increasingly significant in the course of the nineteenth century, the formula of a "nation" became a means for sanctifying old traditions and old hierarchies in a new way. If religious piety, reverence for custom, and popular inertia were no longer adequate to furnish support to kings, nobles, priests, and institutions of property, this might still be made feasible on a new basis—by appealing to a powerful secular ideal of common national identity which, in turn, would sanction these very same hierarchies, institutions, and traditions. It could all be done in the name of the fatherland. Even a rudimentary definition of what nationalists mean by a "nation" is difficult; probably more so than rudimentary conceptions of democracy and socialism. For many of its adherents, the idea of "nation" all but defies definition. It involves the conception of a collective, enduring personality whose attributes are, in any given case, unique and permeated with mystery. In part, at least, it has generally meant a human collectivity linked by ties of history, culture, ethnic lineage, language, religion, and even purpose, into a unity conscious of a common past and a common future, conscious of belonging together. For most nationalists, this consciousness has always been more important than any one set of factors from which it might conceivably derive—hence its somewhat subjective, mystic character. Occasionally, it has existed with only some of the attitudes we have listed but not others.

CHAPTER **3**

Liberal Democracy

Destined to become the most secular and pragmatic of the great doctrines, democracy, as an ideology of the masses, emerged paradoxically from the womb of the medieval church. The ideals of political democracy were always implicit, and long dormant, in church doctrine. The struggle to vindicate popular rule and individual freedom began historically in the realm of the universal, medieval church rather than in the realm of the secular state.

In the tradition of the Bible, since the time of Moses, all men have been seen as equal in the fundamental sense of their relationship to the common creator, God, and in terms of their reciprocal brotherly obligations to one another. As God's creatures and as subjects of his divine will and law, men have been held fundamentally alike whether they were priest, shepherd, or king. To be sure, in earthly life there were many distinctions of rank, status, wealth, and the like; but these were regarded as relatively secondary differences in the here-and-now, infinitely secondary to the universal and equal laws by which God created, maintained, and judged human life. In the legacy of Judeo-Christian tradition, men have been seen as rational beings endowed with the ability to assure their physical survival, maintain communities, contribute to the welfare and betterment of others, and distinguish between right and wrong and between truth and falsehood; with a capacity for compassion, and the ability to pursue virtue and truth in accordance with a divine purpose. By the fact of divine creation and by the nature of their intellectual and spiritual attributes, men were seen as partaking of the sacred worth or value of Divinity itself. What they did and thought as individuals was believed to be of profound importance to God. Each soul was seen as infinitely valuable and capable of an eternal life. Man was the pinnacle of divine creation; violence and abuse directed against man was indirectly thought to be outrage against God.

Not only has there been great emphasis on the value and uniqueness of the individual in the Judeo-Christian tradition but also the notions of man's rationality and value were complemented by an ideal of freedom. The moral man was one who did right not only because he could distinguish between right and wrong but also because he freely chose good over evil and truth over falsehood. The righteous were those who, above all, willed and believed in the right, not those who simply succumbed to force or custom. Freedom to choose was at once the paradox and salient characteristic of the Judeo-Christian tradition. In practice, however, much of this ideological heritage of democracy lay dormant in western Christendom until the period of the Reformation, and the ascendance of a powerful middle class.

Although the doctrine of Judaism and Christianity can and have been used in justification of democratic egalitarianism, much of religious teaching and practice discouraged it. Religious institutions emphasized the role of priestly hierarchy, the sacredness of elaborate rituals, and the preponderant value of an "other-worldly" orientation. To the extent that religious leaders succeeded in convincing people that an afterlife was really more important than the here-and-now, they promoted indifference and acquiescence in contemporary social conditions. The miseries of men's secular, everyday lives were made to seem but a short and all but irrelevant purgatory on the way to a higher destiny beyond. Thus the thrust of religious teaching, as opposed to some of the underlying dogma, was socially quietist rather than activist. Understandably, these practices offended radical reformers and spokesmen of the poor. It was not until the stirrings produced by the economic, cultural, and technological change in the late Middle Ages that the revolutionary, egalitarian potential of religion began to manifest itself.

It was men like Marsiglio of Padua, John Hus, Jean Calvin, and John Knox, among many others, who began to invoke the themes of religious individualism, egalitarianism, and freedom against the monolith of established church authority. But their efforts had far-reaching political consequences, producing what might be called today spill-over-effects. They influenced, and as some saw it, contaminated the political world, too.

The political "dynamite" of Marsiglio's thought, for example, may be appreciated from the following brief extracts from his writings.

On the church:

". . . no bishop or pope can have coercive jurisdiction in this world over any priest or layman unless this is granted to him by a human legislator, in whose power it always remains to revoke this if any reasonable course arises."

On the state:

"The legislator . . . is the people or the whole body of citizens or their weightier part . . . . human legislative authority belongs only to the whole body of citizens or its weightier part . . . acting itself directly or (in trust) to some one or to several. . . ."[1]

It was not until the decline of the medieval church that the ideology of democracy became what might be termed a product of mass consumption. In the words of a famed historian of political ideas, George H. Sabine,

"The discussion of (church reform) may . . . be called the first great movement of popular education."[2]

Opposition to papal power, combined with attempts to find a truly just and proper basis for religious authority, led, in fourteenth-century Europe, to important secular political consequences. The arguments first deliberately and explicitly applied to religious rulers were soon adapted by others to challenge secular rulers as well. In the fifteenth and sixteenth centuries, the momentum of religious reform increased throughout Europe, and its impact on politics grew more direct and formidable. Two themes implicitly dominated religious onslaught on traditional authority: a belief in the essential autonomy of individual conscience, and the conviction that the best foundation for authority in an imperfect world lay with the people in general. Thus, if we but keep in mind the different context of their approach, we find Renaissance churchmen as the first *spokesmen* popularizers of two essentially democratic notions—individual liberty and popular sovereignty (or majority rule and minority rights, in still different words).

The religious notions of church reformers received some specifically political interpretations during the Wars of Religion in France; in the famed *Vindiciae Contra Tyrannos*, an anonymous Huguenot writer defended the religion and civil liberty of subjects against the tyrannical authority of kings.[3] This treatise and subsequent works of the period,

---

[1] Cited from "Defensor Pacis" by W. Y. Elliott and Neil A. McDonald in *Western Political Heritage* (Englewood Cliffs, N.J.: Prentice-Hall, 1957), pp. 312–13, 316.

[2] *A History of Political Theory* (New York: Henry Holt, 1950), p. 314.

[3] On the political tracts of the Age of Reformation in Europe, see J. W. Allen, *A History of Political Thought in the Sixteenth Century* (London: Methuen, 1960). Harold J. Laski (ed.), *A Defence of Liberty Against Tyrants: A Translation of the*

both Protestant and Catholic, developed some of the explicit foundations of a democratic political ideology. They emphasized the theme that the power to govern was one which emanated from the entire body of the people, and that it could be rightfully exercised only as a trust on behalf of the whole people. In a practical sense, churchmen, both Protestant and Catholic, were frequently interested in limiting the sphere of political power so as to prevent persecution by hostile rulers (those who happened to be anti-Catholic or anti-Protestant, as the case might be). The search for safety from persecution thus led to the formulation of a "contract theory" of government; it was assumed that the ends of political power derived from an original agreement between people and ruler, which was limited in nature, and was rationally deducible in the absence of any concrete historical evidence. Government was worthy of obedience *only* if it acted in pursuance of the legitimate limits of its power—the boundary of its presumed contract.

In some cases, notably in that of Martin Luther,[4] the protection afforded the reformer by the princes of Germany led him to abjure all appeal to the people. Luther, suspicious and fearful of the "rabble," looked down on popular power and counseled unconditional obedience to the secular rulers, whom he regarded as far wiser guardians of community than the ignorant and rapacious masses. Even in Luther's case, however, Protestantism made a highly characteristic contribution to the developing ideology of democracy by its emphasis on the sanctity and autonomy of the individual conscience. In spite of Luther's own personal, overtly political views, his ideal of religious liberty, his appeal to the conscience of each human being, had profoundly libertarian implications.

Vindiciae Contra Tyrannos by Junius Brutus (Gloucester, Mass.: Peter Smith, 1963). The authorship of the *Vindiciae* is uncertain and has been variously attributed to Duplessis-Mornay, Beza, Languet, Hotman, and Robert Parsons. Laski believes that the evidence favors Duplessis-Mornay (pp. 57–59). The work was composed at an unknown date, probably between 1574–1576, and probably published in 1579 (p. 58 fin); see also Julian H. Franklin (ed.), *Constitutionalism and Resistance in the Sixteenth Century; Three Treatises by Hotman, Beza and Mornay* (New York: Pegasus, 1969); and James MacKinnon, *Calvin and the Reformation* (New York: Russell and Russell, 1962).

[4] On Martin Luther, see L. M. Waring, *The Political Theories of Martin Luther* (New York: Kennikat Press, 1968). On Jean Bodin (1529–1596), advocate of secular sovereignty in the face of religious strife of his time, see Jean Bodin, *Six Books of the Commonwealth*, abridged and trans. by M. J. Tooley (Oxford: Blackwell, 1955), and Julian H. Franklin, *Jean Bodin and the Sixteenth-Century Revolution in the Methodology of Law and History* (New York: Columbia University Press, 1963). As Waring remarks, for Luther, "each man must determine the meaning of the word for himself. And the inevitable result of this principle is individual liberty" (p. 235). Compare his conclusion, p. 281.

A sphere of spiritual, moral, and intellectual life of man was regarded as lying outside the writ of any earthly authority, political, religious, or whatever. It represented a realm of freedom in which the important element was not any law, custom, or ritual but the subjective perceptions, preferences, and ultimately faith of each man standing in a private relationship to God.

In this respect—in the area of private and individual rights—the Protestant Reformation stimulated the development of secular political counterparts to a religious "private sphere." It thus supported the notion and the cause of "limited government."

Adapted by secular philosophers, of whom the most famous was undoubtedly England's John Locke (1632–1704), the contract theory of government provided a framework of characteristic democratic ideals. The contract was always a fiction since no one could prove when and how government was originally established in any given polity. But the ideal itself was reasonably clear and highly significant. The nature of political power, to the extent that it was proper and legitimate rather than tyrannical, was seen as confined to the performance of certain minimal tasks. As in Locke's version, government was supposed to protect the property and lives of its subjects, provide mechanisms for settling disputes, keep the peace, and defend the polity from external enemies. Beyond these functions, it was supposed to let the people live as they saw fit, with a bare minimum of interference and regulation. The powers of government were all regarded as *instrumental* or justified solely by the concrete ends which they were designed to realize. Power for the sake of power, or for grandeur, or for the imposition of religious ideals, or indeed for any but those tasks necessary to the execution of the original compact was rejected. Certainly, the principles of the compact themselves could never be historically ascertained; they were believed to be discoverable by the agency of human reason. In fact, they were, as with Locke and his American disciple, Thomas Jefferson, widely associated in the eighteenth century with a revived version of a law of nature.

Traceable to Greek and Roman times, and particularly to the Stoic school of philosophy, the concept of natural law contributed a familiar theme to the subsequent treasury of democratic thought, "the law behind the law," as Professor William Ebenstein has called it.[5] In this

---

[5] On the conception of "law behind the law," cf. William Ebenstein, *Today's Isms*, 3rd ed. (Englewood Cliffs, N.J.: Prentice-Hall, 1961), pp. 128–131. On the conception of "natural law" see also Otto Gierke, *Natural Law and the Theory of Society*, trans. by Ernest Barker (Cambridge: University Press, 1934); Carl Becker, *The Declaration of Independence: A Study in the History of Political Ideas* (New York: A. A. Knopf, 1942); Charles G. Haines, *The Revival of Natural Law Concepts* (New York: Russell

conception, all human regulations, ordinances, and decrees are judged in relation to a higher law, an immanent criterion of true justice among men. In the theory of natural law, the validity and value of the actual human laws were judged in the prespective of a higher standard, one that was not spelled out in statute books or court cases, or dictated by local customs, but one representing universal maxims of human conduct. Thus, given particular circumstances, *right reason* would dictate the proper conduct to any well-ordered mind in the world, anywhere, at any time. Insofar as this law of nature related to man and society, it could be called the ultimate moral law. Democratic theory not only appropriated the concept of natural law but also in the theory of John Locke, made it the touchstone of legal legitimacy. An individual's obligation to obey a law, or a government that issued the law, was contingent upon its adherence to the precepts of the law of nature.

This persistent theme in the ideology of liberal democracy has had important practical legal manifestations. In Britain, for example, a fundamental and long-observed principle of the legal system has been the accountability of public officials for wrongs done to others, *even if* these wrongs were done at the explicit command of a duly constituted higher authority. What mattered was not "who gave the order," but whether the order was "lawful" on its own merits.[6] Those who violated the legitimate boundaries of political power, implicit in the contract for the governance of a community, and those who transgressed the laws of nature in the exercise of power, were not entitled to citizens' obedience. They were contract-breakers against whom it was just and rightful to revolt. There was a sphere of private, individual rights with which government could not interfere. Some human rights were so basic and fundamental that their violation nullified the contract whereby rulers rule and subjects obey. Indeed, the denial of these rights necessitated the invocation of the very ultimate right of social self-preservation: the right of revolution.

What began with thirteenth- and fourteenth-century church reformers as insistence on the autonomy of individual conscience and the rights of religious liberty against papal authority, became in the seventeenth

and Russell, 1965); Thomas McPherson *Political Obligation*, (London: Routledge and Kegan Paul, 1965); Yves R. M. Simon, *The Tradition of Natural Law* (New York: Fordham University Press, 1965); Leo Strauss, *Natural Right and History* (Chicago: University of Chicago Press, 1953).

6 See A. V. Dicey, *Introduction to the Study of the Law of the Constitution*, 8th ed. (London: Macmillan, 1926), p. 298: "When a soldier is put on trial on a charge of crime, obedience to superior orders is not of itself a defense." Compare W. Ivor Jennings, *The Law and the Constitution*, 4th ed. (London: University of London Press, 1952), p. 211.

century a secular insistence of middle class philosophers on the sacred rights of property and tolerance of political dissent. The challenge to the papacy gradually engulfed monarchy as well. Just as papal authority could not survive the cultural changes of the Renaissance without challenge, so royal power in Europe, comfortably mercantilist and domineering in sixteenth-century England, was challenged in the seventeenth by an even more virile, confident middle class. In the Middle Ages, merchants looked to kings for protection against nobles and brigands. They welcomed the extension of political power under royal auspices. Grown rich, numerous, and confident in the seventeenth and eighteenth centuries, the mechant bourgeoisie of western Europe resented the remaining shackles of that power, and it believed increasingly in its own capacity to govern. It demanded freedom from restraint where once it called for paternalistic protection.

In the seventeenth century, the concern with individual well-being as the basis for the political order was so dominant, that it even constituted, paradoxically, the foundation of a philosophy of secular absolutism advanced by Thomas Hobbes in England in his famed *Leviathan*.[7] Above all, it culminated in the development of democracy.

The term "democracy" derives from a Greek word meaning rule by the people. Democratic ideology is, in essence, a mosaic of questions and answers accumulated over a long period of time about the nature and uses of political power. It is united by a number of common theories but with wide variations among and between them. What we can do here is simply to sample and illustrate the universe of a broad and rich political tradition.

Probably the most common formula of the democratic ideology is that democracy means "majority rule with minority rights."

This admittedly elementary and ambiguous statement combines two crucial propositions about (1) *who* shall rule and (2) *how*. Presumably, a majority should make decisions for the whole community, but somehow this majority ought to respect the rights of those who are outweighed or outvoted in the process of making decisions.

---

7 On Thomas Hobbes (1588–1679), see his own *Behemoth: The History of the Causes of the Civil Wars in England*, ed. by William Molesworth (New York: B. Franklin, 1963); *De Cive* ed. by Sterling P. Lamprecht (New York, Appleton-Century-Crofts, 1949); *Leviathan* (Baltimore: Penguin, 1968); and, among many secondary sources, Crawford B. Macpherson, *The Political Theory of Possessive Individualism: Hobbes to Locke* (Oxford: Clarendon Press, 1962); Eugene J. Roesch, *The Totalitarian Threat: The Fruition of Modern Individualism as Seen in Hobbes and Rousseau* (New York: Philosophical Library, 1963); Howard Warrender, *The Political Philosophy of Hobbes* (Oxford: Clarendon Press, 1957).

Note that there is nothing at all in this formula about the *ends* which political decisions ought to seek. The two components of majority rule and minority rights both need much explaining, before we can apply them to "real-life" situations. Who, for example, qualifies as a citizen or voter in a given collectivity? Unless we know the answer to this question, we clearly cannot tell what a majority means. Is it, for example, a majority of all men, women, property owners, or "adults"? Is majority rule applicable to decisions in all human collectivities on all issues that are really "political" rather than say "technical," "scientific," or "economic"? What "rights" of minorities must the majority respect? Does this statement refer to some specific rights, or is it rather a broad injunction for self-restraint on the part of all possible majorities? Finally, what about the resolution of conflicts between these two conceivably clashing principles? What if the majority does not respect the rights of a minority? At what point in its disregard of these rights does a collectivity cease being a "democracy"? How can we determine on any given issue that "rights" are being disregarded, apart from claims voiced by the winners on one side, and the losers on the other? In each case, mechanisms and standards for deciding such questions are necessary.

When Thomas Jefferson wrote in the 1776 *Declaration of Independence* that "all men are created equal," he was not only stating one of the oldest themes of democracy but also supplying the historic rationale for the principle of majority rule. The justification for making decisions by recourse to prevalent public opinion—the opinion of a majority—is based on the belief that human beings are, in some essential, fundamental sense, equal. Given this assumption of equality, the votes of three men must always amount to *more* than the votes of two in the same sense that three coins of the same denomination or three packages of the same weight are always "more" than one, two, or two and a half.

However, if we grant that men are equal in *some* supremely important, overriding sense, this would be enough to suggest that no person in the world has a *greater* right to govern others, and to make decisions for them, than anyone else. The logical implications of such a condition, however, fall short of "majoritarianism."

Perhaps *no* person should decide anything for anyone else; if all are equal, each must make his own decision in his own way. Perhaps decisions could only be made by the unanimous consent of all persons in the collectivity. These, in part, are the conclusions of philosophical anarchists based on the purest premise of equality. The proposition that a majority should always have its way requires *additional* premises which may be legitimately regarded as qualifying the principle of "equality."

If the views of X are really inherently as valuable as those of Y, how can we allow Y to prevail over X simply because more people agree with Y? But an additional premise of democratic ideology has usually been that people exist in collectivities, which *must* be ruled according to some shared laws and toward some shared objectives. The absence of common rules and ends is regarded as undesirable if not impossible. Thus the need to make rules and to enforce decisions, for and upon others, is usually taken as an important foundation of any and every human society. In this qualified context, the rule of numbers, of majority over minority, given the fundamental equality of all, appears simply as the least arbitrary way of governing others.

The principle receives still other support from most democratic theorists. If we assumed that all human beings were "equal" but also fundamentally vicious, destructive, and aggressive, the right of a majority to govern the community would be a dubious, if not even an absurd value. It would certainly be no better than anarchy, for men would simply destroy one another in an organized way as readily, if not more so, as they might destroy themselves each on his own. Traditionally, however, democratic ideology combines beliefs in human equality with other positive, optimistic views of man. In common with many religions, including the Jewish and Christian traditions, it holds the view that men are not only equal but that they are capable of cooperating with one another in ways that enhance the welfare of each and of all. Stated in one way, it means that man is "good"; that he possesses certain intellectual and moral attributes for a fruitful social life with shared means and shared ends.

Finally, we should note the most important element, symbolism and, simultaneously, problem in democratic ideology—the Democratic Man. Despite some discouraging results of modern survey research about people as thoughtful, involved political participants, the most fundamental faith and hope of the democrat is in an idealized "average man" and in the collectivity of the "People." The wisdom and virtue of the ordinary individual, multiplied by millions, is at the root of democratic optimism about freedom and, above all, the possibilities of self-government. Ignorance, tyranny, and other causes may only temporarily submerge the democratic man. Both practically and theoretically, democracy would not be viable if people generally did not, at least sometimes, take an active interest in political affairs, if they did not inform themselves about or participate in social and political decision-making. Obviously, elections would not mean much without some candidates, some voters, some issues, or audiences. The number is debatable. Democratic ideology usually assumes that men can tell right from wrong, and that they can choose wisely from among alternatives presented to them by experts, politicians and occasionally pranksters and crooks. It also usually assumes that people care about freedom and will if necessary struggle and suffer for it. If they neither care nor struggle, the democrat faces some real dilemmas.

At this point, let us consider some representative examples of the range of democratic liberal theory—different mixtures of the duality of majoritarianism and libertarianism.

A moderate and particularly influential democratic formula was that of Locke, son of a prosperous lawyer who had fought on the side of Parliament against King Charles I in 1642. In 1690, Locke published *Two Treatises of Government* in which he at once attacked the Divine Right of Kingship and the more modern, nonmystical, utilitarian defense of absolutism which Hobbes had worked out. Using the "contract theory" of government popularized by the writers of the Protestant Reformation, Locke argued that:

1. Ultimately all political power inheres in the people, although ordinarily it may be exercised by representative agents of the people.
2. The legitimate power of governments is inherently a limited one, and that—however constituted—government should not trespass on certain basic individual rights of life, liberty and, particularly, property. If it did, the implicit contract between governors and governed—the exchange of citizen obedience for government protection of these rights—was dissolved and, in the absence of redress, a right of revolution devolved upon the people who were being misgoverned.
3. Individual rights were part of the law of nature whose ultimate origin was divine; these rights were prior both in origin and import to the fiduciary obligations of government. On balance, government was to be dedicated to the needs of individuals, not vice versa.

The type of government that Locke suggested for maintaining equilibrium between a popular sovereignty, individual rights, and effective administration may be described as "mixed." Locke advocated combining an elective legislature with a monarchical executive and he favored the separation of the executive and legislative powers of government. Locke combined the notions of immutable individual rights *and* the rule of the majority in the common fabric of the law of nature which, in his view, ultimately dictated a harmonious coexistence of these two values. Thus he argued that:

"The natural liberty of man is to be free from any superior power on earth, and not to be under the will or legislative authority of man, but to have only the law of nature for his rule. The liberty of man *in society* is to be under no other legislative power but that established by the *consent* of the Commonwealth . . . *according to the trust put in it.*"[8]

Within a century, Locke's ideas about politics were complemented by those of Adam Smith in the realm of economics. Smith, who wrote *Wealth of Nations* in 1776, was the foremost exponent of *laissez-faire.* If Locke may be said to have represented the claims of the newly emergent middle classes in the political sphere, Smith represented them in the economic. He opposed mercantilism by which kings had tried to promote national power through the regulation of business, particularly foreign trade. He argued that the best economic decisions, from the standpoint of society as a whole, would be made only if men were generally left to their own devices to produce, buy, and sell whatever they chose as best they could. Free and open competition would, Smith believed, eliminate the wasteful and inefficient producers. Ultimately, economic exchange, if not tampered with by government, would give the advantage to the best endowed, most efficient, industrious, and inherently profitable operations. All would be for the best, if "nature" were allowed to take its course. The best interest of society and the sum of individual self-interests coincided. In Smith's view, as in Locke's, the proper functions of government were few and simple relating principally to national defense, keeping the peace, and providing machinery for adjudicating disputes. Thus, the democratic-liberal state of the eighteenth century was a distinctly limited, noninterventionist one. In an oft-used phrase, as applicable to Smith as to Locke, it was meant to be but a night-watch-man.[9]

Within a century of Smith, that is, by the time of John Stuart Mill and T. H. Green, liberal-democracy had become identified with more activist, social, economic, and cultural policies. The nature of social problems and the clientele of liberal democracy were drastically changing. The self-confident, self-reliant farmers and merchants of the eighteenth century constituted a very different middle class from the managerial bureaucrats and the blue and white collar workers of later times. The Industrial Revolution brought in its wake cataclysmic social and economic problems all but unheard of in the days of the Puritans. Changing social context thus makes the liberal democrat of the eighteenth

8 John Locke, *Treatise of Civil Government,* cited by William Y. Elliott and Neil A. McDonald, *Western Political Heritage* (Englewood Cliffs, N.J., Prentice-Hall, 1957), p. 569. Italics mine.

9 See so-called Physiocrats, French laissez-faire thinkers of the eighteenth century. E.g. Max Beer, *An Inquiry into Physiocracy* (London: Allen and Unwin, 1939); Henry Higgs, *The Physiocrats* (London: Macmillan, 1897); Ronald L. Meek, *The Economics of Physiocracy* (Cambridge: University Press, 1963).

century seem a staunch "conservative" in the twentieth. Among philosophers of the Enlightenment, Jean Jacques Rousseau may be described as standing to the left of Locke by his greater emphasis of the egalitarian power of the majority, and relatively less concern for the rights, property, and privileges of discrete individuals.

Like other democratic ideologues, Rousseau (1712–1778) believed that political power rightfully belongs to the people as a whole, and that consent is the moral foundation of just government. But unlike Locke, he sought to protect the freedom and welfare of each person *not* by specifying the limits of government through the device of natural law, but by a "proper organization" of the governmental power itself. Rousseau articulated the faith of radical democracy in his vision of the liberation of each man through his active and equal participation in the people's self-rule. His most important political writings included the *Discourse on the Origins of Human Inequality*, published in 1755 and, above all, the *Social Contract* of 1762. His scheme of the General Will literally equated legitimate government, indeed the best kind, with self-government. Rousseau passionately condemned power and representing the will of each citizen through some intermediary, whether legislative or executive. His political philosophy was permeated by distrust of elites and experts, and emphasized the essential virtue, goodness, and wisdom of the common man. In Rousseau's view, these human qualities were submerged and all but lost because of the legacy of misgovernment to which man had been subjected. He believed strongly in the therapeutic virtues of radical democracy. The People, properly constituted, that is, within the framework of the General Will, could do no wrong. Their sense of right and prudence was more to be trusted than the judgment of philosophers, scientists, and all those who set themselves up above the average man.

Rousseau's concept was in some respects concrete, yet in some quite abstract. The General Will was the assembly of all the citizens acting as a legislative body equally and generally on behalf of all. But Rousseau stipulated that the General Will was not to be confused with the "will of all." It required the citizens to dedicate themselves to the general, public interest rather than to the pursuit of private ends through public means. The General Will was or had to be, unselfish; it was the quintessence of public spiritedness. Moreover, the object and modes of its actions had to be general and universal laws, equally applicable to all, rather than specific administrative or legal enactments differentiating between X and Y, not in terms of general roles but as individuals. Rousseau was thus, to all appearances, more interested in setting up a standard for the conduct of the sovereign collectivity than in developing a practical model of the state.[10] Rousseau's special penchant for egalitarianism and his equation of freedom with equality have made him an appealing figure and a kind of fountainhead for many radical democrats, anarchists, socialists, as well as nationalists. The notion that the People, if properly organized, could do no wrong fit well into a formula of "All Power to the People"; its appeals have proved long lasting, and are current even today.

Rousseau's mystic regard for the community which somehow enhanced the judgment and spirit of each of its members proved singularly resistant to obsolescence. The arrival of the Industrial Revolution and the Welfare State made no difference to the underlying formula of the General Will. Rousseau did not attempt to second-guess what rights the collectivity would give to or withhold from individuals or what sort of policies it would pursue. The General Will was eternally omnipotent.

Among philosophers who advocated a strongly populist version of democracy was the great utilitarian, Jeremy Bentham (1748–1832). Author of numerous works, among them *Fragment on Government* in 1776 and *An Introduction to the Principles of Morals and Legislation*, Bentham believed neither in innate rights as did Locke nor in the mystic virtues of a moral community as did Rousseau. All that really "counted" for Bentham was the imperative dichotomy of pleasure-and-pain. Good and evil, right and wrong were understandable, he argued, only in terms of their consequences for discrete individuals. Actions and objects all ultimately involved the sensations either of pleasure or pain. So long as men could really understand whether any given act would produce more pleasure or pain for them, they were the best judges of what was good and desirable and what was not. The art of legislation, for Bentham, was simply to maximize the pleasure or happiness of the largest number of people in the state. Increasingly persuaded that, by and large, each person was the best judge of his own happiness, Bentham enhanced the cause of so-called philosophical radicalism in England, and in the 1820's advocated the extension of suffrage, annual elections, secret ballot and equal electoral districts to facilitate the most forceful assertion of public opinion on government. Interestingly, however, one of his foremost disciples, John Stuart Mill (1806–1873), having initially embraced many of the same general principles and many of Bentham's specific, favorite

10 Thus, Rousseau wrote: "The idea of representation is modern; it comes to us from feudal government, from that iniquitous and absurd system which degrades humanity and dishonors the name of man. . . . The people cannot be represented . . . the moment a people allows itself to be represented, it is no longer free: it no longer exists." *Social Contract,* trans. and ed. by G. D. H. Cole (New York: E. P. Dutton, 1950), pp. 94–96. "Sovereignty . . . cannot be represented," p. 94.

causes is probably best remembered for his defense of the individual's right to be free and different, *against* the potentially intolerant and crushing power of mass opinion. He articulated these themes most notably in *On Liberty* in 1854 and *Considerations on Representative Government* in 1861. Unable to believe that whatever most people wanted was necessarily best, Mill attempted to balance the democratism of Bentham and of his own father, James Mill (1773–1836), by emphasizing human uniqueness and excellence against the rule of mere unmbers.[11] Among influential writers whose thinking reflected a balance between concern for individual freedom and extension of power to the people-at-large was also Alexis de Tocqueville (1805–1859). He was attracted to political democracy, seeing in it the promise of extending liberty from just a few people to all, and as a vehicle for the improvement of human life. Yet he feared that the relentless pursuit of equality might cause democracy to deteriorate into a tyranny of the many over the few, stifling individuality, creativity, excellence, and achievement.[12]

In the seventeenth and eighteenth centuries, the ideology of liberal democracy was enriched and buttressed by the contributions of men who believed in liberty and justice, under law, for the individual but who had little, if any, sympathy for "majority rule."

Those social thinkers who have carried their concern to an extreme may be said to represent the conservative Right in democratic ideology, ultimately preferring enlightened despotism to a democracy. Among the clearest examples of these were Voltaire and Diderot in the Age of Reason. Both were foremost exponents of rationalism and individual freedom, and lifelong foes of religious superstition, bigotry, and obscurantism. Yet both believed that the cause of human freedom, justice, peace and, above all, the progress of science and art would be best served by the leadership of truly learned competent monarchs. They tended to identify democracy with mob rule, and feared the ignorance, superstition, and savagery of the masses. They believed that a strong and wise ruler would act as a safeguard for the values of freedom and civilization.[13]

11 See John P. Plamenatz, *Mill's Utilitarianism* (Oxford: Blackwell, 1949); and Leslie Stephen's monumental *The English Utilitarians*, 3 vols. (New York: P. Smith, 1950).

12 For an excellent account of de Tocqueville's idea on this subject, see Marvin Zetterbaum, *Tocqueville and the Problem of Democracy* (Stanford: Stanford University Press, 1967).

13 On Voltaire (1694–1778), see Peter Gay, *Voltaire's Politics: The Poet as Realist* (Princeton, N.J.: Princeton University Press, 1959); see also Renee Waldringer, *Voltaire and Reform in the Light of the French Revolution* (Geneva: E. Droz, 1959), and C. Rowe, *Voltaire and the State* (New York: Columbia University Press, 1955). On Denis

In more recent times, the great spokesman of *laissez-faire*, Herbert Spencer (1820–1903), gravitated toward such a position when he argued in 1884 in *Man Versus the State* that "the function of Liberalism in the past was that of putting a limit to the powers of kings. The function of true Liberalism in the future will be that of putting a limit to the powers of Parliament."

An eighteenth-century thinker who represented what might be called the Right-wing of the liberal-democratic tradition was Baron de Montesquieu (1689–1755) who, in 1748 published one of the most famous political treatises, *The Spirit of Laws*. Like Voltaire, Diderot, and many other thinkers of this and subsequent eras, Montesquieu was more concerned with liberty for the individual than with majority rule. If he qualifies as a "democratic thinker" at all, it is only because he believed that a measure of popular power—properly balanced—was necessary to secure a government that would respect the liberty of individuals. Where Locke influenced the American Revolution of 1776 on the subject of "inalienable rights of man," Montesquieu stimulated the search for checks-and-balances in the writing of the American constitution.[14]

The cross section of our examples has been drawn from the eighteenth and nineteenth centuries. But the issue of balance between popular power and individual rights is as contemporary as it is ancient. Undoubtedly, it will be fought over in the future also.

In each great ideological mainstream, certain institutions, processes, persons, and events become objects of special emphasis. This is true in two ways. In part, they are singled out for utilitarian reasons, that is, for the realization of some specific cherished values. In part, they are held up for veneration and esteem, in pursuit of affective purposes. They become unifying symbols to rally the faithful. Emotions help to establish and maintain political legitimacy.

In the ideology of democracy, we find that this special emphasis is reserved, first, for institutions connected with representation and communication and, second, for institutions and processes that guarantee individual and group rights. In the first category are to be found legislative bodies and the press; in the second, courts and various solemn constitutional documents, such as the Bill of Rights and the Declaration of Independence in the United States; The Declaration of the Rights of Man and Citizen in France; the Magna Carta or the Bill of Rights in Great Britain, and so forth. In the perceptions of men who share in a

Diderot 1713–1784), see biography by Lester G. Crocker, *The Embattled Philosopher* (East Lansing: Michigan State College Press, 1954).

[14] See Franz Neumann's "Introduction" to Montesquieu's *Spirit of Laws*, trans. by Thomas H. Nugent (New York: Hafner Publishing Co., 1949).

common political tradition, things that are quite mundane and ordinary for other men become transmuted into objects at once practical and sacred.

The respect and even reverence for popular assemblies manifested in democratic ideology are rooted in the values which they are seen to realize. In our own era, Winston Churchill regarded himself as, above all, a House of Commons man. In the nineteenth century, French and British democrats looked upon parliamentary assemblies as fountainheads of political legitimacy. Here, presumably, the will of the people is manifested. Reason, dialogue, and persuasion hold sway. Men are able to represent feelings, ponder facts and information, exchange ideas and negotiate. In sum, all the processes that democracy associates with man as a sociable, gregarious, and reasonable being are here as if on exhibit.

Understandably, for people concerned with 'majority rule,' legislatures and the subjects related to them: representation, their powers, privileges, and procedures, have always been of the greatest interest. To be sure, legislative bodies have existed in various forms in most countries of Europe since medieval times. The so-called estates of clergy, nobility, and townsmen were as common at one time in Spain, France, and Poland as in Great Britain. But not in all countries were they nurtured by widespread supportive political beliefs. Analogously, charters conferring privileges and immunities, such as those obtained by English nobles from King John I in 1215, were not unique either. In Britain, as in the United States, Scandinavia, and other areas of the world, the relationship between various institutions and values of democracy had been mutually reinforcing and interdependent.

In seventeenth-century England, some men—representatives of a numerous and self-confident middle class—asserted the doctrine of parliamentary supremacy over the king. They invoked alleged British traditions and constitutional precedents in support of their claims. These could be, and were, hotly disputed by staunch royalists.[15] But, with each victory of parliamentary supporters over the king, the tradition was becoming more and more substantial until, by the end of the century, it passed from a merely controversial opinion to what in Britain, at least, became an established value. The tradition grew and was continually strengthened.

Institutional traditions and revolutionary victories have made impor-

[15] On the English Civil War, and the historically powerful precedents supporting the king's cause, see, e.g., Joseph R. Tanner, *English Constitutional Conflicts of the Seventeenth Century* (Cambridge: University Press, 1952) on the Hampden (ship-money) Case of 1637, pp. 273–277.

tant contributions to the mystique of popular assemblies in democratic ideology. In the 1640's, it was the House of Commons that focused successful opposition to King Charles I and raised an army to fight and defeat him in the ensuing civil war. The Speaker of the House became a symbol of parliamentary resistance to royal absolutism when, during the 1620's and 1630's, king and parliament disputed the question of power. In the British political system today, the Speaker of the House of Commons has come to occupy a place that is both symbolically and functionally extremely important.[16] Long tradition and a remarkably successful record of performance have made this possible. In the carrying out of his job, the Speaker personally adjusts all of the dynamic tensions of democracy within the walls of the House of Commons: authority and liberty, the right of the majority to carry the vote, and the right of individuals and minorities to have their say.

In the history of the French Revolution of 1789, the transformation of the middle class Third Estate, called in 1788 by King Louis XVI, in to the National Assembly of all France followed by so many dramatic and (to republican believers) heroic deeds, furthered the parliamentary "mystique." It gave republicans and democrats of the nineteenth century, in France and elsewhere, a historical symbol of identification, success, and inspiration, analogous to the Paris Commune of 1871 for Marxist radicals on the eve of the Bolshevik Revolution of 1917.

Thus the basic concepts and forms of the British, French, and American revolutions live on as symbolic as well as utilitarian elements in the creed of modern democracy.

In his famous Gettysburg address, President Abraham Lincoln dedicated the Union's war effort to a government of the people, by the people, and for the people. We can appreciate his remarks as a link in a useful chain of faith that unites believers of different ages. The men, the deeds, and the remembrances of Bastille, Valmy, Valley Forge, Sedan, or Leningrad, for that matter, provide various modern creeds with the spiritual nourishment of distinctive symbols and traditions.

What is of interest also is how ideological considerations translate into institutional concerns. In seventeenth-century England, men quarreled over the powers of parliament to make laws or levy taxes. Democrats wanted to subject the executive to the wishes of parliament: they were eager to protect the members and the proceedings of the House of Com-

---

[16] On the British institution of the Speaker of the House, see the seven-century survey by Arthur I. Dasent, *The Speakers of the House of Commons* (London: John Lane, 1911), and also W. Ivor Jennings, *Parliament*, 2d ed. (Cambridge: University Press, 1957), pp. 14–15 and 61–72. Compare Mary P. Follett's *The Speaker of the House of Representatives* (New York: Longman's Green, 1909).

mons from control or reprisals by the king. They debated the question of franchise, whether property, and how much of it, should entitle a man to vote. Since the nineteenth century, the questions of proportional representation, secret ballot, fair distribution of electoral districts, and women's suffrage have all received much attention. Politicians, publicists and scholars concerned with democratic theory and/or practice have argued the merits of different kinds of voting and different ways of representing voter preferences for centuries.[17]

A classic example has been proportional representation, a perennial issue in democratic thought because it relates to the central concerns about majority rule, minority rights, and the freedom of individuals to articulate their preferences.

The electoral system inherited from late medieval times in Britain, and adopted by American colonists in the seventeenth century, has been the single ballot plurality system. It has been often referred to as a "first past-the-post" method of electing representatives. No matter how many candidates might offer themselves in an electoral district, and no matter what the total vote, the victory (or a seat in the legislature) would go to the person with one more vote than his nearest competitor. Obviously, under this kind of system there may be occasions where the person chosen to sit in the legislature represents only a small proportion of the total electorate of his district. Under the single-member system, this would happen whenever the voters divided their preferences something like this: A gets 10 votes; B gets 9 votes; C gets 8 votes; D also gets 8 votes; E gets 5 votes. Thus, A who gets only 10 out of 40 votes cast is elected. The other candidates' votes are, for practical purposes, "wasted." To some democrats, concerned with popular sovereignty and fairness of representation, such an outcome seems to establish not majority but minority rule. It makes the spokesman of the district someone who can claim the endorsement of only 25 percent of the voters! The remedy for this, they argue, is proportional representation, which would change single-member districts into multimember districts so that, in the example we have used here, not only the supporters of A but even those of E would be represented—in proper proportion to their numbers in the total electorate of the district. This idea has always understandably appealed to those eager to carry the "one man one vote" principle to its ultimate, logical conclusion. If votes are cast, they should all count equally. And the idea has

17 On the subject of proportional representation, see particularly Enid Lakeman and James D. Lambert, *Voting in Democracies; A Study in Majority and Proportional Electoral Systems* (London: Faber and Faber, 1959); John R. Commons, *Proportional Representation* (New York: A. M. Kelley, 1967); and F. A. Hermens, *The Representative Republic* (Notre Dame: University of Notre Dame Press, 1958).

received institutional embodiments, beginning with the practice of nine-teenth-century Belgium and, with particular emphasis on minute propor-tionality, in Germany under the Weimar Republic (1919–1933) as well as in France under the Third Republic (1919–1926) and again in the period from 1946 to 1958 under the Fourth Republic. It has also been used in Scandinavia since before World War II and in Italy since the War, among other examples.

In some instances of its use, however, Weimar Germany and France being the most famous cases, proportional representation reflected and reinforced tremendous social, economic, cultural, and political cleavages in the body politic. The idea of accurate and complete representation of popular opinion became visibly incompatible with another democratic *desideratum*, namely government supported by a majority in parliament. Proportional representation translated the cleavages of society so faith-fully into cleavages among legislators and governors, that it became all but impossible to constitute a reasonably stable political system supported by a majority in Germany of the 1930's or France of the 1940's and 1950's.[18]

What appeared in jeopardy was the very power to govern, to assure law, order, continuity, and progress toward any coherent policy-goals in the society at large. For the democratic ideologue—in countries so divided —it posed the central theoretical, as well as practical issue, of how liberty and order, authority and freedom, could be balanced and reconciled, if at all.

Those attached to Anglo-Saxon institutions pointed with pride to the relative stability of government in Britain and America and argued that their cruder, plurality-based, electoral system provided the necessary balance. Accuracy of representation was not as important as political stability. Moreover, the single-member, "winner-take all" electoral system was likely to moderate voter attitudes, and discourage splinter parties and pure mischief-making which the "generosity" of proportional repre-sentation encouraged. Pointing to the long periods of dominance by two major parties alternating in power in Britain and the United States, these people believed that it was salutary for individual voters to discipline themselves into making choices on the basis of the "least objectionable alternative" rather than perhaps some very esoteric and idiosyncratic ultimate preference. According to these democratic politicians, publicists, scholars, and journalists, political parties themselves would be encour-aged to be broadly representative, to compromise and to negotiate with

18 Note that such problems did not arise in Scandinavia under circumstances of greater social consensus.

all sorts of social interests in order to maintain the kind of unity that victory at the polls would require. Such ideological as well as practical conflicts are part of the inherent dilemma of the democratic creed, of the combining of aspirations that necessarily clash with one another from time to time.

Other illustrations of the ideological characteristics and tensions of democracy may be found, for example, in legislative organization. Democratic ideology generally extols the power of the representatives of the people and the rights of the people to articulate grievances through their elected representatives. But every legislative body faces the acute and practical problem of how to expedite its business with promptness and expertise on the one hand while allowing full weight and expression to popular opinion on the other. In the American Congress the relationship between specialized expert committees and the House or Senate at large has reflected these problems, as has the issue of filibuster.[19] Is it right for a few senators to thwart the wishes of a majority ad infinitum? Is it proper for a majority to deny the minority the right of free and full expression of its views? Who is to decide what constitutes "obstruction" and what is but the "free and full expression" of opinion? Does a majority have a right to impose its views on the minority regardless of the intensity of minority opposition, or is there a degree of underlying consensus that somehow must be kept between the "ins" and the "outs" if democracy is to function effectively?

Surely, the people have a right to petition their government. Democratic constitutions generally guarantee this. But what about the efforts of lobbyists who, thanks to their superior financial resources or personal connections, make the wishes of a few people count for more with the legislators or the bureaucrats than those of perhaps untold millions?[20]

Some of the most difficult and embarrassing problems implicit in the ideology of democracy stem precisely from its well-established regard for the right of petition. Part of the ideology demands that officeholders be subject to periodic elections. Another part, however, safeguards the opportunities of individual members of the electorate to solicit the support

[19] On the subject of legislative functions, organization, and roles see, e.g., George B. Galloway, *The Legislative Process in Congress* (New York: Crowell, 1953); Richard F. Fenno, Jr., *The Power of the Purse* (Boston: Little, Brown, 1966); and Telford Taylor, *Grand Inquest* (New York: Simon and Schuster, 1955).

[20] On activities of interest groups and their "lobbies" in conjunction with democratic legislatures see, e.g., Lester W. Milbrath, *The Washington Lobbyists* (Chicago: Rand McNally, 1963). See also Theodore J. Lowi (ed.), *Legislative Politics USA; Congress and the Forces That Shape It.* (Boston: Little, Brown, 1962). On the more general subject of pressure groups, see Harmon Zeigler, *Interest Groups in American Society* (Englewood Cliffs N.J.: Prentice-Hall, 1964).

of officeholders. In the language of the seventeenth century, every man must be considered entitled to ask for "redress of grievances," and presumably to voice freely opinions, advice, and information to the authorities and the community in general.

Yet the people who approach legislators and administrators for favors, or pressure them into particular positions, are generally self-selected on the basis of specialized interests. They may not necessarily see eye to eye with the electorate. They may not even represent particularly large groups in the electorate. But if they are skillful, well-organized, rich, persuasive, and persistent, their influence is likely to be greater, and sometimes much greater, than the unorganized, the mute, the poor, and those only sporadically involved in the business of politics.

Thus, a legislator may understandably become much more concerned with the attitude of a powerful interest group than of thousands of his "ordinary," or unorganized, constituents. At one time in American history, railroads and other business interests were powerful enough to all but manage numerous House and Senate seats. Most people simply could not match their financial and organizational resources; and these could be used not merely in the crude form of bribes or payoffs, but in the indirect management of public opinion, in effective legislative, administrative, and judicial advocacy, and other entirely legitimate activities, such as good staff work, public relations, legislative liaison, and the like.

In many democracies, efforts have been made to minimize the unequal impact of privileged interest groups. For example, in Britain and West Germany, laws have been passed to limit the amount of money candidates could spend in election campaigns; in some cases, limits have been set on how much business enterprises and trade unions could directly donate for such purposes. Certain lobbying practices have been prohibited as unlawful. Lobbyists' expenses have been subjected to public exposure so as to discourage unethical spending by those seeking favors from government officials. In France and Britain, the availability of television time has been so equalized among the parties at election time as to eliminate the candidates' need for obtaining rich backers in order to employ this medium of persuasion.

But all these devices have not really eliminated differentials in influence among interest groups. So long as people of unequal attributes (abilities, interests, and means, etc.) are allowed to exert efforts on behalf of their particular points of view (or "interests"), the results are bound to be more favorable to some than to others. If direct campaign contributions could be limited by law, various kinds of indirect support could not. If bribery by a lobbyist could be punished as a crime, certainly the employment of articulate lawyers, skilled accountants, experienced stat-

isticians, and persuasive public relations men could not. The sacred organizational rights of democracy—freedom of speech, press, association,
and protection of the law—could all be used to thwart prevalent popular
sentiments.

In the United States, during the last several years, the National Rifle
Association has been widely credited with blocking comprehensive gun-
control legislation in Congress, despite substantial public support for
such a measure demonstrated in numerous national opinion polls. Relatively small organizations of physicians have been influential at various
times in thwarting schemes of publicly supported health care. Representatives of public utility firms have often successfully resisted mass pressures for price and service changes. The list of example could be easily
extended. No democracies, including the more egalitarian Scandinavian
ones, have been able to construe the right of petition, and the related
procedural guarantees of democracy, in such a fashion as to make the impact of interest group representation a wholly equal force for all citizens.

Another ideologically rooted cause of pressure group power has been
democracy's bias toward voluntarism. The belief that the best way of
reaching decisions is by consultation and agreement of those affected,
and with their willing cooperation, has conferred political access upon
all sorts of interest groups. If a democratic government has a policy
toward agriculture, business, or labor, it usually sets up institutional
means for consulting them such as public hearings, advisory boards, appeal boards, and the like. Through all these means, the affected groups
could come forward, offer their views and, in effect, bargain with the
government over its policies. Thus, in Britain in 1948–1949, the Labour
party, thoroughly committed to the principles of liberal democracy, felt
compelled to consult with the industrialists whose property it sought to
nationalize, and with doctors whose services it sought to use in its system
of socialized medicine. The rates of compensation to the former, and the
conditions of service to the latter, were bargained over until mutually
satisfactory solutions could be reached. Frequently, matters of detail and
administration turn out to be more important in such negotiations than
alleged "policy."

The areas of so-called delegated legislation, and legislative control of
the executive, also illustrate the dilemmas of democratic ideology, as
much in practice as in theory. The belief that power to make laws shall
reside in the freely elected representatives of the people is without doubt
one of the commonest hallowed creeds of the democratic ideologue. But
the needs of modern government, with the ever-increasing onrush of
economic and military crises of this century, have made it necessary for
legislatures all over the world to delegate rule-making responsibility to

various executive agencies. Instead of making laws, modern legislators often simply approve frameworks suggested to them by executive agencies for the making of rules if, as, and when necessary. The instruments of delegation generally provide for some forms of *post-factum* audit or control. Such controls are sometimes more symbolic and ritualistic rather than genuinely thorough and effective in nature. Yet the alternative to delegation, painful as it is, may be a *de facto* inability to govern. Again, we are back to the problem of reconciling popular power and freedom with effective authority.[21] In 1861, Abraham Lincoln asked in one of his speeches, "Must a government of necessity be too strong for the liberties of its own people, or too weak to maintain its own existence?" No doubt, this will always remain a pertinent query at the juncture of democratic ideals with democratic institutions.

The protection of individual and group rights is another focus of both symbolic and practical concern of democracy. It is an integral part of the ideology; it, too, presents problems of conflict among the values of (1) individual and group rights, (2) the rights of the majority to determine policy and law, and (3) the ultimate need for an effective government which can keep the peace and keep the community together.

In the words of the American Declaration of Independence, for example: "We hold these truths to be self-evident, that all men are created equal, that they are endowed by their Creator with certain unalienable Rights, that among these are Life, Liberty, and the pursuit of Happiness." One of the most common practical ways of ensuring such rights has been to make them into a supremely binding law of the land—as in the first ten amendments of the U.S. Constitution—and to provide for judicial defense of them through the courts; in the American experience, court protection of the rights of individuals has always been subject to a kind of "balancing act." If the people have constitutional rights as individuals, they also have rights as a collectivity, exercised nationally through Congress and the Executive. The power of making laws and policy resides not in each individual but in the duly constituted organs of the whole collectivity. The judiciary must first straddle a difficult line of demarkation, safeguarding the individual citizen from abuse at the hands of the collectivity without trespassing on the equally important political rights of the collectivity. The courts must also weigh all appeals on behalf of rights—individual, group, or majority—against the exigency of a still larger public interest: the safety and ultimately the preservation of the state itself.

21 On the subject—and problems—of delegated legislation from two geographically and chronologically different perspectives, see E. H. Carr, *Delegated Legislation* (London: 1940) and Theodore J. Lowi, *The End of Liberalism* (New York: Norton, 1969).

During World War II, the majority of the United States Supreme Court made an ideological choice when it refused to interfere with the removal of thousands of Japanese-Americans into internment camps because of an alleged danger to national security. In 1949, in the so-called Dennis Case, the Court decided between those who argued that Communists, like everyone else, were entitled to freedom of speech and those who, again, saw the problem in terms of a threat to the state. In 1970, a federal court stirred considerable controversy when it forbade a Congressional committee from issuing an implicitly censorial list of campus speakers. In the annals of U.S. judicial history, there have been numerous ideological decisions, often conflicting ones, on the "rules of the system." Needless to say, the disposition by courts, legislatures, or other governmental organs of issues central to democratic ideology is fraught with all sorts of perils.[22]

[22] See Robert E. Cushman, *Leading Constitutional Decisions*, 13th ed. (New York: Appleton-Century-Crofts, 1966) and his *Civil Liberties in the United States* (Ithaca: Cornell University Press, 1956) for examples of the reconciliational problems of liberty, order, and power as handled by the U.S. Supreme Court.

CHAPTER **4**

Socialism

The origins of socialist ideas and models of "socialist societies" may be traced to antiquity, indeed to Plato's *Republic*. There are also medieval and Renaissance origins in the writings of churchmen and philosophers, men like Tomasso Campanella and Sir Thomas More, and occasionally religious dissenters in Germany and England.[1] But socialism did not become an important ideological current until the eighteenth century. Modern socialism is a child of the Industrial Revolution. Just as the ideology of democratic liberalism arose from the economic and social stirrings of the Renaissance and the Commercial Revolution, socialism grew under the impact of industrialism.

To the hardy merchant classes of the seventeenth and eighteenth centuries, the pursuit of happiness seemed to require the abolition of governmental controls imposed from above and from without. The good life seemed assurable if men were but left to their own devices and the common good or public interest seemed obtainable by combining (1) the so-called "invisible-hand" principle, that is, the free pursuit of individual advantage, as in Adam Smith's scheme, with (2) voluntary association of men for promotion of objectives that they could freely and mutually agree

---

[1] See, for example, Eduard Bernstein's *Cromwell and Communism: Socialism and Democracy in the Great English Revolution* (New York: A. M. Kelly, 1963), and particularly G. H. Sabine (ed.), *The Works of Gerrard Winstanley* (Ithaca: Cornell University Press, 1941). Winstanley preached the doctrine of communism based on the idea that poverty was at the root of all bondage, and that organized religion was a tool of deception and subjugation in the hands of the rich. See *Works*, p. 569.

upon. It was an ideology that grew out of a basic optimism about society and mankind. The optimism was partly that of an age and partly that of a class. The inarticulate masses of workmen and serfs, to the extent that they possessed a political consciousness, did not always share the attitudes of their more affluent middle class compatriots.

The uneasiness of the poor and the downtrodden became, however, increasingly acute and articulate in the latter part of the eighteenth century. Industrialization, first in England, then in France and elsewhere in western Europe, began to drive the peasants and craftsmen off the land, mobilizing a new urban mass of laborers. These were largely unskilled men, women, and children herded into the squalor and misery of urban slums, mercilessly exploited and exposed to hazardous working conditions for long hours, often at meager pay.[2] In the eighteenth century, governments had not yet taken notice of these new industrial masses, of their plight and their needs. The poor were thus not only uprooted and exploited but unprotected by public agencies against the abuses of private greed or, as some argued, not greed but the mere unfortunate necessities of the market-place. Nevertheless, the urban, industrial poor, no matter how wretched their condition, began to "count," socially, economically, and politically. Their numbers continually grew; they were increasingly the mainstay of the European national economies. Their subjection to similar working and living conditions was bringing about a new kind of mobilization, not simply in numbers but in awareness of their common plight. This new consciousness was, as Karl Marx pointed out, in part an awareness of class, but it was also in a larger perspective increasing political awareness. Men began to look beyond the ancestral home, the village, the family, or the neighborhood, for remedies to what they recognized as pervasive social problems. They turned to the state and to political action for redress and relief. They did so in different ways; some wanted merely to appeal to the state, others wanted to gain possession of it, some wanted to destroy it.

In all cases, certain common themes underlay the aspirations of socialist ideologues:

1. A primary concern with the "economic question," that is, those human activities which relate to the production and distribution of goods and services in a society.
2. An interest, explicit or implicit, in the amelioration or removal of exploitation, of the unfair "taking advantage of" by one man of another.

2 See J. L. and Barbata Hammond, *The Rise of Modern Industry* (London: Methuen, 1966), pp. 84–88, on the enclosure movement and industrial development.

3. The reconstitution of the economy and society so as to banish human want and suffering—within a more egalitarian and communal framework.

Alexander Gray wrote that:

"As the words are commonly understood, socialism is . . . regarded as opposed to individualism . . . but in fact they are not so much opposed as complementary principles."[3]

Indeed, much of the ideology of socialism may be regarded as the emphasis of values shared with the democratic-liberal ideology. The differences between democracy and socialism, in terms of values emphasized, clienteles attracted, and institutional expressions, can be best explained by reference to their origins. The early nineteenth century produced several prominent advocates of socialist doctrines.

The Frenchman, Charles Fourier (1772–1837), for example, was a typically nonviolent socialist. He was an early advocate of voluntary associations of producers; Fourier was interested in humanizing economic life by changing its purpose from unbridled individual profit-seeking to a more secure balance between individual well-being and social stability. He advocated the establishment of so-called "phalanxes" or communes. These were to be primarily agricultural enterprises that would allow people not only closeness to the soil but also escape from the minutely specialized monotony of the division of labor. Individuals would rotate social tasks among themselves. Barter was to replace money and the phalanx was to supply a certain minimum of food, clothing, and shelter, as well as medical, educational, and cultural facilities to all its members. Extraordinary productivity was to be rewarded by profit-sharing. Fourier's ideal phalanx was to include only about 400 persons, thus substituting a virtually face-to-face economic organization for the impersonal bureaucratic factory system. His communes were intended to integrate all the functions of society—work, study, play, etc.—in these small family-like units. Fourier's concern with the physical and mental well-being of people subject to harmful, dehumanizing, or degrading work situations, was a forerunner of much of the Welfare State philosophy of the twentieth century.[4]

[3] *The Socialist Tradition: From Moses to Lenin* (London: Longmans, Green, 1947), pp. 488–489.

[4] See Albert Brisbane, *Social Destiny of Man: Association and Reorganization of Industry* (New York: A. M. Kelley, 1969); *Selections from the Works of Fourier*, trans. by Julia Franklin (London: S. Sounenshein, 1901), and N. V. Riasanovsky, *The Teaching of Charles Fourier* (Berkeley: University of California Press, 1969).

Another example of evolutionary, cooperative socialism based on the appeals of persuasion rather than force was advocated by Robert Owen (1771–1858), British manufacturer and social reformer. Owen believed that man was basically a product of his environment, and he attached particular importance to man's early years. Beginning with some textile mills in Manchester and New Lanark in the early 1800's, Owen combined factory work with comprehensive social and cultural care for his employees and their children. He provided them with low-cost housing, food, and education, and stimulated community self-help among his employees. Owen hoped to improve not only the workers' material conditions but their moral and intellectual faculties as well. In 1815 Owen began to demand nationwide reform of factory conditions in England; he soon generalized his own experience into a universal scheme of community organization based on worker/farmer cooperatives. He believed that people should share work, leisure, and the rearing of children, in small groups of about 1200 persons in each commune. Ultimately, all society could be transformed, Owen thought, into a federation of cooperative work establishments where direct relationships, close-knit work, and cultural contacts would contribute to the security and well-being of each member. Owen's ideas were influential in the trade unions and ultimately also in the establishment of cooperatives among workers, farmers, and consumers.[5] Both Fourier and Owen found numerous followers in the United States but most of the communes founded by them disintegrated within a short time largely because of religious, political, and personal quarrels among the members.

Among the forerunners of socialism's anarchist branch was William Godwin (1756–1836), British author of *Enquiry Concerning the Principles of Social Justice,* published in 1793. Godwin advocated social organization through small autonomous communities based on complete voluntarism of work and the sharing of wealth. Somewhat similar schemes of small-scale voluntary communities replacing the Leviathan state were also developed by France's Pierre Joseph Proudhoun (1809–1865), Russia's Mikhail Bakunin (1814–1876), and Prince Peter Kropotkin (1842–1921) among others.[6]

[5] See his autobiography, *The Life of Robert Owen* (London: G. Bell, 1920); and his *A New View of Society* (Glencoe, Ill.: Free Press, 1948), as well as John F. C. Harrison, *Quest for the New Moral World; Robert Owen and the Owenites in Britain and America* (New York: Scribner, 1969).

[6] Among sources about anarchism, see Alexander Berkman, *ABC of Anarchism*, 3rd ed. (London: Freedom Press, 1964); Irving L. Horowitz (ed.), *The Anarchists* (New York: Dell, 1964); James Joll, *The Anarchists* (London: Eyre and Spottiswoode, 1964); James J. Martin, *Men Against the State: The Expositors of Individualist Anarchism in America*, 1827–1908 (New York: Libertarian Book Club, 1953); S. E.

Among the nineteenth-century prophets of anarchism, Mikhail Bakunin became something of a Russian rival to Marx, vying for the following of the industrial workers. Bakunin advocated revolution not only against the bourgeois state of his time, but against all forms of state and all types of authority by man over man. He accused Marx of substituting a "red" bureaucracy and dogmatism in place of "black" or "white" bureaucracies and dogmas.[7] In the late 1860's, Bakunin tried to win over the International Workingmen's Association (the so-called First International) to his cause of worldwide revolution against all the existing political systems.[8] He exemplified utmost faith in the sociableness of man apart from the state—precisely those conditions which Aristotle believed rendered man a beast. In his methods, Bakunin accepted violence, and paradoxically the need for organizing and, in his case, also directing, revolutionary conspiracies.[9]

Anarchism was to a large extent the cult of the idiosyncratic individual—suspicious of science, technology and, above all, bureaucracy; it was dedicated to the cult of the small community and direct relationships as cures for social conflict, injustice, and the alienation of man from society. It combined individualism and communalism in its rejection of

Parker, *Individualist Anarchism* (London: S. E. Parker 1965); George Woodcock, *Anarchism: A History of Libertarian Ideas and Movements* (Cleveland: World Publishing Co. 1962).

[7] A 1922 anarchist Congress held in Berlin declared that "Revolutionary syndicalism . . . has not for its object the conquest of political power, but the abolition of every state function in social life."

[8] The First International, an association of revolutionary worker groups, was founded in London in 1862; plagued by doctrinal differences, it expired in 1874. The Second International came into being in Paris in 1889, and from 1890 until 1914 had its headquarters in Brussels. It was dominated by the German Social Democrats. Lenin's victory in Russia led to the establishment of a more militant, pro-Soviet body, the so-called Third International from 1919 to 1943. It was dissolved by Stalin during World War II, as a gesture of good will toward his then noncommunist Western allies. Between 1947–1956 the Communist Information Bureau (Cominform) became a successor to the defunct Comintern, ostensibly to promote interparty cooperation. It was made up of Party representatives of the USSR, France, Italy, and the East European parties including Yugoslavia. In June 1948, Yugoslavia was expelled by the Cominform and in 1956 Khrushchev-Tito rapproachment led to the dissolution of this body.

[9] On Mikhail Bakunin, see his *Marxism, Freedom and the State*, ed. and trans. by K. J. Kenafick (London: Freedom Press, 1950); *God and the State* (Indore: Modern Publishers); and E. H. Carr, *Michael Bakunin* (London: Macmillan, 1937); In *God and the State*, Bakunin wrote that all religions are "founded on blood for all rest principally on the idea of sacrifice. . . ." (p. 27). "We reject all legislation, all authority, and all privileged licensed and legal influence, even though arising from universal suffrage, convinced that it can turn only to the advantage of a dominant minority of exploiters against the interests of the immense majority in subjection to them" (p. 40).

all authority, supported by the belief in the spontaneous, innate sociableness of man. These beliefs, as well as a penchant for violence as means to the end, made nineteenth-century anarchism a precursor of some of the extreme radicalism of present-day New Left. Italy and Spain became particular strongholds of anarchism in the late nineteenth and early twentieth centuries.

Among early forerunners of modern communism, advocating abolition of private property in the means of production and distribution—through violence and dictatorship by workers—was Francois (Gracchus) Babeuf (1760–1797). A participant in the French Revolution of 1789, he assumed the role of a spokesman for the disinherited, that is, those who unlike the middle class and the peasants did not improve their economic position in consequence of the Revolution. Babeuf and several of his conspirators were executed by the Directory in 1797 for plotting to overthrow the bourgeois regime. His greatest contribution was to the legacy of radical myths and legends rather than to the theory of society or revolution. Another socialist who closely preceded Marx, though in much less influential advocacy of militant struggle by workers, was the Frenchman, Louis Blanqui (1805–1881), who participated in the bourgeois revolutions of 1830 and 1848, and supported the nineteenth-century prototype of the workers' revolution—the Paris Commune of 1871.[10]

Looking back from the perspective of the 1970's, clearly the most influential socialist thinker and ideologue was Karl Marx (1818–1883). In fact, while disputing his merits, Bertrand Russell nevertheless classified Marx as the single most influential philosopher in all history.[11] As one of his foremost biographers put it:

"Not only the conflicting classes and their leaders in every country, but historians and sociologists, psychologists and political scientists, critics and creative artists, so far as they try to analyze the changing quality of the life of their society, owe the form of their ideas in part to the work of Karl Marx.

. . . Marxism set out to refute the proposition that ideas govern the course of history, but the very extent of its own influence on human af-

---

[10] On Louis Blanqui, see Raymond W. Postgate, *Out of the Past: Some Revolutionary Sketches* (Boston: Houghton Mifflin, 1922), and M. Dommanget, *Blanqui et l'opposition revolutionnaire a la fin du Second Empire* (Paris: A. Colin, 1960).

[11] "For at least one-third of the world's population in the second half of the twentieth century, Marxism provides the official philosophical point of view, or the systematic articulation of beliefs about the world and man's destiny in it." Samuel E. Stumpf, *Socrates to Sartre: A History of Philosophy* (New York: McGraw Hill, 1966), p. 421. Compare Bertrand Russell, *A History of Western Philosophy* (New York: Simon and Schuster, 1959), p. 782.

fairs has weakened the force of its thesis. For in altering the hitherto prevailing view of the relation of the individual to his environment and his fellows, it has palpably altered the relation itself; and in consequence remains the most powerful of the intellectual forces which are today permanently transforming the ways in which men think and act."[12]

Marx himself described several forerunners of his own ideological system as utopian socialists—a term of scorn and condescension. What Marx shared with these Utopians was a preoccupation with economics, a profound resentment of human exploitation and oppression, and a vision of a more just, egalitarian society. But what Marx deplored and attacked in such men as Robert Owen, Charles Fourier, Henri de Saint-Simon, and, earlier still, the likes of Sir Thomas More, was their naïveté. To Marx, these thinkers, writers, and reformers were visionaries, men who lacked the essentials of realism and science. They may have had good intentions as moralists, but they lacked understanding of economic, history, and social change. They could dream dreams and plead for mercy on behalf of the working man; they could, on occasion, call for bloodshed and revolt. But all these strivings were ultimately futile because they were uninformed as to a true theory of action based on a really scientific appreciation of society—not just compassion or reformist zeal.

There was some substance in Marx's view when we compare the ideas of the earlier socialists with his. Utopian socialists, the forerunners of "scientific" Marxian socialism, provided a plethora of remedies for the ills of industrial society and the woes of the wage earners. Men like Owen and Fourier advocated the founding of voluntary cooperative societies by workers sometimes in collaboration and with the assistance of the employers. Such schemes would presumably open up islands of escape, economic havens, to the victims of deprivation and exploitation in the society at large. Some appealed to governments and public opinion for

12 For accounts of the life and ideas of Karl Marx see, among others, Emile Burns, *An Introduction to Marxism*, rev. ed. (New York: International Publishers, 1966); George Lichtheim, *Marxism: An Historical and Critical Study* (New York: Praeger), 1965. Robert Friedman (ed.), *Marx on Economics* (New York: Harcourt Brace, 1961); V. V. Adoratski, *Dialectical Materialism* (New York: International Publishers, 1934); Shlomo Avineri, *The Social and Political Thought of Karl Marx* (London: Cambridge University Press, 1968); Isaiah Berlin, *Karl Marx; His Life and Environment*, 3rd ed. (London: Oxford University Press, 1963); G. D. H. Cole, *What Marx Really Meant* (London: Gollancz, 1934); John H. Jackson, *Marx, Proudhon and European Socialism* (London: English Universities Press, 1957); Karl Korsch, *Karl Marx* (New York: Russell and Russell, 1963) Franz Mehring, *Karl Marx: The Story of His Life* (London: Allen & Unwin, 1936). Pierre S. R. Payne, *Marx* (New York: Simon and Schuster, 1968); Otto Ruhle, *Karl Marx: His Life and Work* (London: Allen and Unwin, 1929).

more enlightened laws to curb the oppression of employees by employers. In their view, the road to socialism was by persuasion. Anarchists such as William Godwin were convinced that the conflict between the "haves" and the "have-nots" could be resolved only by abolition of the system which somehow made men into "wolves" and "sheep," respectively. If the framework of the whole legal-political compulsive order could be removed, men would fall back on their natural reasonableness and kindness. Having assumed that corruption, evil, and oppression were products of the social order, not of the individuals composing it, they desired its abolition. They saw greed as an outcome of the institutions of property, not vice versa.

Certainly, there were some socialists who, like Marx himself, had no illusions about the pitiless character of the class struggle between the exploiters and the exploited. These men did not waste their time appealing to the consciences of the capitalists and hoping for miracles of moral regeneration among them. But even these socialists, presumably, had no appreciation of the laws of economic and social development. Like most subsequent anarchists, Bakunin and Kropotkin, for example, wanted to liberate men from want by merely destroying the instruments of compulsion by which some men could forcibly exploit and oppress others. They did not understand what they were up against, in terms of the nature of capitalism and the state. Moreover, they did not have an understanding of what was possible and what was not in terms of leading workers toward a revolution against their capitalist masters and oppressors.

Indeed, what Marx contributed to the ideology of socialism was a world outlook so broad that it provided general directives and orientations not just toward one or a few objectives but toward virtually every human concern. Marx greatly enlarged the perspective of socialism. His ideology connected mere bias to philosophy, economics, and history for a powerful total amalgam. It has continued to fascinate ordinary men, scholars, intellectuals, and politicians for more than a century since Marx and Friedrich Engels (1820–1895) wrote the *Communist Manifesto* in 1848. In the current communist states, it has been lifted to the position of a ruling "science"—at once truth and dogma for all purposes.

Marx borrowed and adopted from many sources for his cosmic philosophy of history. To begin with, he took a materialist view of man and the world, rejecting all spiritual-religious explanations of human existence on earth; he treated religion and God as contrivances of man, products of human invention reflecting the needs, fears, and hopes of mankind in certain particular (relatively primitive) stages of mankind's development. In this view Marx was influenced by the writings of his contemporary, Ludwig Feurbach, adopting the notion that it was not God who created man, but rather man who created God.

Most of Marx's economic ideas were adopted from the writings of English economists generally identified with the laissez-faire school of thought, among them John Locke, Adam Smith, David Ricardo, and Robert Malthus.[13] Above all, however, the distinctive characteristic of the Marxian philosophy, with which its founder animated all his various concepts and ideas, was adopted from the German philosopher Georg Wilhelm Friedrich Hegel (1770–1831). From Hegel, Marx borrowed the so-called dialectic, which was at once a method of reasoning, a tool of analysis, and a pattern of history.

Reduced to common sense terms, the dialectic envisioned reality as a perpetual struggle and adjustment of opposite tendencies in which, according to the famous expression, thesis confronts antithesis, yields a synthesis and, in turn, assumes a new thesis-antithesis pattern. Each being, human, natural, material, and every kind of process or interaction is thus seen as a moving, evolving continuum: a conflict of affirmation and negation of opposite tendencies going through successive stages of disequilibrium.

For Marx, as for Hegel, reality could only be grasped historically, that is, through the unfolding of the several stages of development of any given thing, phenomenon, or being. One could not understand what an oak was without understanding the acorn, and all the stages between a seed and a mature tree. Thus also, a man or a society were comprehensible only in terms of a total sequence of their developments. Marx typically answered his own question as to what "capitalism" was by saying that it was really its whole history. However, where Hegel was an "idealist" who envisioned history as "God's march through the world"—that is, progress toward an ultimate spiritual realization of man, a fulfillment of divine plan or purpose—Marx claimed to have set Hegel's dialectic right side up.[14]

For Marx, history was the progress of mankind conditioned by material factors, primarily economic ones. Like Hegel, Marx believed that the dialectical process was an *inevitable* one in that given the existence of

[13] Compare, e.g., Bertrand Russell, *op. cit.*, p. 783.

[14] On Hegel's "purposive" interpretation of history, see *Reason in History: A General Introduction to the Philosophy of History,* trans. and ed. by Robert S. Hartman (New York: Liberal Arts Press, 1954). ". . . history represents the rationally necessary course of the World Spirit whose own nature unfolds in the course of the world" (p. 12). "If it is conceded that Providence manifests itself in (animals, plants, and individual lives) why not also in world history? . . . the divine wisdom, or Reason, is the same in the large as in the small" (p. 18). On the variety of Hegel's influences, see Editor's Introduction, pp. ix–x.

certain historical forces, the unfolding of certain social "outcomes"—triumphs for some, disasters for others—could not be avoided. But the basis for all these forces was not in God's will but in the material and particularly economic foundations of man's society. For Marx, as for the men of the Enlightenment, history meant progress but, above all, it meant conflict.

Marx assigned primary importance in all aspects of social development to the forces of production and distribution of the means of human sustenance, that is, as economists would say, of goods and services. At any given moment in history, these forces constituted for Marx the basis of society. These forces, their character and distribution determined the nature of social organization in terms of a class structure. The kinds of wealth that were being produced and exchanged, the resources, technologies, and markets that were associated with them, and the division of the products determined what kinds of social classes would exist and how they would relate to one another. As economic conditions of society changed so did the classes composing it. And with every shift in the class structure, there would be corresponding shifts in what Marx regarded as the social *"superstructure."* The latter included almost everything that could be classified among the political, moral, legal, religious, or cultural aspects of a society. The superstructure included government, church and education, science and ethics, art and literature. For Marx, all of these phenomena reflected the characteristics of the underlying economic system as mediated by the prevailing, corresponding class system. As shifts took place in the foundation, they were bound to follow in the superstructure, too. For Marx, the ruling ideas and practices of each age and place were, as he put it, the ideas of the ruling class or classes. The conflict of ideas and practices, whatever it might seem at first sight, could always be related to the underlying economic conflicts.[15]

Applying this general formula to actual history, Marx believed that mankind emerged from conditions of a primitive, primordial communism when men were few and resources for maintaining life were still relatively abundant into an era of scarcity. Pressure of population upon the

[15] On the class character of ideas, see the Marx-Engels *Manifesto* of 1848: ". . . don't wrangle with us so long as you apply to our intended abolition of bourgeois property, the standard of your bourgeois notions of freedom, culture, law, etc. Your very ideas are but the outgrowth of the conditions of your bourgeois production and bourgeois property, just as your jurisprudence is but the will of your class made into a law for all, a will whose essential character and direction are determined by the economic conditions of existence of your class." See Lewis S. Feuer, *Basic Writings on Politics and Philosophy, Karl Marx and Friedrich Engels* (Garden City, N.Y.: Doubleday, 1959), p. 24. Compare Marx on the same theme in a more general way in his *German Ideology* of 1846. Feuer, op. cit., p. 247.

land led to fierce struggles for survival among men; these manifested themselves partly into crude violence of the strong against the weak; but more than that, they led to specialization of labor and the division of tasks—an attempt to maximize social efficiency in the acquisition and exchange of available resources. The establishment of relatively stable roles and functions and the dominion of the stronger and more skillful over the weaker—in relation to land, weapons, implements, stocks, and the like, resulted in the establishment of social classes. Inasmuch as scarcity has continued to plague human existence since the dawn of history, the establishment of social classes did not result in the abolition of the struggle for existence but rather in the better organizing of it. The struggle for survival became a conflict of coherent social orders animated by common (class) interests rather than one of mere, amorphous individuals.

For Marx, individuals lived and perished ephemerally—with generally little enduring significance; social classes, however, were relatively more enduring; their particular interests, and the institutional expressions of these interests, dominated the lives of societies sometimes for centuries. So long as classes existed, individual lives were contained by the values, institutions, and power relationships of classes. The social unit, not the individual, was truly significant for the way in which society lived and governed itself. Where for Hegel the really crucial "social unit" that determined the quality of human life was the state, for Marx it was class; the state merely represented the ruling classes. Where Hegel allowed the occasional "hero" a dynamic, creative role in social change, Marx (ironically in view of his own subsequent influence) allowed none. The individual was ephemeral; the collectivity was truly real and enduring.

This Marxian view, characteristic also of Leninist adaptations of his ideas, had a strong influence on the ruthless, "no holds barred" ethic of the modern communist movement: on the strategy and tactics of revolution.

Given the obvious centrality of Marx in the development of revolutionary socialism, we are justified in considering his characteristic ideas in greater detail here than those of his socialist contemporaries.

The Marxian method was, above all, historical. Marx built his political, economic, and social philosophy upon a plausible interpretation of European history. He viewed all the events and processes discussed here in Chapter 2 from the standpoint of an unfolding class conflict toward objectives which, though still distant in his own time, were nevertheless implicit and inevitable beyond any man's power to change them.

In the Marxian perspective of history, primitive nomadic societies gradually settled down to land-based agricultural-commercial states of antiquity, such as those of Egypt, Babylon, Rome, and Greece. Among these states, the problem of scarcity was overcome by the application of a particularly brutal form of human exploitation—slavery. As long as the economies of the ancient world kept their essential stability—in terms of what was produced and how, and also in terms of the outlet markets for goods and services—the class structure of the period remained stable, too. Landowners, merchants, peasants, craftsmen, priests, officials and, ultimately, slaves "coexisted" in the several economically analogous societies of ancient times. The conflict among them manifested itself only occasionally or indirectly, almost furtively, most of the time. Sometimes the slaves would rise against their masters-oppressors, and wars would take place between urban-merchant and rural-landed interests. But more often than not, the struggle went on far less dramatically. The ruling classes imposed systems of social, legal, political, and even religious organization which kept the poor at bay, and which promoted the better exploitation of the latter. They, in turn, struggled to maximize such means of livelihood as they could and, often blindly and almost instinctively, sought to loosen the shackles imposed on them by the ruling, possessor classes.

Marx believed that the economy of the ancient world, brought to its apogee of wealth and power by Rome's empire in the centuries immediately preceding and following the Christian era, crumbled from within. Its reach exceeded its grasp; the more it succeeded in accumulating lands, resources, and riches, the more it sharpened the rivalry between those who produced the wealth and those who principally benefited by it, and even among these classes, too.

The decay and "fall" of Rome, led to the establishment of a new economic order in Europe associated with the period of the Middle Ages, or as some called it, Dark Ages, roughly between the sixth and twelfth centuries A.D. The large scale, cosmopolitan, agrarian-commercial empires yielded to many relatively small, primitive, self-sufficient economic units. Since the decline of Rome coincided with the invasions of barbarians from the north and the east, the new economies of Europe tended to insulate themselves from the world at large and in place of trade emphasized autarky often at dismally low levels of subsistence. New classes came into existence with the new economies. The warrior-noble, who could control and defend the land against all invaders, became the nucleus of the ruling class of this period—the landed nobility. The urban merchant class, except for a few places, as in the Italian city-states of Florence and Venice, became reduced to virtual insignificance. In the Middle Ages, trade became a rare and generally dangerous occupation. The Roman legions, which had guaranteed the security of the roads, rivers, and seas, gave way to brigands and feuding warlords. With the decline of the cities, the market for luxuries and exotic goods decreased. The prinicipal basis of the economy was in agriculture but on a more limited and even primitive scale. The principal exploited class was that of the serfs—peasants bound to the cultivation of the land and to the service of their particular noble master in perpetuity. Agricultural cultivators became, like tools or livestock, the virtual property of their owners, usually treated as part and parcel of the given estate or fief. They were inherited and passed on by a noble lord to his heirs, and when occasionally estates changed hands their human operatives went with them. Generally, however, except for changes in ownership resultant from conquest, landed property was not available for purchase or sale on an open market. It was held in fief, a sort of perpetual trust, within a pyramidal social hierarchy. Lesser lords held land, subject to the duty of service and support, of a higher lord, and ultimately, in theory at least, the pyramid of holdings ended with a king at the top. In fact, the system tended to be decentralized.

Complex economic changes, some related to the opening of new markets, new geographic and technological discoveries, new routes, all inducing new wants and new means of satisfying them, undermined the feudal economic order.

In the period of the Renaissance, the importance of land declined, and the cities reemerged once again. Merchants and money became increasingly more important than lords and land. They produced and accumulated great new wealth. In turn, the gathering of capital in the hands of an entrepreneurial class produced both economic and sociopolitical as well as cultural consequences of great magnitude.

A new middle class of merchants and craftsmen sprang up. It was economically dynamic and expansionist, and the more successful it grew in the market place, the more insistent it became upon a reconstitution of the whole social-political order to meet its needs. At first, it sought protection against the anarchic nobles by supporting the power of kings. Ultimately, having curbed the willfulness of nobility and secured law and order indispensable to commerce and industry, it turned upon the kings in the name of liberty. The new middle class sought not only order but also freedom for its economic activities—the right to sell commodities and land freely, the right to carry on trade and industry without hindrance, the right to employ its money and leisure as it pleased. As its economic power grew, the political claims of the middle class grew more irresistible. Conversely, the power of traditionalists—nobles and royalists or clergy—to stop these claims gradually weakened and receded.

Under the leadership and auspices of the (economically) triumphant middle class, the liberal state came into being. A series of revolutions in the seventeenth and, most dramatically in France, in the eighteenth centuries toppled the social and political privileges of the traditional feudal order. Freedom of contract, assembly, and association, the right of property, and of individuals to use it, triumphed politically also. The Great French Revolution of 1789 symbolized this new congruence between economic structure and political superstructure. Those who became dominant economically also became dominant politically.

But inevitable as this process appeared to Marx, it also had another dialectical quality. The more successful the bourgeoisie became, the more it maximized the internal contradictions of the society it created. In the words of the *Communist Manifesto,* the bourgeoisie was creating its own gravediggers—in the very masses who it drew to its factories and workshops. It was only a matter of time before the operatives of capitalism would turn on their masters and overthrow their system.[16]

Parenthetically, we may note that Marx attributed great accomplishments to the workings of capitalism.[17] First, capitalism was steadily simplifying the class structure of every society into which it penetrated—drawing vast industrial legions off the land and into the ranks of the proletariat. The proletariat increasingly faced not many different classes arrayed against it and around it but one class—a small number of wealthy entrepreneurs who controlled all the means of production and distribution. All who were not industrial proletarians in, say, the mid-nineteenth century—that is, men with "nothing to sell but the labor of their hands and brains"—would soon become proletarians, Marx believed. He believed that capitalist economies produced a polarization. Small and inefficient producers, merchants, craftsmen, or peasants were

---

16 "The advance of industry, whose involuntary promoter is the bourgeoisie, replaces the isolation of laborers, due to competition, by their revolutionary combination, due to association. The development of modern industry, therefore, cuts from under its feet the very foundation on which the bourgeoisie produces and appropriates products. What the bourgeoisie, therefore, produces, above all, is its own gravediggers." *Manifesto,* Feuer, op. cit., pp. 19–20.

17 In his writings Marx combined an appealingly "scientific" pose of detachment about capitalism with profound, yet seemingly matter-of-fact condemnation of its workings. Thus, Marx meticulously described in *Das Kapital* the abysmal conditions of manufacture in various British industries—with 5- and 6-year-old children working from 12 to 15 hours, day and night; observed that "Dante would have found the worst horrors of his Inferno surpassed in (such) manufacture"; but concluded that, "Looking at things as a whole, all this does not, indeed, depend on the good or ill will of the individual capitalist. Free competition brings out the inherent laws of capitalist production in the form of external coercive laws having power over every individual capitalist." See his *Capital: A Critique of Political Economy,* Vol. I, trans. by S. Moore and E. Aveling, ed. by Frederick Engels and E. Untermann (New York: Modern Library, 1906) pp. 271–272 and p. 297.

bound to succumb, sooner or later, to the competition of their larger, more efficient capitalist competitors. While perhaps a few of the people in the middle would succeed in becoming capitalists themselves, most were likely to fall by the wayside. Unable to compete, they would join the ranks of an ever-increasing proletariat in the employ of even fewer and richer capitalist masters. The simplified, efficient processes of capitalist production brought about an era of undreamed possible abundance to mankind, Marx believed. Never before could so much be produced so cheaply.

But the fatal flaw in the capitalist system, its major contradiction, as Marx saw it, was between the increasingly *social* character of capitalist production and the *private,* individual, and selfish appropriation of the product by the capitalists. All that the capitalists were doing promoted increasing interdependence of men, of many component parts of the industrial process, indeed even of widely scattered regions. Unlike the medieval craftsman, the capitalist entrepreneur could not even manufacture a single button without involving thousands of people and places in the process; mines, power plants, complex transport facilities, all sorts of auxiliary products and supplies, and possibly raw materials from the four corners of the earth. If anything went wrong with this complex system at any one or several stages, the whole entity could be brought to a standstill. Goods would not be produced, men would lose their jobs, wants would go unsatisfied.[18]

Yet, at the very core of the capitalist economic system stood the private profit motive. Unless the capitalist could continue to make profit on his activities, he would not conduct them, and the effects on the worker would be catastrophic.

Marx believed that, in the long run, capitalists would be unable to harmonize and coordinate their activities. Driven by an inexorable thirst of individual gain, they were bound to collide with one another and miscalculate both markets and profits. Their competition would tend to drive down the profit margins forcing more and more thorough and harsh exploitation of labor—the ultimate source of all profit. Thus, two kinds of experiences lay in store for workers, according to Marx. First, they would be subject to cyclical depressions, periods of unemployment

[18] Marx gave a prophetic vision of the world depression of 1929 in this passage of the *Manifesto*: "In these crises . . . Society finds itself put back into barbarism; it appears as if a famine, a universal war of devastation had cut off every means of subsistence; industry and commerce seem to be destroyed; and why? Because there is too much civilization, too much means of subsistence, too much industry, too much commerce. . . . The conditions of bourgeois society are too narrow to comprise the wealth created by them." Feuer, op. cit., p. 13.

and hence acute misery, even starvation, when the warring capitalists glutted the markets and arbitrarily cut back production. Second, they would be increasingly impoverished on a chronic, secular basis inasmuch as the falling rate of profit would force each capitalist to step up the exploitation of the workers in order to keep his business viable at the marketplace. Borrowing views from the pessimistic British economist, David Ricardo, Marx believed that workers would never achieve, over the long run, a favorable balance of rising wages and declining prices. Like the Manchester School economists, he thought that wage increases would be checked by rising supply of labor and the capitalists' need to cut costs in response to falling profits.

In the upshot of such an untenable situation, Marx believed that the workers would eventually rise up against their capitalist masters and seize control of the marvellously rich but so capriciously disjointed economic system. Having expropriated the capitalists, they would inaugurate a stage of unheard-of material abundance for all.[19]

Although neither Marx nor Engels devoted much attention to the process required, they indicated that capitalism would yield to a brief, transitional stage, which they labeled the dictatorship of the proletariat. In this period, the workers, having seized power, would liquidate the last remnants of the capitalist economic, social, and political system. They would also, in a purely cooperative and voluntary way, organize the economy to produce and distribute even more plentifully than ever before. Ultimately, as both want and class oppression vanished, men would receive whatever they needed for individual sustenance and happiness, while contributing whatever they cared and wanted to contribute to the general welfare of society. Division of labor would at last disappear, thanks to mechanization and opulence.

Instead of doing one job for life, a man might do any number of things that interested him in his lifetime. Work would be liberated from boredom and oppression. Alienation from work and society would disappear.

Marx believed, with the democratic rationalists of the Age of Reason, that man was basically good and cooperative. If only freed from the vexing burdens of social conditions, he would need no stick to guide him along. Politically, the proletarian revolution would put an end to "government" because, as Marx saw it, politics was but an extension of economics. Government, in all its branches, was but an instrument of class oppression. Once that oppression was abolished, the need for government would cease. And while the "dialectic of thesis antithesis-synthesis" would

19 "[Capitalism's] fall and the victory of the proletariat are equally inevitable." Ibid., p. 20.

always go on, the proletarian revolution would end the development in this *one* particular plane—it would signal man's social victory over the domination by his material environment and set the stage for other, different struggles of human development.

Marx had no doubt that the revolution, in his day, was just around the corner. He certainly did not doubt that it was inevitable. But exactly how and when it would come about, he left unclear. He professed the belief that in some countries, singling out England, it could come about peacefully, without bloodshed, and through a gradual ascension of proletarians and withdrawal or capitulation by capitalists.[20] Presumably, elsewhere, the capitalists would resist pressure to give up control and violence would follow. In any case, it was an important part of the Marxian vision that the revolution, no matter how it was carried out, would not come because this or that person wanted it, because it was "good" in some moral sense, but because it was the inevitable consequence of economic and social conditions. These were beyond the control of any given man or group, worker, or capitalist. They could no more be changed than the shape of the earth. On the other hand, in terms of his dialectic, Marx recognized that human volition and action *did* play a role in the process. Boiled down to essentials, that role was one of accelerating or retarding the great cosmic forces at work. The class conscious proletarians, the party activists, and occasionally even a far-seeing capitalist entrepreneur, could contribute to the shaping of history. Generally, however, Marx did not believe that either economic conditions or class attitudes could be really manipulated at will. The framework of development was materially set and given. As he and Engels expressed it in the *Manifesto,* the new society of the future would emerge from the womb of the old—when it was ready. The development of the forces of production constrained human will.

Setting aside social goals and values, let us consider the institutional mechanisms that nineteenth-century socialism, Marxian and otherwise, supported for the realization of its aspirations. The largest part of the socialist movement in nineteenth-century Europe worked out a synthesis between the aspirations of Marxism and the techniques of liberal democracy. The German Social Democratic party was the single most numerous example of this tendency. Analogous syntheses, however, occurred in France, Italy, Scandinavia, Spain, Austro-Hungary, and Russia. In fact, in eastern and southeastern Europe, where the urban middle class was

[20] In his 1886 preface to Marx's *Das Kapital,* Engels wrote that "life-long study of the economic history and condition of England [led Marx] to the conclusion that, at least, in Europe, England is the only country where the inevitable social revolution might be effected entirely by peaceful and legal means." Ibid., p. 32.

not nearly as strong as in the west, it was the socialists who became the principal spokesmen for and defenders of the ideals of liberal democracy. Broadly speaking, the democratic socialists accepted the Marxian analysis of society with its inevitable class antagonisms as well as its goals of worker control of the state, leading to a classless society of the future. They saw their immediate tasks, however, not in hatching conspiracies, but in organizing the power of the working class, developing its consciousness, articulating its social, economic, and political demands and, above all, making its voice and weight felt in the machinery of the state. The socialists struggled to obtain and to extend the suffrage for the masses, and to secure full legal and political rights to workers, trade unions, and worker organizers. They participated in elections, parliamentary assemblies, and local government councils, although at times they shunned cabinet-level participation with representatives of bourgeois parties as too "compromising" or "contaminating." The democratic socialists placed their faith in working class opinion and, concomitantly, in the "naturalness" of the Marxian prophecy. After all, did not Marx insist that violence was but the midwife of social revolution, not its mother? Did he not specifically envision peaceful transition to socialism in some social settings? Above all, if Marx was right about capitalism, in the sense of its inevitable world ascendancy and its accompanying elevation of the proletariat into a movement of the immense majority conscious of its wrongs, why should not socialism triumph by the ballot? The workers were, after all, the class of destiny. When their spokesmen, the socialists, had won the mandate of the people, recalcitrant capitalists —if any then remained—could be appropriately dealt with.

The democratic socialists not only exhibited great confidence in the mechanics of political democracy for winning power, but simultaneously espoused them within, that is, in their own party organizations. In fact, one of the fundamental conflicts between the democratic socialists of Russia (the Mensheviks, as they came to be known) and Lenin's followers (the Bolsheviks), in the early 1900's, was precisely over this issue. The democratic socialists believed in open parties and in leadership accountability to the rank and file of the workers. In Russia, they were revolutionists only because and only to the extent that tsarism did not allow them the opportunities of democratic politics. Lenin, on the other hand, distrusted the masses and doubted the revolutionary efficacy of democracy. (See also Chapter 6.)

Between the end of the nineteenth century and the interwar period of 1918–1939, the democratic socialist movement became increasingly *reformist*. Marxism had given it a tradition and a rhetoric but, in fact, its ideas became less and less significant for the movement with each passing decade. On the one hand, socialists contemplated with satisfaction the enactment of various labor and welfare reforms, for which they had clamored and, on the other, increasingly doubted the imminent disintegration of capitalism. Like the much less numerous Christian socialists, they were increasingly prepared to accept piecemeal reforms within the framework of a capitalist economic system, and to pursue a vaguely consensual vision of social justice rather than power for the working class.

Another highly influential variant of democratic socialism in the late nineteenth century was British Fabianism. Its name derived from that of the cautious Roman general, Fabius. The so-called Fabian Society became the ideological fountainhead of Britain's Labour party and continues as an affiliate of the party even today. Around the turn of the century, it included many prominent British writers and intellectuals, including Graham Wallas, Bernard Shaw, R.H. Tawney, and Beatrice and Sidney Webb. Tied neither to Marxism nor religion, the Fabian socialists were undogmatic humanists. Generally and broadly, they believed that public control and planning of key segments of the economy would ameliorate widespread want and poverty in the society of their day. They rejected rigid notions of an inevitable class conflict between rich and poor, and they expected to persuade people at large that "socialism works," through appeal to reason and by example. The Fabians were interested in promoting greater social equality, in improving the standard of life for the poorest strata of society, and in achieving greater stability and security through concerted social action against the mass hazards of unemployment, sickness, and pauperism. They believed that their ideas would ultimately benefit all classes; their gradualist approach to the realization of public ownership and planning gave rise to the expression "gas and water socialism." The Fabians believed that if socialism could be shown to work in terms of one municipality's public services, the example would spread. In any case, they were prepared to submit to the judgments of the electorate, and to await public acceptance of their ideals however long this process might take.

Since the 1800's, part of the labor movement and of social protest representing the very poor either have not marched under the banner of political democracy, or have done so with significant reservations. Illustrative of these have been anarchist and syndicalist labor groups as well as the communists. The common denominator of their attitudes toward democracy has been the myth of the "bourgeois hoax." Notwithstanding numerous reforms and improvements in the lot of the working man and of the poor in the nineteenth century, the belief has persisted among the radical Left—well into the present time—that democracy cannot solve the problems of the poor. The belief has taken the form of two repudiations of democracy, one partial and qualified, the other extreme and absolute.

The communists have traditionally identified with the first of these repudiations. Beginning with Marx himself, the communists have linked democracy with the rule of the middle class, seeing in it not an instrument for the satisfaction of the demands of all, but rather the institutional expression of bourgeois economic organization of society. Democracy, with its emphasis on individual freedom and extended participation in government, was to Marx and to Lenin a weapon with which the bourgeoisie displaced the old order of royal and aristocratic rule. It was both a popular symbol rallying mass support for the middle class against the old upper classes, and also a convenient and even necessary way of governing society. The middle class wanted to establish freedom of trade and the availability of mobile wage labor. In order to assure these profitable ends, it had to destroy feudal bonds that kept land out of the open market and kept labor tied to the land through feudal customs and restrictions. The freedom of the marketplace presupposed related freedoms in technology, science, the intellectual and cultural as well as ultimately political realms. But in establishing greater freedom and increased participation for the individual, the bourgeoisie could not dare to go all the way; it wanted primarily and above all rights for itself, not really for "everybody." Hence, bourgeois democracy, as Lenin argued at length in *State and Revolution,* was inherently hypocritical; it was a halfway house in which the reality of middle class economic power, expressed in superior capacity for the exercise of democratic rights and in behind-the-scenes influences, kept the whole system from "going too far."[21]

The poor and the rebellious were, in a de facto sense, disqualified or so handicapped that for them the democratic system offered merely the illusion of rights and of participation than the reality. Nevertheless, even Lenin recognized that political democracy did, after all, offer *some* tangible, important gains and benefits to the cause of the proletarian revolution. Unlike the extremely repressive and limited autocracy, it allowed workers and workers' parties (communists foremost, of course) to organize and to agitate and thus to further the development of revolutionary pro-

---

21 As Lenin wrote in his *State and Revolution* (New York: International Publishers, 1943): "In capitalist society . . . democracy is always bound by the narrow framework of capitalist exploitation, and consequently always remains, in reality, a democracy for the minority, only for the possessing classes, only for the rich . . . in the ordinary peaceful course of events, the majority of the population is debarred from participating in social and political life." pp. 71–72.

letarian class consciousness. From the communist point of view, there-fore, politically as well as economically, democracy could be used against its creators, the bourgeoisie.

Both in Marxian and Leninist versions of the creed, however, there is an underlying assumption that the freedoms and opportunities offered by democracy can never extend *far enough* to allow the revolution to be fully consummated. For Marx in most places, for Lenin in all, the bour-geoisie will not allow democracy to be used against its ultimate vital, survival interests. When the revolution becomes genuinely incipient, the bourgeoisie will most likely "strip its democratic mask," and resort to overt, outright force and violence to maintain its economic power in so-ciety. And only corresponding force and violence directed against the bourgeoisie and its outwardly democratic system of government can bring about the revolution.

In the current versions of communist tradition, the Maoists in China and elsewhere still adhere to this view.[22] Other communist movements, including the Soviets since the death of Stalin, profess greater optimism about the possibility of forcing the bourgeoisie to capitulate by forcing concessions short of actual large-scale violence. We may note, however, that this "optimism" is not to be equated with any unequivocal dis-claimers of force, either in principle or on prudential grounds. Rather, there has been a tendency since the 1950's to substitute for Lenin's pre-diction of a certainty of violent conflict everywhere, the probability that in some instances it may be avoidable and unnecessary. This is akin to Marx's nineteenth century view that the proletarian revolution *might* triumph in some countries, like Britain, without recourse to arms.

As to the inherent values of such democratic rights as freedom of ex-pression, communist attitudes have been traditionally ambivalent. They range from the belief that these rights are indeed valuable but only partially realized and that only under communism can they be meaning-fully extended to the proposition that they have been so vitiated through bourgeois treachery, subterfuge and hypocrisy that they are hardly any good at all. This view led George Orwell to observe once that through communist "reductionism" there is no longer any difference between a half a loaf of bread and no bread at all.

To the extent that the communists have identified their own revolu-tionary tradition of 1917 and, hence, as sequels to the democratic revolu-tions of the seventeenth and eighteenth centuries, they have developed an ideological rationale for occasional policies of cooperation with the

[22] This rationale also underlies much current New Left discussion of an inevitable repression in American society today.

less equivocal supporters of the democratic system. These policies have been expressed in the so-called united front alliances as in the 1930's, during World War II, and in some cases even more recently. These same ideological premises have led the communists to accept the value of democratic structures and processes in a purely instrumental and temporary sense—as battering rams, as it were, against the bastions of established socioeconomic power facing them.

No matter how differently communist groups may "use" democracy, depending on the occasion, their fundamental aim is antipolitical. Their goal is not to create societies in which all men could participate more equitably in politics but rather to abolish the very process of politics altogether.

In the process of transition from capitalist rule to the classless society, it would be a crime and a folly for the proletariat to allow the bourgeoisie the use of political weapons against itself. Hence, *bourgeois democracy,* which does allow different interests to articulate their positions, must, in the communist view, be replaced by a proletarian democracy that would not.

The allowable dialogue must become narrowly circumscribed by the Party as the leader of the proletariat, and every discussion within or without the Party must take cognizance of the Party's aims. To the communists every form of government, including their own, though hopefully only temporarily and transitionally, is concealed class oppression of the exploited by the exploiters. The end of exploitation will also signal the end of government and of politics, in their view, and the ultimate goal of nonpolitical self-rule by the workers.

Anarchists and syndicalists of the nineteenth and twentieth centuries sought either the direct abolition of government—thereby skipping the communists' dictatorship of the proletariat phase—or the conquest of political power by trade unions: apart from and against the institutions of democratic government. In both these movements a deep-rooted suspicion of the bourgeoisie and its institutions was characteristic. It led to the view that under no circumstances could parliamentary or electoral processes really serve the cause of workers' liberation. The bourgeoisie was too powerful and too cunning in the uses of the political apparatus to allow this. Workers elected to bourgeois legislatures were sure to be bribed, corrupted, and in any case stymied in their efforts. Only direct action against the state, not within it, could realize the anarchist and syndicalist goals. Implicit in this view was also an impatient and mistrustful rejection of the appeal to public opinion at large. Viewing the "class enemy" with intense hostility, these workers' movements discounted the possibility of persuasion and progress from "some" to "more" and "more yet"—within the framework of the established order. So long as the bourgeoisie had its vested interests, and controlled the institutions of power, only direct action, not moral appeals or reforms from within, could dislodge its hold. Appeals for change, they believed, would fall on deaf ears so far as the bourgeoisie was concerned. On the other hand, the labor movements of the extreme left also displayed deep pessimism that those who *ought* to oppose the bourgeoisie—the workers, the landless, the poor—could ever be won over to the cause of change by the ballot so long as the bourgeoisie was allowed to keep them in ignorance and restrain their actions through its own overt and indirect influences. The masses had to be freed in spite of themselves, the radicals maintained, since they could not ever do so themselves within the framework of the middle class society, with all its inducements to quiescence and acceptance of the status quo. These arguments, too, are currently revived by new Left ideologues.

The socialist extremists from Marx to Bakunin differed in their views on the tactics to be employed to overthrow the existing order; and they, above all, differed on the arrangements to follow its overthrow. They shared, however, a profound hostility toward and suspicion of bourgeois institutions—including political democracy—and doubted the ability of the common man—within a bourgeois order, to be sure—to understand and follow "correct" revolutionary policies which they advocated.

In reviewing the ideals and methods of the nineteenth century, we confront some of the great paradoxes of politics. The socialists, who essentially relied on reason and persuasion to achieve a more humane society, did, in fact, influence public opinion and public policy. The Welfare State of the twentieth century and a long list of piecemeal reforms in many countries in the 1800's—factory legislation, abolition of child labor, old age pensions, unemployment and health insurance, worker representation in industry, collective bargaining—all these testified to their success in considerable measure. Moreover, all these reforms were brought about in western Europe, Scandinavia, and North America without the sacrifice of political and legal freedoms of citizens. Many of the claims of nineteenth-century socialism gradually became accepted by wider publics—by people who did *not* think of themselves as "socialists." In the most technologically advanced, industrial nations of the world, moderate, democratic socialists were the ones who gained by far the larger following, not the radical revolutionists of Marxian, anarchist, or syndicalist persuasion.

On the other hand, the anger and intolerance of militant Marxian revolutionism proved much more successful in the relatively backward, economically archaic societies.[23] Wherever Marxian revolutionism tri-

[23] See William Ebenstein, *Today's Isms*, 3rd ed. (Englewood Cliffs: N.J.: Prentice-

umphed, the costs of its reforms invariably entailed the sacrifice of individual freedoms—the right of free speech, association, equality before the law, and the security of each man's life and, within the law, his property.

The doctrine that Marx propounded as the philosophy to end all philosophy—that is, as THE ultimate "scientific" truth about man and society—was built upon a number of plausible ideas. It drew its strength from the very adroitness with which it combined a hard-bitten historical and economic realism, even cynicism, with a powerful moral appeal. It cried out against and vowed an uncompromising struggle against the exploitation of man by man, against injustice, against the alienation of man from his work and his society. Yet, it was actually no more "scientific" than the rest. Marxism, like all ideologies, rested upon certain fundamental axioms or assumptions which were not really "scientific" in an empirical sense but which were metaphysical. Ultimately, like Thomas Jefferson, Karl Marx appealed to self-evident truths. His system of ideas, more or less plausibly, singled out and envalued certain aspects of man's social existence. Some things were "fundamental," "basic," and "important"; others were not. Unlike a researcher in the physical or biochemical sciences, Marx could never rigorously demonstrate what the relationship between X and Y (say, "economic development" and "political power") was, or how and why it might vary under any specifiable conditions. How can we tell, for example, that economic factors determine religious beliefs in a society? Or that class conflict is more *fundamental* than ethnic conflict? Or that the organization of the means of production and distribution *determines* the *basic nature* of a society's literature? Are some of these relationships occasionally reversible, and if so, how, when and why? Is "inevitability" (such as death, for example) the test of "right"?

Notwithstanding the great uncertainty involved in such questions, the contemporary followers of Marx, even more than Marx himself, have been willing to quash dissent by force of arms,[24] and to sacrifice the lives and happiness of millions of people to future gratifications theoretically posited by his doctrine.

Hall, 1961), p. 208. He reports that in 12 West European states between 1946 and 1960 Communist electoral strength increased only in one: Italy. On the other hand, significant declines occurred in Austria, Belgium, Denmark, France, West Germany, Great Britain, Netherlands, and Norway.

24 Compare George H. Sabine, *A History of Political Theory* (New York: Henry Holt, 1950), p. 798: "Karl Marx once said of himself that he was not a Marxist. This remark referred in part to his own comparative indifference to the doctrinal completeness of his social philosophy and the misgivings with which he and Engels in their later life regarded the dogmatism of some of their disciples."

CHAPTER **5**

Nationalism

Eighteenth-Century democracy was, above all, concerned with unshackling the individual and creating a viable state based on a maximum amount of personal freedom. The primary concern of socialism combined material abundance (or at least "sufficiency") and equality among men, with communal reintegration of mankind. The contribution of nationalism may be described as most directly integrative. Democracy emphasized individuality and competition; socialism emphasized conflict between the poor and the rich; nationalism historically sought to restore the wholeness of society in the name of certain shared values and symbols. It attempted to unite men around "flag and country" and—in the case of its more conservative varieties—around the traditional, inherited political, social, and economic institutions of particular countries.[1]

Democracy channeled men's aggressive impulses toward individual competition—from the premises of equal opportunity and freedom for all—toward economic, social, or cultural preferment based on each man's merit and hard work. Socialism channeled aggressive impulses toward class conflict in combating the unjust power and influence of the rich.

[1] Among works dealing with the phenomenon of nationalism in the nineteenth century, particularly interesting ones include Carlton J. H. Hayes, *The Historical Evolution of Modern Nationalism* (New York: Macmillan, 1948); his earlier *Essays on Nationalism* (New York: Macmillan, 1926), and his *Nationalism: A Religion* (New York: Macmillan, 1960); Elie Kedoure, *Nationalism* (London: Hutchinson, 1960); and Hans Kohn, *The Idea of Nationalism* (New York: Macmillan, 1944), and his *The Age of Nationalism* (New York: Harper, 1962).

Nationalism, on the other hand, channeled aggression toward outsiders, emphasizing the cohesion and unity of the members of the national "in-group." It identified dangerous enemies among members of other national groups and those subservient to them. It demanded vigilance and dedication against the enemy without and their alleged agents within.

In its genesis, nationalism stands in particular debt to the Great French Revolution of 1789. The French Revolution dramatically brought to the attention of Europe and the world the ideas, slogans, and institutional expressions of nationalism. Here, it was originally associated with the idea of human equality, of inclusive citizenship, freedom, and social solidarity. The passionate manifestos of the French National Assembly, the heroic example of the "People-in-Arms" fighting and winning against the interventionist armies of reactionary Austria and Prussia at Valmy in 1793 under the leadership of a civilian-turned-soldier, Lazar Carnot—all these acts represented an inspiration and an example to people elsewhere. Moreover, the armies of Napoleon I, which conquered the bulk of the European continent in the three decades between the Tennis Court Oath and the Battle of Waterloo, carried the message of nationalism for them.

The concept of nation has always been an elusive one. Race, religion, language, common domicile, possession of a definable territory, a shared past, a shared aspiration to achieve and maintain statehood, as in the case of modern Zionism before 1948, have all been used to identify various national groups.[2]

In a nineteenth-century definition by Frenchman, Renan:

"A nation is a soul . . . A nation is a great solidarity, created by the sentiment of the sacrifices which have been made and of those which

---

[2] On nationalism in a contemporary perspective see Karl W. Deutsch, *Nationalism and Social Communication* (New York: Wiley, 1953); David E. Apter (ed.), *Ideology and Discontent* (London: Free Press of Glencoe, 1964); Barbara Jackson (Ward) *Nationalism and Ideology* (New York: Norton, 1966); Leonard W. Doob, *Patriotism and Nationalism: Their Psychological Foundations* (New Haven: Yale University Press, 1964). See also Louis L. Snyder, *The New Nationalism* (Ithaca, N.Y.: Cornell University Press, 1968); Wilfrid Knapp, *Unity and Nationalism in Europe Since 1945* (New York: Pergammon Press, 1969); and K. Symmons-Symonolewicz, *Modern Nationalism: Towards a Consensus in Theory* (New York: Polish Institute of Arts and Sciences in America, 1968). Definitions of nationalism have always been notoriously imprecise, largely because of the great variation among, and the mystical subjectivity in, all nationalisms. Karl W. Deutsch reports a rueful European definition that "A Nation is a group of persons united by a common error about their ancestry and a common dislike of their neighbors." *Nationalism and Its Alternatives* (New York: A. A. Knopf, 1969), p. 3.

one is disposed to make in the future. It presupposes a past; but it resumes itself in the present by a tangible fact: the consent, the clearly expressed desire to continue life in common. The existence of a nation is a plebiscite of every day, as the existence of the individual is the perpetual affirmation of life."[3]

All men, rich and poor, noble and common, were seen as belonging to this common entity—the nation. In turn, the nation was regarded as the ultimate summit of human loyalties, a spiritual, cultural, and material possession akin to home and family, and a source of the most worthy and inspiring values. The collective entity of the nation was seen as the ultimate dispenser of civilization, morality, law, and prosperity.

If the French Revolution may be credited with the positive contribution of a forceful, successful example of nationalism, it also acted as catalyst in a negative sense. As a giant mobilizer of dormant masses, the French Revolution was as frightening to some people in Europe as it was inspiring to others. Courtiers, noblemen, many clerics and wealthy bourgeois did not relish the specter of a popular tiger at the gates— masses of people demanding power and equality against the whole established pattern of past conventions.

To many of these people it was clear that to stem the tide of revolution and reform associated with popular power, they would have to learn from, and somehow adapt the elemental force of mass mobilization that the Revolution represented. In a sense, one could say that the reactionaries had learned something from the experience of 1789–1815.

They adapted nationalism so as to combat democracy all the more effectively. Actually, the uses made of democracy by labor and widely held expectations as to the consequences that democracy was likely to have, rallied opposition to it from among many diverse interests.

Among those who conspicuously feared and opposed the extension of "democracy" to the masses were the one-time middle class liberals. The merchant class and the peasant proprietors who in the seventeenth and eighteenth centuries fought royal absolutism and demanded freedom and equality for all became alarmed in the nineteenth century over the social and economic consequences to themselves, to their property, and to their social status, as a result of a democratic revolution through the extension of suffrage and de facto power to the "great unwashed." Nineteenth-century European liberals tended to become conservatives when threatened with the power of the masses. Many feared that the rights which they had once championed for themselves would now be used

[3] From a definition published in 1887 and cited by Hans Kohn, *Nationalism: Its Meaning and History*, rev. ed. (Princeton; N.J.: Van Nostrand, 1965), p. 139.

against them. Freedom of speech and association could be used not merely for the dissemination of philosophic doctrines but, very practically to "stir up the poor," possibly to bring about the expropriation of wealth, and the destruction of all social distinctions. Nationalism gradually gathered a conservative clientele.

Many individuals who were otherwise well educated, tolerant, and open-minded became nevertheless political conservatives in the sense that they supported efforts to curb or limit the power of the masses or the "mob," as they saw it. The values of law and order became either paramount to them or at least assumed the position of coordinate importance with the values of libertarian free expression and full representation. Many increasingly gravitated to the camp of integral nationalism.

The rationale employed by liberals who had grown wary and conservative frequently emphasized a peculiarly aristocratic guardianship of liberal values, not their rejection. They took the view traceable in thinkers ranging from de Tocqueville and Mill in the nineteenth century to Ortega y Gasset in the twentieth, that the "masses" would trample on liberty if given unrestrained power.[4] This is turn gave rise to a succession of ingenious schemes for keeping the impact of popular power in balance or at some safe maximum, short of really equal and full representation of all adult males (let alone females) in the political community.

Government by the majority of the people would be class government argued the conservative critics; it would tyrannize over the minority and would be particularly intolerant of individuals who did not fit the common mold of the mass man. The average man did not yet possess the requisite skills and therefore the wisdom to rule the community. If he was poor, there was every chance that he would behave "irresponsibly" toward those who were not. And it would be difficult, if not impossible, argued the erstwhile liberals, to raise so great a multitude of the poor to a level of intellectual and moral attainment that would allow them to be judicious, tolerant, and wise.

Therefore, they argued, suffrage should be limited or at best extended

---

[4] See John Stuart Mill's discussion of the conditions under which representative government is "inapplicable" and of the "infirmities and dangers to which (it) is liable" in Chapters 4, 6, and 7 of his *Considerations on Representative Government* (London: Park, Bourn, 1884). Mill feared "a low grade of intelligence in the representative body, and in the popular opinion which controls it" as well as "class legislation on the part of the numerical majority" (p. 131). Note that Mill himself did not draw the nationalist-conservative or reactionary conclusions from such views as many other middle class intellectuals did.

only gradually and within the framework of governmental institutions themselves. Safeguards ought to be provided which, in the form of an aristocratic second chamber, an executive veto, and dispersal of power would check the impetuosity and rash willfulness of a legislature representing the masses.

While any study of the history of the nineteenth century will disclose a dialogue along these lines in Europe and in the United States, the pattern is by no means so antiquated or so confined. The constitutional struggle to limit the power of the masses has been repeated on a large scale, with numerous interesting examples, in the aftermath of the Versailles Treaty in Europe and again following World War II. The more conservative political groupings—in terms of their socioeconomic interests and clienteles—became the spokesmen of bicameralism, judicial review, strong executive power, qualifications of suffrage and, frequently also federalism. The more radical groups generally supported unicameralism, unrestricted and frequently proportional representation to men and women, old and young, and generally also a smooth and direct articulation of power relationships between the national legislature based on such representation, and the executive and the administrative branches of government.[5]

If many liberals became "conservatives" in their attitude toward the extension of popular power, the conservatives of the eighteenth and nineteenth centuries—the supporters of Kings and of Established Churches, of the Nobility and Landed Wealth, however reduced in numbers and influence—became the reactionaries of the twentieth century. If they had found the still relatively limited middle class revolutions of 1642, 1775, and 1789 unacceptable, the demands of radical democracy appeared even more outrageous to them. In their efforts to restore eighteenth century status quo ante, they generally wished not merely to delay the extension of popular power, or to buttress it with limiting safeguards, but to abolish it. They became the advocates of "turning the clock back" (in terms of a popular political slogan used against them) to the rule of hereditary monarchy and aristocracy. They

[5] See Hans Rogger and Eugen Weber, *The European Right: A Historical Profile* (Berkeley: University of California, 1965) on the conservative institutional aspirations of various nationalist parties in Europe both in the nineteenth and twentieth centuries. See also Malbone W. Graham, *New Government of Central Europe* (New York: H. Holt, 1924); Gordon Wright, *The Reshaping of French Democracy* (New York: Reynal, 1948); and Arnold J. Zurcher (ed.), *Constitutions and Constitutional Trends Since World War II* (New York: New York University Press, 1951), for information on constitutional cleavages between various segments of European "Left," "Right," and "Center."

became spokesmen for the restoration of a political order which, in practical terms, was becoming increasingly obsolete and rare in the modern world.

To these groups, the norms of democracy were anathema in principle, where to erstwhile middle class liberals they seemed fraught with danger but nevertheless still "negotiable." For the eighteenth-century conservative and modern reactionary, the right of political participation was neither inherent in every man nor developable in some cautious, gradualist fashion. It inhered only by birth and prescription, that is, in terms of such monarchical, aristocratic, feudal, and ecclesiastical traditions which constitute the true and legitimate order of society. To the reactionary, any departure from this true order has constituted varieties of crime and folly.

But, in the nineteenth century, telling the people to "keep their noses out of politics" and follow the orders of their superiors clearly was no longer enough. The mobilization effected by the French Revolution influenced not only those sympathetic to liberty, equality, and fraternity but also those most opposed to it. For these people, conservative nationalism became the answer to the threat of popular power and popular revolution.

Popular aspirations had to be harnessed; they certainly could no longer be safely ignored. If ancient privileges were to stand, they could do so only on the basis of a new acceptance by the masses.

The last great ideologue of the "Old Order" in Europe, after the French Revolution, was undoubtedly Joseph de Maistre (1753–1821). He was an aristocratic exile from revolutionary France, who had become an ambassador to the court of the Russian tsar at St. Petersburg from the Kingdom of Piedmont. De Maistre was a great exponent of the conservative tradition; he extolled the virtues of social stability and continuity, and viewed the Revolution of 1789 as an act of enormous villainy. He regarded its intellectual prophets, spokesmen, and sympathizers, men like Locke, Rousseau, and Voltaire, as dangerous rogues. Unlike the devices of modern nationalists, however, de Maistre's palliative was to restore the spirtual supremacy of the Universal Church of the Middle Ages. Author of *Du Pape* in 1819, de Maistre wanted to anchor stability, continuity, and tradition in the ultimate spiritual authority of the Pope. In retrospect, he found even the harsh discipline of the Inquisition salutary.[6]

But the developing mainstream of those who sought cohesion and

[6] See Joseph M. de Maistre, *Works* (New York: Macmillan, 1965), Claude J. Gignoux, *Joseph de Maistre: Prophet du Passe* (Paris: Nouvelles Editions Latins, 1963), and Robert Triomphe, *Joseph de Maistre* (Geneva: Droz, 1968).

stability above all else looked to the state rather than to the church. The growing ideology of nationalism was appropriately, modernistically, secular rather than religious.

Among those who did not necessarily or particularly think of themselves as "nationalists," but whose ideas were nevertheless pressed into the service of nationalism, were Jean Jacques Rousseau (1712–1778), Edmund Burke (1729–1797), and Georg William Friedrich Hegel (1770–1831).

Hegel's historicism and his dialectic were major contributions to Marxian socialism; Rousseau's passionate concern with equality and his formulation of the concept of the General Will made him an important theorist of democracy. But beyond this, Hegel, Rousseau, and Burke shared a common "organic" view of society which made their ideas useful to the proponents of integral nationalism.

Rousseau advocated the concept of a closely knit community in which the business of the state was really everyone's business, and by implication, at least, also the reverse. Unlike Locke and Smith, Rousseau gave scant attention to each individual's "private sphere." What really counted was the collectivity and its duties. He preached patriotism and public spritedness on the model of a Greek city-state. Rousseau's ideal was not the modern, commercial, and materialistic society in which everyone might ask: "What's in it for me?" but rather one in which the individual would always feel that no sacrifice on behalf of the common weal could possibly be too great.[7] Moreover, he attributed a mystic wisdom and rectitude to the human collectivity subsumed in the state which, somehow, was infinitely superior to the qualities of its several parts.[8]

[7] In Rousseau's own words: "The better the constitution of a State is, the more do public affairs encroach on private in the minds of the citizens. Private affairs are even of much less importance, because the aggregate of the common happiness furnishes a greater proportion of that to each individual, so that there is less for him to seek in particular cares. In a well-ordered city every man flies to the assemblies: under a bad government no one cares to stir a step . . . . As soon as any many says of the affairs of the State *What does it matter to me?* the state may be given up for lost." Jean Jacques Rousseau, *The Social Contract*, translated with an introduction by G.D.H. Cole (New York: Dutton, 1950), pp. 93–94.

[8] "When in the popular asembly a law is proposed, what the people is asked is not exactly whether it approves or rejects a proposal, but whether it is in conformity with the general will. . . . Each man, in giving his vote, states his opinion on that point; and the general will is found by counting votes. When therefore the opinion that is contrary to my own prevails, this proves neither more nor less than that I was mistaken, and that what I thought to be the general will was not so. If my particular opinion had carried the day I should have achieved the opposite of what was my will; and it is in that case that I should not have been free." Ibid., p. 106.

Hegel professed to see the progress of history as the development of the idea of freedom. History was, for him, the march of God through the world. But Hegel's writings made the state into the vehicle of that gradually unfolding idea. Thus the state was the highest and the most complete vehicle of human civilization and the most advanced expression of human freedom in his day. Here, order and freedom, Hegel thought, found their best temporal synthesis. Hegel's philosophy thus tended to sanctify the notion of the state for modern nationalists—making it at once the most worthwhile of temporal aspirations to attain and/or preserve. Hegelianism also endowed the state with all the mystique that nationalists found so practically useful. If it really was all that Hegel believed, then the "selfish and willful" interests of individuals, classes, and groups could be justifiably subordinated to this higher value.[9]

The contribution of Burke, akin to both Hegel and Rousseau, was the belief in the natural evolution of human society, such that most of its institutions, rules, and hierarchies could be looked upon as the product of centuries of social history. What developed gradually over the ages, Burke argued, represented the collective wisdom and experience of many generations; only those who were rash and foolish would tamper with the natural, organic heritage of their societies, each shaped in a different and uniquely appropriate fashion. Reforms, changes, and even adaptations from abroad might be occasionally useful. But prudent men would always recognize the overriding importance of their indigenous heritage. Society was, in Burke's celebrated expression, not a contract in the sense conveyed by a commercial exchange, but an immutable pact between the dead, the living, and those yet to be born.[10] Chaos and evil were likely to befall those who rashly tore at the roots of their society. This was the

Here we have Rousseau's contribution to the notion of a "totalitarian democracy," nationalist or socialist, in which the individual is free by submitting to the higher wisdom of the collectivity.

9 In Hegel's fulsome words: "The state in and for itself is the ethical whole, the actualization of freedom. It is the absolute end of reason that freedom be actual. . . . When reasoning about freedom one must not start from the individual self-consciousness, for whether one knows it or not, this essence still realizes itself as an independent power in which the single individuals are only elements: it is the course of God through the world that constitutes the state." *The Philosophy of Hegel*, edited with an introduction by Carl J. Friedrich (New York: Random House, 1953), pp. 282–283.

10 See W. J. Bate (ed.), *Edmund Burke Selected Works* (New York: Random House, 1960), p. 407. Burke extolled the state as a "partnership in all art; a partnership in every virtue, and in all perfection . . . . Each contract of each particular state is but a clause in the great primaeval contract of eternal society, linking the lower with the higher natures, connecting the visible and invisible world . . ." Ibid.

fate, in Burke's view, as set out in his *Reflections on the Revolution in France*, in 1790, of the Frenchmen who contemptuously rejected traditional wisdom, usage, prescriptive rights, and the historic hierarchy of rank and property in their own country in 1789.

Thus, in the genesis of the ideology of nationalism in Europe, we can ultimately discern three stages. First, the idea actually emerged in association with egalitarianism and democracy as an instrument of change; second, it became a popular creed essentially for the support of traditional privilege in opposition to far-reaching social change. In its final European version, nationalism achieved the extreme-radical form given to it by Benito Mussolini (1883–1945) in Italy, and by Adolf Hitler (1889–1945) in Germany.

In its original version, nationalism was exemplified by men like the heroes of Italy's *Risorgimiento*, Giuseppe Mazzini and Giuseppe Garibaldi; France's—and America's—Count de Lafayette; and Poland's—and America's—Tadeusz Kosciuszko and Kazimierz Pulaski. These men espoused the cause of individual liberty no less ardently than the cause of the nation. To them nationalism and an open society were wholly compatible values.

Nationalism and internationalism were not opposites at all but rather indissolubly complementary parts of one fabric of a just human society. In the words of the Polish patriots fighting in George Washington's Continental Army of the 1770's, the struggle was "for your freedom and ours." All nations were entitled to freedom. Nationalism had not yet become a "zero-sum" game in which X's gain was bound to be Y's loss.

Thus, Giuseppe Mazzini (1805–1872) was a spokesman of European federalism and domestic liberty but with national independence (for Italy) as a prerequisite to both. For Mazzini, socialism was far too materialistic, overly concerned with rights instead of duties, putting too much emphasis on class division instead of on the unifying element of national identity.[11]

The second phase is exemplified by such men as France's Charles Maurras (1868–1952), founder of *L'Action Francaise* in 1908, and Poland's influential Roman Dmowski (1864–1939). To these men, liberal democracy was highly suspect.[12] The disciplined subordination of the

[11] See Giuseppe Mazzini, *The Duties of Man* (London: Chapman and Hall, 1862). N. Gangulee (ed.), *Mazzini: Selected Writings* (London: L. Brummond, 1945); William L. Garrison, *Joseph Mazzini* (New York: Hurd and Houghton, 1872).

[12] See Michael Curtis, *Three Against the Third Republic: Sorel, Barres and Maurras*, (Princeton, N.J.: Princeton University Press, 1959). Samuel M. Osgood, *French Royalism Under the Third and Fourth Republics* (The Hague: Nijhoff, 1960). Jean de Fabreques, *Charles Maurras et son "Action francaise"* (Paris: Perrin, 1966).

individual to the welfare of the nation was paramount. They, and others like them, extolled integrative institutions and symbols, such as the Church, the Army, or the Crown, in order to maintain an undefiled national identity. They feared erosion and alienation of the people from the integrative values represented by such institutions. To them, liberalism and laissez-faire were wanton anarchy. Socialism was an evil assault upon the spiritual values and traditions of the nation. They were morbidly suspicious of foreigners and foreign influences, and were vitriolically anti-Semitic.

After the defeat of France in the Franco-Prussian War of 1870, the nationalists of both Germany and France typically focused public attention on the armed forces.[13] In Germany, the army became the ultimate symbol of the national interest. The military were glorified and worshipped with heedless abandon.[14] In France, the nationalists looked to the army to avenge the humiliation of Sedan and to rally the patriotic spirit of the people. In the 1880's, they even hoped that a popular War Minister, General Boulanger, would rescue them from the perils of parliamentary democracy.

In 1896, the values of nationalism and democracy ilustratively confronted one another with worldwide impact in the drama of one man's life. Captain Alfred Dreyfus, a Jew and a dedicated staff officer in the French Army, was accused of espionage on behalf of Germany. The accusations ultimately turned out to be false, but on the strength of forged evidence, Dreyfus was sentenced to exile on Devil's Island by a French military court. A 10-year struggle was required to clear him.

Dreyfus' champions, men like Emile Zola and Georges Clemenceau, defended his cause on the grounds that the rights of even one man—whatever his background and station—were of the highest importance to the democratic republic. Equal justice for all was to them a nonnegoti-

---

See also Alexander Groth, "Dmowski, Pilsudski, and Ethnic Conflict in Pre-1939 Poland," *Canadian Slavic Studies,* Vol. 2, June 1969, pp. 69–91.

[13] On nationalist concern with the power and prestige of the army see, e.g., Eugen J. Weber, *The Nationalist Revival in France, 1905–1914* (Berkeley: University of California Press, 1959) pp. 106–119.

[14] Speaking before the German Reichstag in 1887, Field Marshal Count Helmuth von Moltke "modestly" summarized the military role in these terms: "The Army takes the first place among the institutions of every country. It alone makes possible the existence of all the other institutions. All political and civil liberty, all the creations of civilization, the finances, the State itself, stand and fall with the Army." See Munroe Smith, *Out of Their Own Mouths* (New York: Appleton, 1918) p. 150–51 for this and many similar pronouncements. Compare Adolf Hitler in *Mein Kampf* "What the German people owes to the Army may be summed up in one word, namely, everything."

able principle. They believed the Dreyfus case to be a test of the French Revolution's famous Declaration of the Rights of Man and Citizen.

To conservative French nationalists, the paramount interest was the prestige and integrity of the army. After all, the army maintained national power and domestic tranquility. It expressed and symbolized the traditions of French patriotism and unity. The cause of France was clearly more important than that of an obscure individual. Besides, Dreyfus, the Jew, symbolized the alien influences in high places against which the nationalists had so long inveighed. The men who annually covered the Statue of Strasbourg (a city lost to Germany in the 1870 war) with black crepe, were not about to risk the reputation of the army on behalf of one Jewish officer.[15]

The worship of the military—its uniforms, jackboots, insignia, traditions, codes, and legends—was not confined to France or Germany. Militarism and nationalism became closely linked elsewhere, too. It was not until the twentieth century, however, that the fullest confluence of these values was brought about in fascism and nazism.

These ideologies, as espoused by Mussolini and Hitler, have much in common, and we can profitably outline the common denominators of these two doctrines before we review their differences. First, they provided an element of popular involvement, an adaptation to the mass politics of the age of democracy. In each case, however, this involvement combined participation with a very lopsided subjection of the masses to the elite, and particularly to the leader—Fuehrer or Duce. Both Hitler and Mussolini were held to be extraordinary personalities, imbued with the qualities of seers, genuises, and heroes and thus not subject to the considerations that bind and limit ordinary mortals. With respect to participation, fascism and nazism transcended the idea of merely telling millions of ordinary people to remain apolitical or have faith in the leaders, because they act for the good of nation. Instead, they demanded that each man, woman, and even child be an active fighter and promoter of the Leader's cause, albeit in a clearly subordinate role. The organizational idea, as it were, of fascism and nazism, was that of a military phalanx. Mussolini's motto, "Believe, Obey, Fight," also applied to nazism. In both cases, people were expected to belong, to march, to work and shout at the beckoning of the Leader and his lieutenants. There was no room for detachment from the cause, for neutrality, or for the luxury of being a mere spectator. Hitler and Mussolini sought to draw people en masse into their respective movements.

15 See Guy Chapman, *The Dreyfus Case* (London: R. Hart-Davis, 1955); Nicholas Halasz, *Captain Dreyfus* (New York: Simon and Schuster, 1955); and particularly Douglas W. Johnson, *France and the Dreyfus Affair* (New York: Walker, 1967).

Although outwardly nazism seemed different from fascism because of its emphasis on "Race" rather than upon the "State," both were alike in glorifying the national self. Mussolini could be regarded as more Hegelian in that his movement was dedicated to the notion of a powerful state, allegedly embodying all the highest values and aspirations of civilization.[16]

Mussolini and his followers, men like Alfredo Rocco and Giovanni Gentile, preached the idea that the state was a law unto itself. No higher or more binding standard of moral obligation existed for the individual. Humanity and mankind were meaningless terms—amorphous conceptions. The judgment of individuals represented only anarchy. The state was a concrete organic institution whose will was law. Its interests were superior to those of any of its lesser constituent entities. For the rightly ordered state was the concrete embodiment of the nation—the sum of those institutions through which it expressed its historic individuality and continuity; the agency through which it asserted its will, its power and, as the Fascist propagandists would say, its distinctive genius. The vitality and greatness of the state was the most important condition of civilization itself—of its value and quality. The paramount interest of the state justified the sacrifice of the individual and of all other lesser, corporate interests to it. Mussolini, like Hegel, not only believed that the state's interest justified the resort to war but that the capacity and will for war were signs of the state's vitality.[17] Some of these ideas were popularized in the Fascist slogan, "all in the state, nothing against the state, all for the state."[18] In line with Heglian vitalism glorifying violence, Mussolini asserted that "war was as natural to man as childbirth to woman."[19]

Outwardly, Hitler professed indifference to the idea of the state, identifying it with a "lifeless bureaucracy." The Nazis refined the idea of the nation to the conception of race and relegated the state to the role of a mere tool of the race. In substance, however, the attributes associated with the political collectivity headed by a Fuehrer were remarkably like those of the collectivity led by the Duce.

The distinctive genius of fascism and nazism alike consisted in the exaltation of the key values of conservative nationalism in combination with an appealing, though largely spurious social radicalism.[20]

16 This claim is disputed by many students of Hegel's ideas, inasmuch as Hegel perceived the state as the embodiment of reason; the Fascists worshipped unreason.

17 See Herman Finer, *Mussolini's Italy* (Hamden, Conn.: Anchor Books, 1964), p. 174–181.

18 Compare A. James Gregor, *The Ideology of Fascism* (New York: Free Press, 1969), pp. 172 and 189–190.

19 Finer, op. cit., p. 175.

20 The full name of the Nazi party was the National Socialist German Workers

Thus, both fascism and nazism managed to exalt the idea of authority to an all but supernatural degree. They succeeded in making the average person, Italian or German, feel insignificant vis-á-vis the leadership at home while simultaneously instilling the notion that every German or Italian was vastly superior to his neighbors. The idea of shrinking the image of the citizen at home and blowing it up in relation to foreigners was carried out to its extreme. Both Mussolini and Hitler openly despised the egalitarian ideals of democracy and socialism as unworkable and pernicious. The masses, they argued, possessed neither the intelligence nor the courage to decide the fate of the polity. Only the hero-genius was fit for such tasks. The idea of human equality and rationality even in some minimal sense was explicitly and implicitly rejected by fascism and nazism. Hitler clearly expressed his contempt for the average person. The masses were swayed by emotion, he argued; their cognitive and reasoning powers were slight. They were weak and vulnerable, both intellectually and morally. The Nazi rejection of parliamentary democracy was symptomatic of their general contempt for the capacity of the ordinary people.[21] The Fascist view of the Duce's leadership and of the man-in-the street was not really different. Both leaders preached extreme forms of national aggrandizement. If hatred of foreigners could serve as a lightning rod for social discontent or an outlet for pent-up aggressions, fascism and nazism excelled in its deployment.[22]

Fascist propaganda pictured Italy as a successor state to the Roman Empire; Mussolini talked of turning the Mediterranean into "Mare Nostrum" (Our Sea), and tirelessly advocated Italy's right to be imperialistic. Considerable evidence cast doubt on the proposition that colonies did really benefit Italy in the nineteenth century; or that the

Party (NSDAP) founded in 1919. Its so-called "unalterable" program of 1921 had several radical anticapitalist provisions and among Hitler's early supporters, men like Captain Ernest Roehm and the Strasser brothers, there were quite a few who hoped for an anticapitalist revolution under Hitler's leadership. By the mid-1930's most of these men were purged; the rest, like Dr. Joseph Goebbels, generally moderated their anticapitalism. On the radical beginings of Mussolini's Fascist party in 1919 and its analogous "Turn to the Right," see Gaetano Salvemini, *The Fascist Dictatorship in Italy* (New York: Fertig, 1967), pp. 1–120.

21 "A majority . . . is always the advocate, not only of stupid, but also of cowardly policies; and just as a hundred fools do not make one wise man, an heroic decision is not likely to come from a hundred cowards." See *My Battle*, abridged and translated by E.T.S. Dugdale (Boston: Houghton Mifflin, 1933) p. 35.

22 See Franz Neumann, *Behemoth: The Structure and Practice of National Socialism* (New York: Oxford University Press, 1942), pp. 187–210, on Hitler's use of the "proletarian nation" concept. As Mussolini put it in one of his speeches, "Fascism demands more ample outlets for Italians, who are the most proletarian of peoples," cited by Pietro Gorgolini in *The Fascist Movement in Italian Life* (Boston: Little, Brown, 1923), p. 184.

density of her population was the basic cause of Italy's economic hardships; or that indeed aggression was the best way to relieve overpopulation and unemployment at home. But the Fascists preached expansion by force against Italy's neighbors and especially against Africans, attributing superiority to Italians over backward peoples—such as the Albanians and Ethiopians as well as the Slav and Greek inhabitants of the Balkan peninsula. Nothing less than a great empire and the role of arbiter of world politics would satisfy Mussolini. These claims provided the theme of some twenty years of Fascist propaganda, and education.[23] In the realm of deeds, Mussolini matched words with a pronounced emphasis on militarism and the maintenance of expensive and relatively large, even if not particularly effective, armed forces. School children, youth, and public officials were put into military or quasi-military uniforms, trained for combat and subjected to military discipline. The model Fascist citizen was the conquering soldier—valiant and obedient.

Hitler's imperialism was, if anything, even more grandiose. The Nazis openly proclaimed the aspiration to an empire (Reich) of some 250 million Germans which, Hitler said, would last a thousand years. Their propaganda frequently alluded to no lesser objective than world conquest. Hitler's great territorial aspirations centered upon eastern and southeastern Europe with vistas of Ukrainian wheatfields and Rumanian oil as well as countless laborers and captive markets at Nazi command.[24]

Moreover, the stereotypes of the foreign enemies surrounding Germany and the exaggerated image of the Germans as the super heroes of the human race stood in stark and explosive contrast to one another. Nazi race theory identified the German people—or *volk*—as the world's master race, endowed with the choicest human qualities among the so-called Nordic Aryans. These Germanic Aryans, said to be descended from the mythical island of Atlantis, were viewed as possessors of unusual intelligence, valor, creativity, loyalty, physical beauty, and moral integrity—all far surpassing other ethnic groups.

Nazi racism was elaborated into a very practical, and at the same time lethal theory, in two basic works. The first of these was Hitler's *Mein Kampf*, which was written in 1924–1925, when the would-be Fuehrer served his short prison sentence for his 1923 attempt at the violent

---

[23] See Herbert W. Schneider and Shephard B. Clough, *Making Fascists* (Chicago: University of Chicago Press, 1929), on Fascist propaganda themes as imparted to youth.

[24] On goals of Hitler's foreign policy, see *My Battle*, op. cit., pp. 260–288. "The frontiers of 1914 mean nothing in respect to Germany's future" (p. 279). "When we talk of new lands in Europe, we are bound to think first of Russia and her border states" (p. 281).

overthrow of the democratic Weimar Republic. The second was the work of his close advisor and collaborator on racial subjects, Alfred Rosenberg. It was titled *The Myth of the Twentieth Century* and appeared in 1930.

Between them, Hitler and Rosenberg built racism into the very core of Nazi doctrine and political system. The Nazis constructed a racist theory of history in which success and failure, good and evil, virtue and vice, were all derived from the relationship between racial *quality* on the one hand, and racial *purity* on the other. Going all the way back to antiquity, Nazi ideologues saw the source of grandeur in the Roman and Greek civilizations in the purity of the Germanic-Aryan elements allegedly dominant there. When these pure elements declined, by inter-marriage and racial mixture with lesser, inferior peoples, the states that they had once founded and led to glory disintegrated and perished. All subsequent history, according to the Nazis, followed the same pattern, and the moral was clear. In order to achieve greatness or excellence a society had to cultivate its racial stock, both in quality and purity. Nazi theory classified races into three basic categories and several subcate-gories. The highest was the Nordic Aryan of which one subgroup, the Germanic, was the most gifted and distinguished. It was the category of "culture-creators" according to the Nazis. This group included the Scandinavians and Anglo-Saxons but, of course, its very best specimen was the German contingent. According to the Nazis, all cultural and scientific achievements, all religious-spiritual inspiration, all martial triumphs, in a word all things worthwhile, ultimately owed their being to Nordic-Aryan origins.

With all the abundant evidence of Germany's own mixed racial stock accumulated in the course of centuries, and his own deviant physique, Hitler insisted that Nordic Aryans were distinguishable by their blond hair, blue eyes, long legs, and short torsoes. These qualities the Nazis identified with beauty and strength, which contrasted starkly with the allegedly squat, round-faced Slavs, the swarthy Semites, and the grotesquely bowlegged, potbellied, odiously hooknosed Jews. Elite Nazi organizations, particularly the crack paramilitary SS units (Schutzstaffel or security guards), heavily emphasized the recruitment of members in accord with the racial criteria of the Party. Hitlerism literally trained its blond beasts to unloosen upon the world-at-large. With a cynical and heavy-handed subjectivism, Nazi theoreticians "proved" this proposition by arguing that if (a) something was great or excellent it *must* have been invented or inspired by Nordic Aryans or (b) if it was clearly and un-equivocally of non-Nordic origins, then it *could not* have been either great, excellent, or worthwhile. Thus, Rosenberg, Hitler, and other Nazi racists argued, for example, that the discovery of gunpowder by the Chinese in the fourteenth century was indeed a great discovery. Since it was so, however, it could not have been possibly discovered by the Chinese, at least as we know them today. It must have been discovered by the few Nordic Aryans scattered amongst them. No further proof of the racial origins was seriously attempted. In the same vein, without any effort at systematically tracing his geneology, the Nazis argued that Jesus Christ was really of Nordic-Aryan origins. Admittedly, he lived among Jews and had been generally considered Jewish, but since they did regard him as an inspiring religious figure (albeit with many, many reservations on the allegedly Jewish-influenced "misrepresentations" of his teachings), how *could* he have been anything but Aryan? Hitler credited the world famous music of German composers such as Beethoven, Wagner, and Mozart to their superior racial quality. In the case of the German-born, but nonetheless indisputably Jewish composer, Felix Mendelssohn, Nazi ideologue Rosenberg declared that Mendelssohn's music was not worthwhile—it lacked a sense of honor![25]

Below the Nordic-Aryan culture-creators, in the Nazi reckoning, stood the vast bulk of humanity. They were classified as culture-bearers. They possessed varying degrees of Nordic-Aryan admixture but, by and large, they represented a mosaic of lower racial strains. They possessed neither the beauty, the intellect, the courage, the virtue, or the creativity and energy of the ultimate master race. For heterogenous elements, the Nazis also used the appellation "Aryan" only to distinguish them from the one small but ultimately evil and depraved category, the Jews.

The non-Nordic, non-Germanic culture-bearers included such diverse peoples as the eastern Slavs, the Mediterranean peoples of Italy, Spain, France, and the Balkans, the Semitic Arabs and the modern Indians, Chinese, and Japanese, as well as African blacks.

As a whole, Nazi theoreticians regarded this category of human beings as capable only, in varying degrees, of copying the Nordic Aryans in all sorts of achievements—cultural, economic, and military. They were not really able to invent and create—except for the Nordic-Aryan impulses and influences among them.

Left wholly to themselves, they were given to brutish sloth, cowardice, and apathy. The best among them, such as Nazi Germany's allies, the Japanese, owed their great successes in art, commerce, and war to Germanic, Aryan-Nordic racial elements in the racial stock of the people.

[25] On the theme of Nazi racism, see particularly A. R. Chandler, *Rosenberg's Nazi Myth* (New York: Greenwood Press, 1968); Ashley Montagu,, *Man's Most Dangerous Myth: The Fallacy of Race*, 4th ed. (Cleveland: World Publishing Co., 1964); and Louis L. Snyder, *Race: A History of Modern Ethnic Theories* (New York: Longmans, Green, 1939).

The worst among these people, such as the blacks or the Gypsies, according to the Nazis, were so inferior that Nazi propaganda and practical policy scarcely differentiated them from the object of Nazism's ultimate hatred—the Jews. This final category was regarded as not simply inferior but actually as an antirace, that is, a kind of destructive racial bacillus which, injected into other racial groups, caused havoc and destruction in the host society. In *Mein Kampf*, Hitler did not explicitly call for the physical extermination of the Jews but he provided virtually every premise necessary to it.[26]

The operative thrust of Nazi racism was twofold. First it demanded the subjugation and exploitation of the lower races by the higher, and ultimately by the highest race. In Nazi reckoning, just as man naturally ruled the world of beasts, so also a higher kind of man had to dominate the lower kind. It was at once physically inevitable, natural, and also therefore proper or rightful that the strong, skillful, and brave should rule over the slothful, docile, and weak. Second, it was necessary to cleanse society everywhere, and in Germany first and foremost, of course, of those racial elements that polluted, contaminated, and weakened the master race.

Nazism thus carried the arguments about the "right of the strongest," and the hatred of out-groups, already well established in most brands of conservative nationalism (and Mussolini's fascism, of course) to their ultimate depths. These principles found operational outlets partly in Nazi foreign policy, which called for the absorption of living space and labor resources from the inferior races of the world, particularly those of Russia and eastern Europe. In fact, Nazi racialism was expressed in the differential, appreciably more lenient treatment of the peoples of northern and western Europe who had fallen under their rule in the period between 1939–1945. A measure of self-government, for example, was allowed to Norwegians and Danes but not to Poles, Russians, Ukrainians, or Belorussians. And on the whole, Nazi policies of extermination, impressment into slave labor, executions, and similarly primitive-repressive operations—harsh and cruel as they were—proceeded with more disguises and with greater restraint. In the case of the Jews, they led first to the establishment of rigidly isolated ghettoes in Eastern Europe into which the Jewish population was herded. Between 1939 and 1942 Jews were "merely" robbed of their possessions and exposed to the ravages of starvation, overcrowding, and epidemics. Between

[26] "If the Jew, with the help of his Marxian creed, conquers the nations of this world, his crown will be the funeral wreath of the human race. . . . Eternal Nature takes inexorable revenge on any usurpation of her realm. . . . by fighting against the Jews I am doing the Lord's work." *My Battle*, op. cit., p. 25.

1942 and 1945, largely under the auspices of Himmler's SS and Gestapo units directed by SS Colonel Adolf Eichmann, the so-called Final Solution was implemented. Jews were gassed, shot, or burned en masse, men, women, and children. These operations, at the explicit orders of the Nazi state authorities, were carried out either in the gas chambers or execution sites of such notorious death camps as Auschwitz, Belsen, Dachau, Majdanek, Teresienstadt, Treblinka, and numerous others, or simply through the work of SS execution units (*einsatz-gruppen*) operating in the countryside, villages and towns of Nazi-occupied eastern Europe.[27] In adition to some 6 million Jews who were thus exterminated, perhaps as many as 10 million non-Jewish civilians, representing other "reprehensible races"—Gypsies, Poles, Russians, Serbs, Greeks, among many others—met a similar fate. One of the largest categories of victims were Soviet prisoners of war whom the Nazis destroyed hundreds of miles from the war zone, en masse, both for racial-political as well as economic reasons. They preferred to expend bullets rather than grain while also getting rid of undesirable *"untermenschen"* (subhumans).

In domestic policy, racialism led to a systematic extermination of those Germans who, in the eyes of Nazi party experts, exhibited undesirable racial characteristics including physical disabilities, mental ailments, and occasionally simply a tendency to displease the Party. Various institutes and research activities under the Nazi party auspices were established which catered to such esoteric pastimes as digging up gravesites to measure skull and bone features of various racial types; blood tests were devised and administered for the purpose of classifying persons according to the proportion of Nordic-Aryan, or other, blood residue they might possess.

Nazi racial science generally had as much relation to rigorous empirical inquiry as astrology has to astronomy. It provided jobs for faithful Party hacks and, above all, gave the regime the needed symbols of cohesion for the ingroup by differentiation—however scientifically spurious and untenable—from hated out-groups. For while Hitler sponsored his various eugenic institutes, sterilization programs, bans on racial intermarriage and intercourse, and physical extermination of the lower races, the Nazis blithely proclaimed the ultimate subjectivity of race. "Race is soul looked at from within" wrote Alfred Rosenberg, while Hitler, Goering, and other Nazi chieftains invoked a capricious private right to decide "who is or is not a Jew." Subjective criteria,

---

[27] See Raul Hilberg, *The Destruction of Eureopean Jewry* (Chicago: Quadrangle Books, 1961) and Gideon Hausner, *Eichmann in Jerusalem* (New York: Harper and Row, 1966) for account of Final Solution activities of the Nazis.

arbitrarily established by Nazi leaders, set aside all the "objective" yardsticks of blood type, bone size, skull shape, and all the rest.

The gas chambers, concentration camps, and execution squads of nazism—its Gestapo, its SS formations, and its gendarmerie—were all rooted in an intense hostility to those outside the chosen core-group. And, like the far milder sanctions of more moderate forms of nationalism, they had their utilitarian objectives.

The rejection of tolerance, persuasion, and compromise as generally desirable virtues on the extreme Left, was in the twentieth century matched by the ideologies of fascism and nazism on the extreme Right.

In their approaches to political participation, fascism and nazism represented an "extreme" in the sense that they stood ideologically committed to a form of dictatorship so thorough and pervasive as to go beyond the wilder visions of nineteenth-century reactionaries. The power of medieval and Renaissance kings was also always understood to be qualified by certain traditional privileges of the subjects depending on the estates to which they belonged. Even the extremist assertions of royal prerogative under the Stuarts in Britain and the Bourbons in France did not *wholly* negate this principle because the claims of royal absolutism did not seek to reshape the political institutions around the monarch but rather to assure him the power of having the last word, if and when he chose to use it. That the monarch's ultimately independent power would be used to *destroy* existing political, economic, social, or religious institutions, was, if anything, assiduously denied by the pronouncements and the spokesmen of James I or Louis XIV.

The ideologies of nazism and fascism, however, vested supreme power in a leader whose own title was not prescriptive, that is, hereditary and traditional, but derived from his unusual genius, his superior insight, and magnetic, personal power to command his followers and the whole nation. This power was to be exercised not for the purpose of presiding over an old and established order of things but to forge a new, total order in place of the old. The purpose of the new order in each case was to destroy an existent parliamentary democracy, with all its paraphernalia, and to establish a more cohesive national entity, united behind the Leader, and dedicated to the grandiose missions of achieving national power and greatness in the arena of world politics. The annihilation of foreign foes (within and without), imperialism and, ultimately, war became at once cherished values and objectives. The very idea of rules and restraints upon the leaders elicited the contemptuous sneers of Nazi and Fascist ideologists and propagandists. Unlike traditional autocracy, however, the Fascist and Nazi regimes sought to realize the objectives of grandeur, not by telling the masses to remain "as they were," passive and inert, leaving politics to a traditional aristocratic class, but by involving the masses politically. There was not to be any turning back of the clock. Unlike the spokesmen of reaction, the Fascists and the Nazis boldly confronted the results of the technological, social, and political changes of the nineteenth century. They bowed to the already existent and therefore inevitable politicization of the masses. The Fascist and Nazi movements actually resorted to an intensive mobilization of the masses *on behalf of dictatorship*. They preached not withdrawal but intense subject-participation for the ordinary man. He was to be, almost literally, a soldier in the quasi-military phalanx into which all society was to be transformed, marching behind the Leader in a direction that the Leader would choose. Thus, paradoxically fascism and nazism addressed themselves at once to the creation of power at the "top" far exceeding that of the age of absolutism, but also with intensive subject-participation at the "bottom" far greater than anything practiced or imagined in the days of traditional oligarchy.

The social and economic *purposes* of that power and the ecology of the popular mobilization behind it, constituted the links between fascism and nazism on the one hand and the forces of the traditional "Right" on the other. To the elites of the old pre-Fascist and pre-Nazi order, Hitler and Mussolini were men who could "deliver" or "engineer" popular support.

The purposes of an egalitarian reshaping of society played very little part in the ideology and propaganda of these movements. Their revolutions were directed toward social and economic objectives that appealed most openly to the lower middle class but without seriously offending the upper strata. There were occasional denunciations of monopoly and finance capitalism which threatened the shopkeepers and white collar employees but the brunt of Nazi-Fascist attacks was directed against Marxists, trade unions, and assorted socialist levelers of society. Unlike the Communists, they did not seek to abolish private property in land or other forms of wealth and did not dedicate themselves to an ultimate vision of universal material prosperity and classless equality. They denounced such visions as unrealistic and worthless. Instead it was the intangibles of heroism, martial virtues, loyalty to the Leader, and above all, power and grandeur for the nation and the race which they upheld as supremely worthwhile.

In terms of their sources of support, fascism and nazism were, as movements before the seizure of power, and as regimes in power, dependent on alliances of groups ranging from the lower middle class to the upper strata of conservative nobility, even royalty and landed wealth.

We must also recognize the fact that much of the *attractiveness* of fascism and nazism to the upper classes, the privileged of their respective societies, stemmed from the very ingeniousness of the antidemocratism and antisocialism of these movements. They sought and attracted considerable popular support while preaching abolition of mass influence on decision-making. In each case the leaders demanded power on behalf of policy goals which, like imperialism, warmaking, unity and order, were shared by conservative and reactionary strata. Many of the Nazi and Fascist slogans were also the traditional watchwords of conservative nationalism which, in the nineteenth century, sought to channel the restlessness of the masses in adventures *outward* rather than reforms *inward*.

There is every evidence that the rise of integral nationalism, fascism, and nazism in the twentieth century has been closely connected with a remarkable shift of allegiancce among the middle class. The shift can be understood only in the context of changed circumstances for the small landholder, shopkeeper, businessman, and salaried professional. The remarkable crossover of the bulk of middle class vote from the democratic parties to the Nazis in Germany within a period of five years, dramatically hinted that the abandonment of the one for the other involved some profoundly instrumental considerations. Was the middle class voter seeking to secure his income and status by casting his lot with the Nazis? Was he convinced that law and order could not continue under democratic rule in the context of a great depression and communist clamor? That a great change of mind occurred among those who, other things being equal, are regarded as the social bulwark of democracy, we do know. Precisely why it occurred is not empirically certain. In the Marxian view, the answer is, of course, simple enough. Where "pressed to the wall," the bourgeoisie did not hesitate to sacrifice the superstructure of liberty for the underlying reality of pocketbook interest. For many erstwhile democrats who voted for Hitler in 1930 or 1932, it may well have been as simple as that. For others, it probably did not appear so simple, after all. It was not a callous, coldly rational calculation of self-interest but perhaps the wave of psychological and emotional change that swept these millions into the Nazi fold. Yet, the fact remains that the political realignment took place in conjunction with very substantial changes in the "real world," outside the minds of the participants, and that this realignment did not take place at an equal rate among all social classes of Germany.

As Seymour Martin Lipset has shown with reference to election trends under the Weimar Republic, the middle classes that had supported democratic political parties *until* 1928 had shifted in proportionally large numbers to the totalitarian, antiliberal Nazi movement *between* 1928 and 1933. The greatest proportional defections to Hitler's nazism *before* 1933 occurred from among the lower middle class, the upper bourgeoisie, the rural proprietors, and the nobility who had supported the conservative Nationalist party and only lastly from among the members of the working class parties.[28]

In order to establish a general middle class propensity to desert democracy when that class is treatened economically, we would have to see whether authoritarian movements analogous to Hitler's made increased headway among middle class supporters under similar circumstances of depression elsewhere. Even in countries with long traditions of democracy behind them, like Britain and the United States, the onset of the depression produced an increased "pull" on the middle class vote by the various fascist and authoritarian movements. But the increased defection was in many cases so marginal in the sum total of the electorate, as to be effectively insignificant. The propensity apparently needs to be qualified by other factors, such as the effects of national heritage or traditions influencing the political culture of a people, and of the subcultures within it.

The carnage and devastation inflicted by Nazi rule in Europe (with Italian Fascist support and acquiescence) have been so great as to deserve a unique *sui generis* place to Hitler and Hitlerism in the minds of many observers. But, in many respects, these movements have had their antecedents, their successors, and some would-be heirs as yet waiting in the wings.

Both Italian fascism and German nazism arose as responses to pervasive social upheaval, and to the "threat from the Left." To be sure, like all large political movements, they attracted all sorts of people into their ranks—but not equally by any means. Fascism and nazism gradually developed distinctive profiles of support which may be used to differentiate them from other political parties or movements. To the extent that we can find similar sources of support, similar ideology, organization, and political style elsewhere, we can extend the Nazi-fascist classification to political groups operating under different names in other countries.

The Nazis and the Fascists both set out to mobilize the lower strata, that is, broadly speaking, workers, peasants, and the lower middle class into anti-Marxian, nationalist political movements. They promised to synthesize national unity with social justice under the total power of the

---

[28] On 1930–1933 election trends in pre-Nazi Germany, see Seymour Martin Lipset *Political Man* (Garden City, N.Y.: Doubleday, 1960), pp. 140–152.

movement. Their rhetoric was directed not only against the radicals of the Left—communists, socialists, and liberals—but in part also against the rich, the industrial-commercial bourgeoisie, and the nobility. But the thrust of Fascist and Nazi rhetoric, the content of their propaganda and policy were weighed far more heavily against the Left than against the Right. While using the language of the embittered poor, Fascist and Nazi leaders cultivated the friendship and support of those who had much to lose by a Red revolution and who were interested in purchasing political "protection" or "insurance" from Mussolini and Hitler. Thus, over and beyond relatively small proportions of the urban and rural poor, fascism and nazism recruited substantially middle and lower middle class followings, as well as the tacit, covert, and sometimes even quite open support from the "highest" social strata: the entrenched socioeconomic elites of both Italy and Germany.[29]

After the Fascists had gained power in Italy in 1922, and the Nazis in Germany in 1933 their domestic policies in each case confirmed and emphasized a generally right-of-center political orientation. In material terms, industrialists, financiers, and landlords lost less by Nazi and Fascist rule than did workers, landless peasants, or even small businessmen. In general, the doors of opportunity—economic, cultural, educational, social—either remained where they had been before the economic crises that brought Hitler and Mussolini to power or even appreciably narrowed. In a sense, these regimes may be said to have kept the "lid on" at home while pursuing an aggressive foreign policy abroad. They maximized and improved upon the model of conservative nationalism— glorious conquests abroad, repression at home—with a vengeance.

The combination of authoritarianism, imperialism, socioeconomic conservatism, anticommunism, *and* political mass mobilization have had their counterparts elsewhere; some of these are still evident in the world today. But most Fascist or Nazi-oriented political organizations have exhibited only some, not all of these major traits.

Thus, for example, the Japanese militarists of the 1930's, led by Tojo, were authoritarian, conservative, and imperialistic but they did not promote mass political mobilization through a party or movement like the Nazi NSDAP or the Fascist party and their several affiliated youth, labor, cultural, and social organizations. In domestic matters, the regime eschewed systematic ideological guidelines. In these respects, the

[29] On the performance of the Nazis and Fascists in terms of social, economic, and cultural consequences, see the previously cited works of Neumann and Salvemini; also David Schoenbaum, *Hitler's Social Revolution* (Garden City, N.Y.: Doubleday, 1966), and, among others, A. J. Groth, *Comparative Politics: A Distributive Approach* (New York: Macmillan, 1971).

Japanese warlords were more like reactionary nationalists of nineteenth-century Europe. On the other hand, the system established by Juan Peron in Argentina in the 1940's was more akin to the Fascist-Nazi model in its emphasis on mass organization, and its explicit doctrine (Peronismo). The latter also combined elements of nationalism and xenophobia; these enabled Peron to rally Argentinian opinion against "Yankee imperialists," just as Hitler and Mussolini rallied their publics against sundry aliens and foreigners. But Peron also evinced considerable aspirations to leveling out social and economic inequalities in Argentina and improving the lot of the urban worker. This substantial reliance upon and appeal to the working class rendered his movement considerably more "leftist" than those led by Hitler and Mussolini.

Among regimes and orientations surviving in power in the 1970's, racism strikingly characterizes the ruling Nationalist party of the Union of South Africa. It is embodied in an explicit ideology, law, and public policy of the state.[30] It enables a minority of about 3 million whites to dominate and exploit a majority of some 9 million nonwhites of African, Indian, and mixed parentage.

Nationalism has traditionally catered to the human urge for belonging, for group solidarity, for rootedness in an age of social upheaval. It has also served as a cloak and excuse for oppression of those outside one's core group and for the suppression of economic and social conflict within one's own society. As with other ideologies, nationalism has "learned," borrowed, and adapted from the other creeds. Mazzini sought to combine it with democracy; Hitler adapted to it the slogans and nomenclature of socialism; today's "Third World" nationalists have linked nationalism and socialism even more closely. In some ways the most mystical and irrational of the three ideologies, nationalism has demonstrated great power where it has tapped latent reservoirs of popular sentiment. But, like democracy and socialism, its appeals have widely fluctuated in time and place and its attempts to integrate societies have often produced results directly contrary to its aspirations.

In Chapter 10 we shall return to the discussion of nationalism as it has evolved since World War II in the newly independent states of Africa, Asia, and Latin America.

[30] On South African racism and policies of Apartheid, see Legum and Margaret Colin, *South Africa: Crisis for the West* (New York: Praeger, 1964); Pierre L. Van den Berghe, *South Africa: A Study in Conflict* (Middletown Conn.: Wesleyan University Press, 1965); Peter Calvocoressi, *South Africa and World Opinion* (London: Oxford University Press, 1961). See also Basil Fuller, *South Africa—Not Guilty?* (London: Jarrolas 1957); Goran A. M. Mbeki, *South Africa: The Peasants' Revolt* (Baltimore: Penguin Books, 1964); and Mary Benson, *South Africa: The Struggle for a Birthright*, rev. ed. (London: Penguin, 1966).

CHAPTER **6**

Communism Under Lenin and Stalin

Many claimed the legacy of Karl Marx but none proved ultimately more influential than Vladimir Ilich Ulianov (1870–1924), best known to us under his revolutionary pseudonym of Lenin.[1] Lenin interpreted and adapted the teachings of the master to his own purposes and his own considerably different social, economic, and political circumstances.

Had it not been for the triumph of the Bolshevik Revolution in Russia in 1917, the merits of "Leninism"—that is, Lenin's version of the Marxian creed—might conceivably have gone unnoticed. Even in his homeland he was overshadowed for many years by other would-be heirs or interpreters, particularly Plekhanov. But Lenin's success in a great revolution of which he assumed direction, and the far-reaching consequences of that revolution, established his enduring significance. In an appropriately Marxian fashion, the importance of ideas was vindicated not by the rules of logic but, historically, by the test of events.

It is not certain, in retrospect, what specifically impelled Lenin to become, early in life, a phenomenally zealous, energetic, and uncompromising revolutionist, although a number of plausible reasons have been

[1] For biographies of Lenin, see the semiofficial, recent *Vladimir Ilyich Lenin: A Biography* (Moscow: Progress Publishers, 1965), edited by P. N. Pospelov, V. Y. Yevgrafov et al. (eds.), and the more critical accounts by Robert Payne, *The Life and Death of Lenin* (New York: Simon and Schuster, 1964); Stefan Possony, *Lenin: The Compulsive Revolutionary* (Chicago: Henry Regnery, 1964); and Leon Trotsky, *Lenin* (New York: Milton, Balch, 1925)

put forth.[2] We do know that Lenin's life was consumed by a pursuit of power inextricably linked with thoroughgoing change in Russia and ultimately throughout the world. The revolutionary ideas that he developed, and that have been used since as models or prototypes by other communists, were designed very functionally and pragmatically. His writings were dominated by the pursuit of power, not by abstract scholarship, ideas for ideas' sake, or detached studies of history or economics. Where Marx and Engels doubted, hesitated, or qualified, Lenin resolutely pressed forward.

Leninism may be appreciated in terms of four characteristic aspects: the organization of the revolutionary party; the concepts of imperialism and of the dictatorship of the proletariat; and the ruthless strategy and tactics that he advocated for the revolutionary party.

In discussing Lenin's uses of Marxian ideas, it is necessary to remember the contextual differences between them. Marx wrote in and for the industrialized society of western Europe, in which the proletarians were numerous, and capitalism itself had been well-established for many years.

Russia of Lenin's day, particularly during his formative years, was a classically underdeveloped country. Overwhelmingly peasant, lacking all forms of modern industry, technology, and communications, she had abolished serfdom only seven years before Lenin's birth. The masses of Russia's peasantry, given few cultural and educational opportunities, were steeped in ignorance and illiteracy with but scant awareness of the larger social and political world about them. Apart from occasional outbursts of violence, they were given to inertia and sullen resignation.

Unlike Marx, Lenin understandably had little faith in the spontaneous revolutionary capabilities of the masses. He did not want to consign the hope of revolution to a long process of economic and social development that eventually might produce in Russia the conditions that Marx witnessed and envisioned in the industrialized west.

To be sure, with increasing industrialization of the 1880's and 1890's, important mobilizational changes were taking place in Russian society. But at least until the abortive Revolution of 1905, massive modernization could still be regarded as fairly remote.

Thus, Lenin's conception of the proletarian revolution greatly tilted the balance between the workers and the workers' party. It made the

2 Compare David Shub *Lenin* (Garden City, N. Y.: Doubleday, 1948), pp. 5–19, and Bertram D. Wolfe *Three Who Made a Revolution* (New York: Dial Press, 1948), pp. 24–38; see also an earlier official apologia of the Marx-Engels-Lenin Institute, *Vladimir I. Lenin: A Political Biography* (New York: International Publishers, 1943), pp. 6–17.

party into a catalytic elite of intellectuals who would teach, organize, and lead the masses toward revolutionary objectives. The party was to be the vanguard of the proletariat in a very creative sense. While Lenin was careful—for purposes of maintaining his Marxian legitimacy—to keep up all the verbal appearances of the importance of objective socio-economic conditions, his idea of the party was that of a disciplined, elitist corps of social modernizers. The party would seek to dramatically hasten the course of Marxian prophecy, and even telescope the course of social developments by all possible means, rather than merely await them.

In order to serve these purposes, Lenin argued—in opposition to other Russian and European Marxists—the party had to be a relatively closed organization, led by dedicated, skilled, and experienced leaders. It had to be protected from debilitating rank-and-file influences, and guarded against becoming a mere debating society, torn asunder by factional disputes. If society at large, the peasantry, or the working class in particular, were steeped in inertia, the role of the party was to overcome this, not faithfully reflect it. The Leninist ideal of the party was, in fact, more suitable to a secret paramilitary society than to a political party in the generally accepted west European or American sense. If the party needed to resort to illegality, violence, and all sorts of stratagems, Lenin believed the judgment of history would ultimately vindicate it. But the questions of strategy and tactics, as well as organization, were the business of an elite of Marxist experts, not of the masses. And Lenin expected that recruits from the middle class intelligentsia, not production-line workers, would give the party this required expertise.[3]

The enduring consequences of Lenin's thinking are currently reflected in the practices of most of the world's ruling and oppositional communist parties. Their common characteristics may be described in terms of Lenin's "democratic centralism."

The democratic principles of discussion and election are part of the organizational pattern. But the discussion is very carefully restricted and confined, and elections are usually no more than ratifications by the rank and file of decisions already made for them by those at the top of the power pyramid.

An illustration and model of communist procedure emerged from the 14th Congress of the Communist Party of the Soviet Union in 1921, the

[3] On the ideas of non-Leninist Social Democracy, see George Plechanoff, *Anarchism and Socialism*, trans. by Eleanor Marx Aveling (Chicago: Charles H. Kerr, 1920); Giles Radice, *Democratic Socialism* (London: Longman's Green, 1965); Israel Getzler, *Martov: A Political Biography of a Russian Social Democrat* (Cambridge: University Press, 1967).

last congress of Lenin's life. At that time the Party formally adopted the rule that "factionalism"—that is, organization of an interest or issue-oriented group within the Party—was a breach of discipline. The Party also forbade dissent and opposition to its decisions—on pain of censure and expulsion—except insofar as these may be voiced within the duly constituted party bodies and at appropriate policy-making meetings. Democratic centralism thus requires the party minority to abide by the decisions of the party majority, and makes it mandatory for *all* members of the Party to support *actively all* of its decisions. Thus, not only is there no room left for organizing opposition to the policies of the Party leadership, but even withdrawal, a selective support of policies, according to what each individual might recognize to be the merit of a particular measure or action, is ruled out.

As for elections, democratic centralism relies heavily on two procedures, both of which substantially dilute the impact of rank-and-file influence. First, elections are indirect. Typically, as in the Soviet Union for about the last 50 years, the total membership of the Party votes only for a national congress of some 2000 delegates which assembles only once every four years.[4] The Congress, in addition to hearing speeches and reports and passing some general resolutions, elects a Central Committee, usually of about 200 members; the Central Committee then elects its own standing executive and policy-making body, currently called the Politburo in the USSR. This body is the smallest, containing anywhere from about 10 to 20 members, usually with a few nonvoting, so-called candidate-members. It represents the core leadership of the Party. Together with several auxiliary, bureaucratic adjuncts, such as the Party Secretariat and the Control and Audit Commissions, these relatively few top functionaries form the only continuously active decision-making organs in the party. Their offices or memberships are usually interlocking. The Central Committee may overturn the decisions of the Politburo, and the Party Congress may ultimately overturn all the intervening decisions of both, but (a) there is no recourse from the decisions of those higher Party organs *between* such convocations; and (b) the crucial decision to convoke is itself a carefully guarded prerogative of the so-called higher organs.[5]

[4] During Stalin's rule, no Congresses were convoked between 1939 and 1952!

[5] "(Wide) discussion on a national scale of questions of party policy must be so organized as to prevent it leading to attempts by an insignificant minority to impose their will on the majority of the Party, or to attempts to form factional groupings, which break the unity of the Party, attempts to cause splits, which may shake the strength and stability of the socialist system". Article III, par. 28 of the Party Rules in effect since 1952; See John N. Hazard, *The Soviet System of Government* (Chicago: University of Chicago Press, 1957), p. 230.

"(Congresses) are convened by the Central Committee of the Party on its own initiative or at the demand of not less than one third of the total membership

Moreover, the process of elections at all levels requires an intervening procedure of nomination by Party organs which are either of a higher or at least equivalent rank. This procedure supports the co-optation of those "below" by those "above." To be sure, all higher organs are elected by lower organs. But the Party organization determines who shall be nominated to the Party Congress; the Central Committee offers lists of candidates to the Congress for election to the Central Committee, and the Politburo similarly screens elections from the Central Committee to its own inner councils. So long as the Party does not sanction "unauthorized" candidacies, it is impossible for dissenters to present, let alone elect, alternative leaders to positions of power and responsibility within the Party.

The acceptance of these Leninist rules in Russia, and throughout the communist world, has had an important practical consequence. So long as the top leadership remains reasonably united, at least outwardly, it is all but impossible within the communist movement itself to bring disputes into the open from below or to oust the leaders.

Lenin wanted the Party to be heavily oriented to popular participation in the sense of involving and guiding the masses, and winning them over. He argued that these were indeed indispensable party obligations. Lenin believed that without gaining and maintaining popular following, none of the Party's revolutionary tasks could be performed. But, at the same time, Leninism connoted controlling and manipulating the masses, rather than responding to their wishes. The Leninist concept of the Party rested on the assumption that the Party, through its mastery of Marxist doctrine, knew the course of history and had an obligation to pursue it. Marxism equipped it with the true knowledge of social problems and an insight into the correct methods for solving them. The Party would lead the oppressed peoples of the world to liberation from the yoke of imperialist oppression because it knew the right course. It would be impermissible, indeed criminal, for the Party to yield its mission to the ignorant wishes of the people-at-large, even the workers. Lenin was concerned not only with the effects on the Party of what might be called the "well-meaning ignorance" of such people, but significantly also with the effect of possible penetration of the Party by bourgeois elements, hostile to its mission and seeking to subvert it by dissension from within.[6]

represented at the preceding Party Congress. . . . The basis of representation at a Party Congress is determined by the Central Committee." Article IV, par. 29, Ibid.

[6] The enduring significance of the concept of "democratic centralism" is attested by the prominence given to it in Red China's recent ideological "Bible"; see *Quotations from Chairman Mao Tse-tung* (Peking: Foreign Language Press, 1967), pp. 116-117. "The leading bodies of the Party must give a correct line of guidance . . . . All decisions of any importance made by the Party's higher bodies must be promptly transmitted to the lower bodies and the Party rank and file. . . ."

In the course of World War I, Lenin also elaborated his influential concept of imperialism, designed to justify imminent revolution throughout the world, and specifically to gain allies for a possible revolution in Russia. For several decades before 1914, and during the first few years of the war, the ideal of a proletarian revolution in western Europe seemed even more remote than in Russia. Particularly after the Franco-Prussian War of 1870, it seemed that the prophecy Marx made about an increasing immiseration of the proletariat failed to materialize. The workers were becoming increasingly better off, rather than worse off, under the capitalist system. Somehow, their real wages were rising, not falling, and working conditions and social security arrangements were also becoming better. When World War I began, European workers, to Lenin's dismay, generally displayed the solidarity of patriots in their individual countries rather than the revolutionary internationalism which radical Marxists had hoped for.

From these developments, one might have concluded that Marx's analysis of capitalism was pessimistically incorrect; or that socialist tactics of persuasion and pressure, short of revolution, produced desirable effects. Lenin, however, developed an explanation intended to justify revolution, not an acquiescence to the status quo of capitalism or acceptance of piecemeal reforms.

Borrowing from the ideas and the scholarship of his contemporaries, Lenin argued that the character of capitalism had undergone profound changes since Marx's time.[7] Marx believed that capitalists would be forced to increasingly exploit their workers—extract greater amounts of effort for less pay—in response to a continually diminishing rate of profits. The effect of competition among capitalists, driving down prices, was making this decline in profits unavoidable. The progressive "immiseration" of labor was thus an immutable characteristic of capitalist production according to Marx. Lenin did not deny the fact that the lot of many workers in Europe in the several decades since the *Manifesto* of 1848 had improved, contrary to Marx's prognosis. Instead, however, he argued that capitalism had transformed itself in most of the so-called developed, or highly industrialized, countries into an international, predatory, and monopolistic system of production and distribution.

The new capitalists, or imperialists, were men who temporarily, at least, could "rig" the market and assure themselves high profit. They could pay high wages to workers at home by their ability to control and exploit

---

[7] For Lenin's ideas on this subject, see his *Imperialism, the Highest Stage of Capitalism* (New York: International Publishers, 1939). Rudolf Hilferding's *Das Finanzkapital*, and J. A. Hobson's *Imperialism: A Study*, originally published in 1906, were the principal forerunners.

monopolistically markets, raw materials, and labor power abroad. Thus, Lenin viewed colonialism as an indispensable manifestation of capitalism in its advanced stage of imperialism. He ascribed the "gunboat diplomacy" of the late nineteenth century, the striving for territorial and commercial acquisitions by such nations as Britain, France, Germany, and Italy in Africa and Asia to the very basis of capitalist economy. Claiming that imperialist tendencies did not gain real momentum until after the Franco-Prussian War of 1870, Lenin argued that the capitalism Marx and Engels knew was still a relatively young and progressive form of economic organization. Notwithstanding the sacrifices it demanded of workers, it furthered expansion and modernization of economic life. It had not grown truly parasitic and destructive until a quarter of a century after the *Manifesto,* and presumably Marx, who had died in 1881, was not yet able to diagnose the true nature of this change, as was Lenin.

Lenin asserted that imperialism suffered from certain fatal flaws—or inner contradictions—which were bringing about its own inevitable destruction. These contradictions centered on the conflicts engendered (1) among the imperialists themselves, (2) between the imperialists and the colonial peoples, and (3) between the imperialists, the workers, and other oppressed classes at home.

Lenin believed that the tendency among capitalists to form various types of cartels, trusts, and monopolies to eliminate profit-destroying competition was bound to succeed only partially, and therefore only temporarily. Certainly, it meant that capitalists would compete in a more collective, cohesive, and large-scale way. But the rise of national and regional, or even international monopolies, was likely to result in the creation of competing national and international monopolies. Thus, far from eliminating competitive conflicts, imperialism, according to Lenin, would mean larger conflicts and, if fewer in number, they would be all the more disruptive and destructive in their consequences. The imperialists were using states, perhaps X, Y, or Z with all their political-military instrumentalities, to assure themselves control of particular markets, sources of raw materials, and investment opportunities. But the monopolists of other states of course, would not sit idly by watching. Eventually, they would challenge their competitors using the same powerful instruments of military force, diplomacy, economic and political pressure, blackmail, and the like. Because of these magnified economic struggles, Lenin saw the capitalist (imperialist) system as basically highly insecure, unstable, always in danger of war, and always forced to prepare for or anticipate war. It would always need vast quantities of armaments, standing armies, and police bureaucracies. As long as outward peace and monopolistic domination continued, all would seem well in the imperialists' home domain.

They could afford to pay workers good wages out of their protected profits. They could also, more or less openly, bribe the leaders of the working class with the rewards of temporary affluence. Sooner or later, however, the bottom was likely to drop from the comfortable floor of imperialism's prosperity, with war, carnage, and widespread suffering resulting from the predatory competition.

If imperialism was rendered brittle by its failure to eliminate competition and conflict on a world scale, it was also vulnerable because of the resentment and opposition engendered among its principal victims. The colonial peoples—in Lenin's time, the Indians, the Chinese, and the Africans—could not be expected to accept indefinitely their subjection to economic exploitation by the imperialists. The maintenance of protected markets and raw material supplies, the exploitation of cheap labor, and the contingent maintenance of military-political domination abroad, were all, Lenin believed, ultimately self-defeating. The colonial peoples would not tolerate indefinitely the burden of paying high prices for foreign goods and foregoing economic development at home, so as to produce only what the imperialists demanded and to avoid competing with the manufactures and commerce of their masters. They would balk at the low wages and hazardous working conditions imposed by the greedy imperialist masters. And to the extent that these heretofore backward, largely non-Western preindustrialized peoples realized—like the Marxian workers—their common problems and grievances, revolution was sure to come. The very effectiveness of capitalist domination was also a guarantee that it would eventually awaken and solidify opposition to imperialism where it did not as yet exist.

Finally, Lenin believed that the working class in the imperialist nations themselves was also bound to oppose its masters, if and when it realized the illusory nature of imperialist prosperity, the risks and the consequences of war, and the continuance of exploitation both at home and abroad. For while Lenin did not dispute the relative improvement of living standards among many wage earners, he made the most of the inequalities and deprivations still widely evident even in the most advanced, industrial states; the miseries of the unskilled, the landless, the homeless; the discrimination against and the lack of opportunity for the poor, women, and other "marginal" elements of capitalist society. An understanding of these conditions, Lenin believed, would make the working classes properly revolutionary. That is, they would act in accordance with their own true class interest—in opposition to the imperialist bourgeoisie.

Simultaneously, however, Lenin believed that the false prosperity of imperialist economics tended to weaken worker appreciation of the real nature of imperialism. Revolutionary consciousness among workers tended to wane. Relatively good times made the workers an easy mark for opportunistic trade union and social democratic leaders, who taught them to accept the bourgeois-capitalist system, work within it, and eschew revolution as impractical and unnecessary. At most, workers would be able to develop what Lenin called a "trade union mentality." Failing to realize and act against the fundamental evil of imperialism, these workers might simply content themselves by extracting local, piecemeal economic concessions. Their activity would focus wholly on the amount of wages, length of working hours, and conditions of labor without challenging the overall legitimacy of the imperialist socioeconomic-political system.

Even with respect to the West, Lenin was much less optimistic than Marx about translating, automatically, the socioeconomic conditions of capitalism into revolutionary fervor and action. He believed that an intermediate agency was necessary for this, and he assigned the role of revolutionary mobilizers to dedicated party workers. They, fortified by thorough and sophisticated knowledge of Marxism, could lead an otherwise apathetic working class. Moreover, these party organizers would be able to bring about the necessary alliances between workers and other oppressed and discontented groups—the colonial peoples abroad, and various impoverished elements, like the poor peasantry or the petite bourgeoisie at home. Quite frankly, and in a sense paradoxically in the context of Marxian thinking, Lenin expected the leaders of revolution to come not from the ranks of workers but from the bourgeoisie. He believed that the intellectual skills needed to lead the masses would be more likely found among the learned and privileged "defectors from the bourgeoisie" (of whom clearly he was one) than among the impoverished toilers. The idea of revolution fostered and led from above had its plausibility, but it seemed to many people that in his emphasis on the professional intellectuals, Lenin was standing Marx on his head. They wondered what had happened to the natural and inevitable impact of economic development. Was the revolutionary elite to be just a midwife of revolutionary change or its creator? Could the power of knowledge, persuasion, organization, and sheer will suffice to overcome the handicaps of adverse "objective economic conditions"?[8] Lenin never theoretically denied the basic Marx-

8 See Lenin's *What Is To Be Done?* (New York: International Publishers, 1929). On the history of the Bolshevik seizure of power and the early days of Bolshevik rule, see John Reed, *Ten Days that Shook the World* (New York: Boni and Siveright, 1919); Albert Rhys Williams, *Through the Russian Revolution* (New York: Boni and Siveright, 1921); Edward A. Ross, *The Russian Bolshevik Revolution* (New York: Century, 1921); Maxim Litvinoff, *The Bolshevik Revolution: Its Rise and Meaning* (London: British Socialist Party, 1918); Paul N. Miliukov, *Russia To-day and To-morrow* (New York: Macmillan, 1922).

ian tenets of the controlling force of man's socioeconomic environment. But he elaborately manipulated the presumed effect of this force in the working details of his program, and in his approach to the problems of the here-and-now.

The Leninist view of imperialism made what Marx had identified as capitalism a much more currently comprehensive, worldwide phenomenon. Marx could speak of mature capitalism only in Europe or North America; Lenin claimed to see the tentacles of a mature monopoly imperialism spread throughout the whole world. On the eve of World War I, in 1914, no part of the globe, however backward, was in his view free of imperialist domination—directly or indirectly. In Russia, Lenin saw international finance, particularly the bourgeois bankers of France and Britain, lurking behind the throne of the Tsar, manipulating the government and resources of the Russian people in behalf of a corrupt coalition. Native landlords, bureaucrats, and bourgeoisie aligned with foreign capitalists to exploit jointly the labor and wealth of the Russian lands. Similar alliances between the local rich and the foreign monopolists existed elsewhere. And Lenin believed that these imperialist international-local coalitions could and would be opposed by analogously broad antiimperialist coalitions.

Like Marx, Lenin preserved the essential "place of honor" for the workers. In his scheme, they still continued as the destined class of history in the sense that the inevitable development of industrialization and large-scale business organization assured the eventual primacy of wage earners everywhere. The small independent producers, in land, services, or manufacture, seemed ultimately doomed to extinction so far as both Lenin and Marx were concerned. But, for Lenin in the crucial here-and-now period, the objective conditions—given the nature of imperialism—encouraged a revolutionary struggle against it by many classes, not just workers, or even primarily workers.

By the fact of their exploitation and by their growing awareness of it, the peasants and the petite bourgeoisie of colonial nations were capable of revolutionary warfare against imperialism, and workers could find them useful allies in a common cause. To be sure, these classes would not share, Lenin argued, the same far-reaching revolutionary objectives that the working class could maintain. Some of the nonworker elements would simply want to substitute local, native masters (or exploiters) for foreign ones; others would seek to reduce the burdens and restrictions on their land and property; some might want to redistribute them though without wishing to give up ultimately their own particular holdings to a future socialist collectivity. Yet, all such groups might well support and even initiate the first, indispensable struggle to destroy imperialist, monopoly domination over their particular country or region of the world. And as

Lenin put it, the imperialist chain would break in its weakest link. When it did, the consequences would be international, even if the breach occurred in some relatively backward domain of this predatory international capitalism. Writing in the midst of World War I, Lenin expected the consequences of that conflict to be revolutionary. The strength of imperialism would be sapped; discontent aimed against its rule was likely to rise both at home and abroad. Communist leadership was bound to take advantage of these circumstances and certain to profit by them. Thus, Lenin believed that even in Russia, if the strains of the war proved great enough, there would be every opportunity for a resolute revolutionary party to prove victorious.

The success of a revolution would depend on the strategy and tactics that the Party pursued. Specifically, Lenin urged the wooing of the vast masses of Russia's peasantry by promising them a more equitable distribution of land but without "scaring off" rural supporters by premature slogans of collectivization. Above all, he emphasized the overriding issue of war and peace. People of all classes grew weary of war with the great human and material losses that it entailed for Russia. By refusing to partake of the patriotic nationalist approach to the war current even among many left-wing political leaders, Lenin maximized the "peace issue" for the Communists. He branded Russia's conflict with Germany and Austria-Hungary as an imperialist war in which the working people of *any* country, on either side, had no stake. Contemptuous of the arguments that Russian lands held by conquering German armies had to be won back, or that Russia's obligations to her Western allies were a matter of national honor, Lenin urged his followers to call for an immediate end to the war. He believed and openly avowed that the defeat of the Tsarist regime would facilitate a Russian, and ultimately a world revolution.

Certainly, Lenin continued the general Marx-Engels panorama of human history. The development of capitalism, even in its imperialist version, would still lead to the overthrow of the capitalists; the workers as the class with "nothing to lose but its chains" would lead all humanity into the Marxian equivalent of paradise—a classless society. Just as Marx did earlier, Lenin believed that the end of capitalist exploitation would usher in an era of great material abundance for all people, and that the "state," in the form of various coercive social institutions, would disappear together with want and exploitation. For, just like Marx, Lenin argued that abundance and the disappearance of economic classes based on differentials of wealth and the division of labor, would obviate the need for some people to keep other people "in check" or "in tow." Like Marx, he assumed that most vexing problems of human behavior such as resort to violence, stealing, deception, or propensity to sloth, derived from man's socioeconomic conditions. All these problems would either disappear or be reduced to minuscule proportions—Lenin believed with Marx —once oppression and want have been effectively banished from earth. Continuing in the Marxist tradition, Lenin did *not* believe that such paradise-on-earth changes could be brought about simply because some, or many, people wanted them. He espoused the view that only a confluence of objective economic circumstances, *and* substantial, corresponding human action could bring about the change. Without the tremendous economic forces engineered by capitalism, there could be no working class, no world revolutionary consciousness and, last but not least, the material perquisites on which a communist society could arise after the defeat of the capitalists.

Granted all this, however, Lenin emphasized not the apparently distant classless world, in which men would work much as they pleased and obtain what they might wish, but rather the more immediate, practical problem of getting there. And, for Lenin, the road inevitably led through a significant period of social construction, the dictatorship of the proletariat. Lenin's ideas on this subject became something of a blueprint for the fledgling Soviet Union of the 1920's with later applications in other parts of the world.

In the writings of Marx and Engels, the concept of a dictatorship of the proletarial received virtually no mention. According to the *Manifesto,* it was to be a transitional period between the downfall of the bourgeoisie and the commencement of a communist, truly classless society. Essentially, the workers would seize power and initiate measures socializing the means of production and distribution. Presumably, of course, in the original Marxian scheme, an anticapitalist revolution would occur only when the immediate circumstances for it were sufficiently ripe. Capitalism would be highly developed; the wage earners numerous, conscious, and experienced; the material perquisites of abundance bursting from factories, mines, granaries, and warehouses whence profit-greedy capitalists had hoarded, dumped, or simply withheld them.

But within his framework of world imperialism as the target and the enemy of the Communist revolution, Lenin saw the problem differently. If the "imperialist chain" did indeed break in one of its weaker links, as Lenin particularly hoped in Russia, the material as well as the social and thus presumably also the intellectual-cultural foundations of a communist society remained to be built. There could be no quick and easy transition from dire poverty, illiteracy, and technological primitivism to the Marxian utopia. The distributive formula of communism, "from each according to his ability, to each according to his needs," would be a mockery of human freedom, abundance, and fulfillment. Moreover, if imperialism was the world-craving predatory phenomenon Lenin believed it to be, could *a* communist-led revolution socialize whatever there was and then simply fold its tent? Could the revolution sustain itself without a "state" to develop the economy, train the people, and defend against the presumably fierce and inevitable imperialist attempt at restoration?

An essential aspect of Leninism was its decisive rejection of these alternatives. In the wake of the Revolution, Lenin called on the Party not to abandon the instruments of power, once won, but to strengthen and consolidate them. He also called for intensive economic and cultural development of Russia, under the Party's auspices; for ruthless suppression of the Party's enemies and utmost vigilance against bourgeois (or foreign-imperialist) inspired attempts to sabotage the Party's rule from within. He also foresaw, and sought to prepare against, violent confrontations between the emergent Soviet state and the surrounding capitalist states. Ultimately, Lenin believed, armed conflict was inevitable between the newly founded base of a worldwide proletarian revolution, and the imperialist states that would not reconcile themselves to Russia's revolutionary role.[9]

Thus, Lenin anticipated an indefinite period of the "lower phase of communism"—alternately styled socialism or the dictatorship of the proletariat. During this phase, men would work according to their ability but earn still only according to the value of their work—until such time as material scarcity and capitalist resistance had been fully eliminated. The state, in the hands of the Party as vanguard of the working class, would not only remain strong but possibly even stronger than under capitalism. To unleash the energies and resources needed for the building of communism, and to prevent the restoration of imperialist rule from within or without, the Party would exact sacrifices of the individual. There would be no democratic rights and freedoms for the enemies of

---

[9] In the wake of the Bolshevik seizure of power in Russia, Lenin declared: . . . "(It) is inconceivable that the Soviet republic should continue to exist for a long period side by side with imperialist states. Ultimately one or the other must conquer; meanwhile a number of terrible clashes between the Soviet republic and the bourgeois states is inevitable." See *Collected Works*, Vol. XXIV, p. 122. Interestingly enough, Stalin took up a somewhat more hypothetical line on the issue of war in his *Foundations of Leninism* (New York: International Publishers, 1939), p. 56: ". . . in the remote future, if the proletariat is victorious in the most important capitalist countries, and if the present capitalist encirclement is replaced by a socialist encirclement, a 'peaceful' path of development is quite possible for certain capitalist countries, whose capitalists, in view of the 'unfavorable' international situation, will consider it expedient 'voluntarily' to make substantial concessions to the proletariat. But this supposition applies only to a remote and possible future. With regard to the immediate future there is no ground whatsoever for this supposition."

the revolution, no toleration of bourgeois opposition or bourgeois influences. Lenin's system implied strong police rule and a closed society, ever fearful of contamination, a breach from without.

When Lenin died 1924, a struggle for power ensued among his principal lieutenants. Lenin's own testament suffered from the grievous defect of criticizing in some way virtually all possible successors and making no choices. Between 1924 and 1929, the man who had held the as yet obscure position of General Secretary of the Party at the time of Lenin's death, Joseph Stalin, emerged as Lenin's heir. He became the undisputed chief of the Soviet Communist Party and in this role was soon regarded as the leader of most of the world communist movement, too.[10]

The history of Russia under communism between 1924 and World War II is largely the story of Stalin's increasingly autocratic and cruel rule. It is also a history of great economic, social, and cultural changes brought about, however, with very little regard for the lives and suffering of millions of people.

The power struggle in Russia was wrapped about ideological issues. One basic choice confronting the Russian Communists in the 1920's was whether to devote attention primarily to their newly won domains, or press on with the tasks of an international revolution, sweeping Europe and ultimately the rest of the world. Each alternative, as a choice of emphasis, had some possible practical and theoretical advantages. Stalin made himself the spokesman of the "Russia first" orientation. His principal rival for power, brilliant polemicist, writer, orator, and organizer of the Red Army, Leon Trotsky, advanced the "internationalist" orientation. Trotsky believed that unless the Russian revolution was accompanied, or at least shortly followed, by revolutions in the economically more advanced Western nations, it would degenerate for lack of mass worker support at home and abroad. It would become a nationalistic-bureaucratic-military dictatorship, he warned, all but divorced from the Marxist vision of an equalitarian communist society. Stalin did not dispute the commitment to an international revolution. Aided by an understandably parochial preference of Russians for Russia, however, and armed by the failure of communist insurrections in Germany, Hungary, and Poland, he argued that the first duty of the Party was to build and fortify the one bastion that it had won. Moreover, he discounted the prognosis that the Soviet system was bound to degenerate and falter without the aid of foreign revolutionaries. Stalin committed the Party to building socialism in one country—USSR—first and foremost. To the extent that his policy

[10] On Stalin's career, see the biographies by Isaac Deutscher, *Stalin: A Political Biography* (New York: Oxford University Press, 1949); Robert Payne, *The Rise and Fall of Stalin* (New York: Simon and Schuster, 1965).

was predicated on the assumption that the more powerful the Soviet Union became the more effectively it would aid revolutionaries throughout the world, Stalin's line was widely accepted abroad as more than simply a policy of Russian self-interest.[11]

Another power struggle issue was essentially developmental. The Russian revolution triumphed with the tacit and active support of the peasantry which responded to Lenin's call for bread, land, and peace. But, could the Party construct socialism and ultimately communism without collectivizing the land? During the so-called NEP period, private owners had been allowed to keep their farms and to sell their products on the open market. In 1921 Lenin had argued that the Russian economy badly needed a breather. Famine and malnutrition stalked the land. The tremendous losses and dislocations of the 1914–1921 period made it imperative, above all, to restore productivity to the Russian economy. If concessions to private enterprise were the price of survival, Lenin was willing to make them—temporarily, at least.

In the late 1920's Stalin prepared to renew the revolution in the countryside by seizing land from the peasants and turning it into collective state-run or state-controlled farms. Since the Party had already taken over industry, transport, utilities, mining, and virtually all sorts of commercial-service facilities, the seizure of the land would complete its control of the economy. It would no longer depend on a rural middle class. It would be able to direct all resources into the task of intensive industrialization.

Stalin assumed that whatever breather the Soviet economy required it had already received, and he was determined to proceed with collectivization without delay. Other party leaders—foremost among them Nikolai Bukharin—urged caution and a gradualist, voluntary approach to the problem.

Stalin managed to picture his opponents on the issue of collectivization as treasonous, anti-Marxist, defenders of the Kulaks—the rural bourgeoisie. With shifting majorities within the top leadership of the Party, Stalin thus gradually eliminated and destroyed all his opponents: first, the Trotskyites on the issue of "socialism in one country"; then the Zinoviev-Kamenev "Left" on the issues of premature collectivization and industrialization; finally, the Bukharin, Rykov, and Tomsky "Right" precisely on the necessity of forcible collectivization and industrialization just a few years later.[12]

---

[11] For the concept of communist parties around the world representing one organizational monolith—still widely held in the 1950's—see Robert Strausz-Hupe et al., *Protracted Conflict* (New York: Harper, 1959) particularly pp. 56–59.

[12] On USSR economic development in the 1930's see G. Warren Nutter, *Growth of Industrial Production in the Soviet Union* (Princeton, N. J.: Princeton University

After 1929, the USSR became thoroughly and singularly Stalinist. Without reviewing the whole intricate history of the years between Stalin's consolidation of power and the outbreak of World War II, we may nevertheless note some of the salient features of "Stalinism."

First, in the liquidation of the Kulaks, Stalin may be said to have set the mark for his regime. It was a process in which almost certainly several millions of Russians perished, either through outright execution or the consequences of exile and starvation. In taking over the land, Stalin maximized force and minimized persuasion. A veritable civil war in the Russian countryside accompanied collectivization. Within about five years, some 90 percent of the land was torn out of the hands of private proprietors, but the cost in destroyed livestock, crops, buildings, and, above all, human lives, was nothing short of appalling. Along with the campaign to take over the land, Stalin inaugurated his ambitious industrialization schemes in several successive five-year plans. Russia, Stalin said, had to catch up with the advanced imperialist powers of the West within a few years or perish at the hands of her enemies.

The five-year plans aimed to bolster Soviet output in two principal areas: in the creation of capital goods and energy resources for further industrialization; and in the creation of an advanced military capability. Stalin set out to sacrifice butter to guns, steel, and hydroelectric power plants. The consumer was being sacrificed in the scheme of industrialization. Housing, food, and clothing were subordinated to the production of metals, machinery, coal, oil, cement, tractors—and tanks. Whatever the sacrifices, the Party quickly pressed on with its task of industrialization. And the results obtained on the eve of World War II were unmistakably impressive.[13]

While the Soviet Union progressed economically, Stalin intensified police terror and increasingly turned it against the Party itself. The late 1930's became known as the Era of the Purges. The Soviet secret police under N. Yezhov and Lavrenti Beria arrested, tortured, killed and exiled hundreds of thousands of members of the Communist party suspected of disloyalty, and sometimes merely potential disloyalty to Stalin. In 1936 began the so-called Purge Trials in which Stalin's relentless prosecutor, Andrei Vishinsky (later Soviet Ambassador to the UN), sent a number of prominent ex-leaders of the party to execution by a firing squad. Among those killed were most of Lenin's top collaborators—save for Stalin, of

---

Press, 1962); on collectivization see Andrew Rothstein, *Man and Plan in Soviet Economy* (London: Muller, 1948); see also Harry Schwartz *Russia's Soviet Economy* (Englewood Cliffs, N.J.: Prentice-Hall, 1954).

[13] On Soviet industrial progress in the 1930's, see Nutter, op. cit., pp. 188–199. Industrial production rose by some 12 percent a year between 1928 and 1933.

course. Kamenev, Zinoviev, Bukharin, Rykov, and Tomsky all met death after dutifully testifying to their own allegedly treasonous guilt in the Moscow show trials.[14] Stalin also drastically purged the Soviet armed forces, killing or jailing most of the top commanders of the 1920's and 1930's. Among the victims was Marshal M. Tuchachevsky, probably best known and most popular of the Soviet generals, who had led the Red Army against Poland in 1920–1921.

Sentenced to death in absentia was the founder of the Red Army, and Stalin's arch rival, Leon Trotsky. The sentence against Trotsky could not be immediately carried out, however, because he had been exiled from the USSR in 1929. It was not until 1940 that Trotsky died—of an axe blow to the head. It was inflicted upon him in his carefully guarded Mexican retreat, by a French Communist named Jacques Monnard who had wormed his way into Trotsky's entourage.

Thus, Stalinism connoted a number of things in its domestic aspects: intensive industrialization at the expense of the consumer; violent seizure of the land; and terror against all sorts of opposition, within the Party as well as without. However, it also connoted a measure of social progress and opportunity for millions of people exceeding anything that they had experienced thus far. For while Stalinism involved consumer austerity in food, clothing, and shelter, it also meant much larger school enrollments than ever before in Russia's history, both in relative and absolute terms.[15] It meant a great expansion of social service, welfare, public health, and recreational and cultural facilities for the masses of Soviet people. It also connoted opportunities for women and minority groups which, at least, greatly exceeded those available under Tsarism. To be sure, the Party was intent on reaping all the propaganda advantages possible from these benefits, but political, mobilizational exploitation did not negate the very substantial impact of these policies. It would be undoubtedly both false and callous to say that the Russian people "did not mind" Stalin's terror because they had never really known freedoms on the Western, democratic model. But, clearly, the tolerance of Stalin's police rule was conditioned by Russia's age-long experience of autocracy, and ameliorated by numerous benefits of the Soviet system.

[14] On Soviet secret police and its various institutional "accessories" see David J. Dallin and Boris I. Nicolaevsky, *Forced Labor in Soviet Russia* (New Haven: Yale University Press, 1947); Robert Conquest (ed.), *The Soviet Police System* (New York: Praeger, 1968); Herbert McClosky and John E. Turner, *The Soviet Dictatorship* (New York: McGraw-Hill, 1960); see also the incomparable fiction work by Arthur Koestler, *Darkness at Noon* (New York: Modern Library, 1941).

[15] See, e.g., Nicholas DeWitt's massive *Education and Professional Employment* (Washington: United States Government Printing Office, 1961) and Deana Levin, *Soviet Education Today* (New York: Monthly Review Press, 1964).

In the domain of foreign policy, Stalinism initially connoted a go-it-alone policy. Communists around the world were called upon to shun contacts not only with the bourgeoisie but even with working class and peasant organizations that operated under alien (noncommunist or anti-communist influences). Stalin espoused the doctrine of a "capitalist encirclement of the USSR."[16] In this view, all governments outside Russia were seen as either actually or at least potentially hostile to the Soviets. Stalin called for vigilance against "bourgeois wreckers and saboteurs" both at home and abroad. Foreign communists were counseled to maintain ideological-organizational "purity" and, above all, to attack and "expose" the most covert enemies of the working class—the socialists. Socialists were attacked for "duping" the workers with Marxian revolutionary language which they used—according to Stalinists—only so they could all the more effectively mislead the proletariat: win it away from the cause of revolution and turn it against the very bastion of that revolution—the USSR.

This line of policy and propaganda was used with particular emphasis in Germany in the 1930's where the Communists had a substantial following. The position of the German Communist party was that while Hitler and his Nazis were evil, the social-democratic opposition to Hitler was really no better. Perhaps it was even worse, because Hitler, according to the Communists, was a relatively blunt and straightforward oppressor and reactionary; the Social Democrats were lackeys of monopolistic capitalism, too, but they hid behind hypocritical phrases about democracy, workers' rights, equality, justice, and the like. Thus, the Communist hope in Germany in the early 1930's appeared to be *not* to prevent Hitler from coming to power by cooperating with others opposed to him; on the contrary, the Communists seemed to support the idea that "the worse things are, the better they are." Presumably, the workers had to be educated to the need for revolution by exposure to the very worst political consequences of monopoly capitalism—as the Communists defined fascism and nazism. This exposure was more likely to speed up the revolutionary reaction among workers.

All such hopes, however, came to naught in 1933. Hitler proceeded not merely to take power, but to make it far more durable and successful than the Communists had ever anticipated. Most of their leaders, as well as those of the Social Democrats, simply wound up in concentration camps. There simply was no revolutionary fervor or popular outbursts among Germans that the Communists could somehow exploit.

Faced with the demise of the Communist party in Germany, and the

16 Stalin, loc. cit.

dangerous anti-Russian designs of Hitler, now buttressed by his dictatorial power, Stalin called a major turn in Soviet foreign policy. He moved from a policy of isolation to one of alliance.

Between 1935 and 1939 the Soviet Union entered a period of so-called United Front policies.[17] Stalin, and the world communist movement loyal to him, called for a united, all-out struggle against fascism. The common danger and the common enemy were declared more important than the differences that divided various anti-fascist groups from one another. The communists professed to see virtues in parliamentary democracy, as opposed to fascist dictatorship, which all but escaped them a year or two ago. The apogee of Stalin's anti-fascist policy was his support of the Spanish Republic in 1936 against the Falanga-nationalist revolution of General Franco. While Britain and France remained timidly neutral, Stalin materially and militarily aided the Spanish Republicans. Since both Hitler and Mussolini were helping Franco on an even greater scale, the Spanish Civil War soon assumed the proportions of a major ideological conflict. The Republicans finally lost in 1939, but Stalin's policy won him the following of a considerable worldwide public opinion and, very significantly, made the Spanish Communist party the principal power in the steadily shrinking domains of the Spanish loyalist state.

Another result of these policies was a great electoral victory in France in 1935 in which, with Communist support, the Popular Front Government of Socialist Leon Blum took power. The Communist party itself won an unprecedented number of votes in this election on its new antifascist, unity platform.

Nevertheless, in 1939, Stalin imposed still another "freeze" on Soviet foreign policy with far-reaching consequences abroad. In a delayed reaction to Western policies, capped by the Munich agreement of 1938, he concluded the Nazi-Soviet Non-Aggression Treaty of August 1939, a major turnabout in world diplomatic history.

On the theory that the Soviet Union would not, as Stalin put it, "pull chestnuts out of the fire" for others, the communists of Europe and the world assumed a neutral stance toward nazism. Actually, Soviet propaganda saved its sharpest reproaches for Britain and France; for two years, Stalin did his utmost to keep Hitler in a stance of neutrality. Ideologically, the communist movement under Stalin reverted to the proposition that

17 See Franz Borkenau, *The Communist International* (London: Faber and Faber, 1938); Gunther Nollau, *International Communism and World Revolution* (New York: Praeger, 1961); Peter Mayer, *Cohesion and Conflict in International Communism* (The Hague: Martinus Nijhoff, 1968); Julius Braunthal, *History of the International*, Vol. II, 1914–1943 (New York: Praeger, 1967); Elliot R. Goodman, *The Soviet Design for a World State* (New York: Columbia University Press, 1960).

all wars by and among "imperialists" are equally damnable from the standpoint of the interests of the international working class. There was no reason for the USSR as the champion of this class to support either side.

On June 22, 1941 Hitler shattered Stalin's calculations of sitting out and thus possibly profiting from the conflict. The Nazis launched Plan Barbarossa—a massive strike into Russia. The consequences of this event are discussed in Chapter 7. The changes produced by World War II so profoundly affected the configurations and supports of the major ideological-political systems of the world that they clearly require separate treatment.

The Impact of the Second World War

Thus far, we have outlined some of the historical circumstances surrounding the rise of the great secular faiths in post-Renaissance Europe. We shall now consider the new background of ideology in the period following the Second World War, inasmuch as certain recent developments are, in large measure, the consequences of that conflict. These are, above all, the Cold War between the United States and the USSR, with its various tributary or "spillover" effects; and heightened processes of social mobilization. Both of these developments have had a tremendous impact on the nature of ideological conflict in the last three decades.

Essentially, the conflict between two great powers, for the first time in human history, has become an issue in one way or another for every political movement and articulated belief-system in the world. This is not true merely in the choosing up of sides between "communism" and "democracy," but most of all in the fact that no one could afford to see himself uninvolved in a nuclear confrontation, and no part of the earth has been seen as "off-limits" by the Cold War protagonists. Thus, Cold War politics has become, in some sense, part of every ideological program of our era.

As for social mobilization, its consequences can be appreciated most readily with reference to the so-called developing or underdeveloped nations. By destroying or undermining the power of European colonialism, World War II has ushered in an era of unprecedented nationalist mobilization throughout Asia, Africa, and Latin America. Once the "old gods" of European power and prestige disintegrated,[1] the need arose for new ones. Technological and communications advances, coupled with the decline of colonialism, and the ferment of a true world politics, spurred a search for new identifications in these countries. Nationalist and independentist movements, which had existed sometimes in merely minuscule fashion in the 1930's sought and gained multitudes of new adherents in the 1940's and 1950's.

From the rise of British liberalism in the seventeenth century to the rise of Marxism and integral nationalism in the nineteenth, Europe occupied the center stage of world attention. She was the seat of ruling wealth, power, and cultural influence. The rest of the globe played the role of a periphery, usually reacting and adapting to actions, ideas, and events that centered in Europe and radiated outward. Until the outbreak of World War II, when one spoke of the "Great Powers" the reference was primarily to Europe. The United States and Japan were late entries, around the turn of the century, into an exclusive European club. Britain, France, Germany, Russia, Austro-Hungary, and even Italy, were regarded as the great powers on the eve of World War I in 1914. Save for the defunct Austro-Hungarian monarchy, the line-up was the same in 1939.

When Hitler's Nazi armies crossed the frontiers of Poland on September 1, 1939, the war began—just as it had in 1914—as a European war. In fact, the scale of the conflict still seemed deceptively limited. Unlike 1914, Russian remained neutral. Germany was opposed only by France and Britain in the West. At first even this opposition was militarily little more than a token one.

Having "ingested" the Rhineland, Austria, and Czechoslovakia during the 1930's without drawing serious opposition from France and Britain, Hitler and the men around him hoped that even after the quick conquest of Poland in September 1939 peace could be restored—on Nazi terms. But neither the French nor the British were willing to believe any longer in Hitler's promises of "no more conquests after this one." The war continued.

In 1940 the Nazis overran Denmark, Norway, the Netherlands, Belgium Luxemburg, and finally France. The French government, now headed by the aged Marshal Petain, concluded an armistice with Hitler's Germany. Only a few French emigrés, led by an energetic young general, Charles de Gaulle, fought on. The mighty Third Reich was now opposed by only one major power—Great Britain. Although Hitler did not succeed either in dissuading the British from further resistance (as "useless")

---

[1] On this theme, see particularly the concise but excellent account by Hajo Holborn, *The Political Collapse of Europe* (New York: Knopf, 1951).

or in defeating them, the Nazi juggernaut continued to sweep Europe. With the conquest of Yugoslavia and Greece in the spring of 1941, Hitler's domination of the Balkans was all but complete. Hungary, Rumania and Bulgaria became virtual satellites of Nazi Germany. Field Marshal Rommel's armies swept to the vicinity of Alexandria and the Suez Canal. American sympathy and lend-lease help to the British notwithstanding, the prospects of Hitler's eventual victory still looked excellent; many thought it was all but assured.

However, on June 22, 1941, in defiance of Bismarck's dictum that Germany should not fight two-front wars, and despite grave misgivings of his own military, Hitler launched an all-out attack on his ally of the last two years—the Soviet Union. The scope of the war was vastly expanded. Within hours of Hitler's attack, Winston Churchill, life-long foe of communism but also Prime Minister of beleaguered Britain, welcomed Stalin to an alliance that was destined not only to destroy Hitler but to reshape the character of world politics for decades. In a broadcast of June 22, 1941, Churchill declared:

"The Nazi regime is indistinguishable from the worst features of Communism. It is devoid of all theme and principle except appetite and racial domination. It excels all forms of human wickedness in the efficiency of its cruelty and ferocious aggression. No one has been a more consistent opponent of Communism than I have for the last twenty-five years. I will unsay no word that I have spoken about it. But all this fades away before the spectacle which is now unfolding. The past, with its crimes, its follies, and its tragedies, flashes away. . . . can you doubt what our policy will be? We have but one aim and one single, irrevocable purpose. We are resolved to destroy Hitler and every vestige of the Nazi regime. . . . any man or state who fights on against Nazidom will have our aid. Any man or state who marches with Hitler is our foe . . . we shall give whatever help we can to Russia and the Russian people. We shall appeal to all our friends and allies in every part of the world to take the same course and pursue it, as we shall faithfully and steadfastly to the end."[2]

Within a few months of Churchill's speech, the Grand Alliance of World War II was completed. The Japanese attack on Pearl Harbor on December 7, 1941, brought the United States into the war against all the Axis powers—Hitler's Germany, Mussolini's Italy, and Tojo's Japan.

In what turned out to be the most destructive conflict in human history (the Soviet Union alone is estimated to have lost some 20 million

[2] Winston S. Churchill, *The Second World War: The Grand Alliance* (Boston: Houghton Miffin, 1950), pp. 371–372.

lives), the alliance of Britain, Russia, and the United States decisively defeated the three Axis states. In the process, however, only two of these states did not succumb to attrition. The United States sustained relatively few casualties on the battlefield in relation to its population while its economic and technological resources, already enormous in 1939, became overwhelming in comparison to other states by 1945. Not the least of these, of course, was the, as yet, sole possession of atomic weapons and the largest navy and air force on the face of the earth. The Soviet Union, while enormously depleted in manpower and economy, not only managed to retain its great land mass and natural resources (one-sixth of the earth's surface) but also succeeded in capturing most of east-central Europe. About 120 million people passed under its control. The Red Armies seized Berlin and Vienna. In the summer of 1945, Stalin fielded the world's largest army in the very heart of Europe. Simultaneously, the conclusion of the war against Japan brought Soviet troops into Manchuria at relatively little cost, enabling Stalin to turn over valuable land, resources, population, and weapons to the control of Mao Tse-tung's Red guerrillas. A substantial step toward the eventual communist conquest of China was thus consummated.

For four years, from 1941 until 1945, the anti-Axis alliance had maintained a public image of unity. Stalin bickered with Churchill and Roosevelt over the timing and volume of material aid to Russia; over the opening of a so-called "second front" in Western Europe to relieve Nazi pressure on Russia; and over his relations with the Polish government-in-exile in London. Suspicions and doubts were still balanced out, however, by the common purpose of winning the war. The rifts and conflicts became publicly apparent only in the aftermath of the war.

In the light of what was known about communist ideology until the formation of the Grand Alliance in the Second World War, certain pessimistic conclusions about collaboration with Stalin's Russia were all but inescapable. If Stalin and his regime were *really* committed to the doctrines of Marxism-Leninism, then Soviet cooperation with the capitalist states of the United States and Great Britain was bound to be a short-term "marriage of convenience." Moreover, it was simply a question of the right time and opportunity before Stalin would resume a position of enmity, and a no-holds-barred conflict, with the bourgeois states of the West. Marxism-Leninism did not sanction the identification of the democratic capitalist powers, to use a colloquial expression, as the "good guys" and the fascist-Nazi capitalist powers as the "bad guys." These were but two varieties, or two faces, of one foe. What it did sanction was an utmost tactical flexibility that would support communist alliances with anyone at any time, Hitler or Roosevelt alike, in pursuit of the Party's world-revolutionary objectives. Naturally, the Soviet Union was likely to benefit if its leaders did not articulate such a position directly and openly to their allies while they maintained a particular alliance. Thus, in August 1939, Stalin cheerfully drank to the health of the German Fuehrer at a Kremlin banquet given in honor of the Nazi Foreign Minister, Joachim von Ribbentropp. In the 1940's he lavishly entertained Churchill, Roosevelt, and other Western dignitaries from whom he asked, and received, vast amounts of armaments, food, clothing, vehicles, ammunition, and sundry supplies. He also asked, and received, various formal and informal guarantees concerning postwar boundaries and zones of influence in Europe.[3]

The critical question was: Would victory over the Axis lead to an era of world peace and reconstruction based on great power cooperation, or would the Soviet Union use its resources and position to move from the solution of one global conflict on to another?

A discussion of the "might-have-beens" of the Second World War, from Munich to Potsdam, while interesting and possibly profitable, goes well beyond the scope of our survey. To the extent, however, that ideological differences permeate the East-West conflict since the 1940's, it may be useful to reflect on just how much ideological factors were disregarded and minimized in Western expectations of that period. In 1938, Chamberlain came to believe that Hitler had "transcended" Hitlerism; in the 1940's similar hopes, or illusions, were widely articulated by Western leaders with respect to Stalin. In both cases, those who suffered disappointment minimized the influence of ideology on international politics. They tended to project their own pragmatism onto others; understandable hopes, and the adroit personal diplomacy of the dictators contributed to their illusions.

During one of his wartime speeches, President Roosevelt declared:

. . . We are now working, since the last meeting in Teheran, in really good cooperation with the Russians. And I think the Russians are perfectly friendly; they aren't trying to gobble up all the rest of Europe or the world. They didn't know us, that's the really fundamental difference. . . . They haven't got any crazy ideas of conquest. . . . And all these fears that have been expressed by a lot of people here—with some reason—that the Russians are going to try to dominate Europe, I per-

[3] See Winston S. Churchill, *Triumph and Tragedy* (Boston: Houghton Mifflin, 1953), pp. 226–28, on how Churchill and Stalin divided "shares of influence" in various Balkan countries in October 1944 in Moscow.

sonally don't think there's anything in it. They have got a large enough "hunk of bread" right in Russia to keep them busy for a great many years to come without taking on any more headaches.[4]

Winston Churchill, though given to occasional doubts, similarly declared in May of 1944:

"Profound changes have taken place in Soviet Russia. The Trotskyite form of Communism has been completely wiped out. The victories of the Russian armies have been attended by a great rise in the strength of the Russian State, and a remarkable broadening of its views. The religious side of Russian life has had a wonderful rebirth. There is a new national anthem . . . the terms offered by Russia to Rumania make no suggestion of altering the standards of society in that country, and are . . . generous. The Comintern has been abolished which is sometimes forgotten . . . these are very marked departures from the conceptions which were held some years ago, for reasons which we can all understand." (Sic!)

On August 2, 1944, he told the House of Commons:

"I still hold to the view . . . that as the war enters its final phase it is becoming, and will become, increasingly less ideological."[5]

Almost two decades after the collapse of the alliance, Churchill's wartime Foreign Secretary, Anthony Eden, recorded this in his memoirs about his relations with Stalin:

"Though I knew the man to be without mercy, I . . . felt a sympathy which I have never been able to analyze. Perhaps this was because of Stalin's pragmatic approach. It was easy to forget that I was talking to a Party man, certainly no one could have been less doctrinaire. I cannot believe that Stalin ever had any affinity with Marx, he never spoke of him as if he did.[6]

During the years of alliance, the prevalent views developed among British and American leaders were that either (1) the Soviet Union, under Stalin's leadership, had been misunderstood, or (2) that the Soviet Union had changed. In the first interpretation, it was believed that

---

[4] The speech was delivered to an Advertising War Council Conference on March 8, 1944. *The Public Papers and Addresses of Franklin D. Roosevelt, 1944–45,* Vol. 13. (New York: Harper, 1950), p. 99.

[5] *The War Speeches of Winston S. Churchill,* compiled by Charles Eade (London: 1952), III, pp. 150, 196.

[6] *Facing the Dictators* (Boston: Houghton Mifflin, 1962), p. 171.

Marxism-Leninism with its worldwide, messianic, revolutionary implications was simply ritualistic verbiage so far as actual Soviet behavior was concerned. The Russians were presumably "no different from everyone else." They wanted to assure themselves a measure of national power, prosperity, and security from external attack. Soviet foreign policy was thus not fundamentally different from that of any other country, except insofar as certain particulars of geography and resources dictated it. To be sure, Stalin paid lip-service to various communist ideals and slogans partly as a way of rationalizing the rule of his Party in Russia, and partly to gain some external support for Russia's traditional aspirations. Concretely, however, his policy, like the Tsars, dictated concern with such practical questions as secure outlets to the Baltic and Black Seas and a buffer zone in the Balkans and Poland as shield against Germany aspirations. Given reasonable assurances on such issues there was no reason to believe that Stalin would not be a "good citizen of a world community." In this view, suspicions of Soviet motives and intentions vis-à-vis the West were based on false stereotypes, a misapplication of propagandistic rhetoric to a far more modest and sober Russian reality. If such suspicions had persisted as long as they did, this was partly because of an innately Russian (not necessarily "communist") penchant for secrecy that had rendered Russia unnecessarily mysterious to Western eyes; it was also, in part, the fault of Western prejudice, ignorance, and ill-will.

In the second view, the doctrines of Marxism-Leninism were not dismissed quite so readily but it was assumed that the experiences of the war, and indeed of the alliance itself, were sure to modify Soviet behavior. It was hoped that the meetings and exchanges between Stalin, Churchill, and Roosevelt would instill mutual confidence. Stalin, particularly, would not continue to operate on the seemingly paranoic premises of Western imperialism and malevolence toward the USSR after his first-hand experiences of successful wartime cooperation with Western leaders.[7]

Between 1941 and 1945 the Soviet Union and her Western allies readied a series of agreements for the governance of the postwar world on the assumption that, once the war was won, they would continue to cooperate in establishing a new, durable world order. At successive summit meetings of British, Soviet, and American leaders in Moscow, Teheran, Dumbarton Oaks, Yalta, and Potsdam a number of commitments were undertaken. Among these were the decision to establish the United

[7] See A. J. Groth, "On The Intelligence Aspects of Personal Diplomacy," *Orbis*, Vol. VII, No. 4, Winter 1964, pp. 833–48; and "Churchill and Stalin's Russia," *Bucknell Review*, Vol. XIV, No. 1, March 1966, pp. 74–94, for a discussion of these issues.

Nations to safeguard international peace, divide Germany into separate zones of occupation by the victorious powers, and establish new governments in east-central Europe. The meaning of all these agreements, and the good faith—or lack of it—behind them became the theme of a bitter "Cold War" that eventually enveloped the whole world shortly after the conclusion of hostilities in Europe and Asia.

As the Soviets moved westward, beyond the frontiers of the USSR in 1939 and 1941, Western leaders became increasingly alarmed about Stalin's apparent intention to establish communist dictatorships as far as his armies could reach. The Russians arrested and executed anticommunist leaders in countries under the Red Army's control; installed communists in key positions in local and national government organs, generally with only token representation for noncommunists. In many instances, they showed no regard for popular wishes by disqualifying anticommunist opponents from all electoral and political activity, alleging such opponents to be simply "fascist collaborators" and "traitors." They quickly proceeded with far-reaching domestic reforms, typically including nationalization of industry and redistribution of land in advance of any elections. And, when elections were held, the combined tactics of terror, intimidation, and disqualification of opponents made them all but meaningless. It soon became obvious that what the two sides meant by terms such as "democracy," "free elections," "peace," and the like was vastly different.

The Soviets distinguished between "democracy" in its unacceptable, decadent, bourgeois form, on the one hand, and its progressive, proletarian, or specifically people's democratic character on the other. Democracy, Soviet-style, meant freedom for the working people to follow correct leadership promoting historically justified and inevitable objectives. It meant suppression rather than tolerance for the "reactionary bourgeois forces seeking to turn back the clock of history." Freedom meant the opportunity and duty of ending exploitation by the rich. On the whole, the interpretations given by Stalin and his allies to such terms as "elections," "freedom," "democracy," and the like were consistent with Lenin's definitions of *State and Revolution* and Russia's Stalin Constitution of 1936, rather than with the interpretations attached to them by most Western diplomats, politicians, and journalists.[8]

The People's Democracies were an amalgam of the Soviet concept of

---

[8] See the accounts of Stanislaw Mikolajczyk, *The Rape of Poland* (New York: Whittlesey House, 1948); Jan Ciechanowski, *Defeat in Victory* (Garden City, N. Y.: Doubleday, 1947); and particularly Edward Rozek, *Allied Wartime Diplomacy* (New York: John Wiley, 1958).

the dictatorship of the proletariat, with some outward trappings of multiparty democracy. To be sure, these so-called People's Democracies grew out of the United Front tactics that the communists had pursued between 1941 and 1945. Trying to broaden their base of support, the communists had sought alliances with socialist peasant, and middle-class democratic groupings. As in the 1930's,—before the Molotov-Ribbentropp Pact—the communists everywhere argued that all anti-fascist forces should cooperate for the common cause of national liberation. The Party's future goals were usually kept vague. It deliberately made itself the spokesman for several generalized ideals that were shared by many other parties. They emphasized, for example, a commitment to democracy, equality, national independence, land reform, and the amelioration of the social and economic conditions of the people. Such political ideals and slogans were shared by virtually all political groupings in Eastern Europe that could be described as left-of-center. Moreover, the communists still tended to camouflage the primacy that they actually assigned to themselves. Other parties were pictured as allies rather than subordinates to the communists. These United Front tactics not only helped the Party to broaden its support in behalf of particular objectives, such as, for example, waging guerrilla warfare on Nazi supply routes to the eastern front; they also helped to establish the Party's legitimacy in the eyes of the people—in countries like Poland, Czechoslovakia, Yugoslavia and Hungary. By these alliances the communists sought to dispel the popular notion that they were simply "Moscow agents," and show that, in fact, they were like everyone else—only more so—patriots, reformers, democrats. These tactics also helped the Party's legitimacy in the eyes of Russia's allies, the Western powers. By convincing the United States and Britain that they were simply one among many left-of-center native parties, the communists could insure themselves against political interference by the West, occasionally receive material aid (by which Tito had very significantly profited in Yugoslavia) and eventually get Western recognition of coalition governments in which the communists would be the *de facto* leaders.

Between 1945 and 1948, the first phase in the building of the People's Democracies was completed. In this immediate postwar period, the communists subordinated or purged all of their coalition allies and put an end to genuinely multiparty elections in Eastern Europe. The days of preparation and window-dressing were over. After 1948, the role of the ruling communist parties (sometimes merged with democratic socialist elements under new names, such as Poland's PZPR or Polish United Workers' party) was everywhere defined as that of the leader. The tasks of the Party were everywhere spelled out in measures unmistakably similar to those of the USSR.[9] Between 1948 and 1953 the dictatorship of the proletariat was being rapidly unfolded in Eastern Europe under the label of People's Democracy.

Thus, the division of Germany into four zones of military occupation, and the quadripartite rule of Berlin (American, British, French, and Russian) turned into a hard-frozen political-economic breach between the Soviet zone in the East and the three occupation zones in the West.

Stalin attempted to force the Western powers out of Berlin, imposing a blockade on all road and rail traffic in and out of the city. American offers of economic aid to the Eastern as well as Western European nations embodied in the so-called Marshall Plan were denounced by the Soviets as a device of American imperialism. Communist ministers in France and Italy quit coalition governments with noncommunists, following Moscow's new antiimperialist, anti-American line. A wave of strikes by communist-led trade unions brought both countries to the verge of paralysis in late 1947 and early 1948.

Gone was the camaraderie of the war. The Soviet government imposed the most stringent restrictions on the movement of persons and goods from East to West, and its lead was followed by the pliant communist regimes of Eastern Europe. Soviet propaganda harshly denounced the West, above all the United States, replacing the Nazis with the Americans as symbols of aggression, expansionism, and sundry political evils.

The lines of demarcation between friend and foe hardened on both sides of the Iron Curtain. Worried about the prospects of a communist seizure of power in Italy, the United States waged a quasi-official campaign in behalf of the pro-Western Christian Democrats there in 1948. The division of Germany became institutionalized in 1949 in the new West German Federal Republic and the East German Democratic Republic, respectively. The United Nations became a battleground of Cold War propaganda and invective. The power of veto in the Security Council, originally conceived as a safeguard of great power unanimity, became a frequent Soviet blocking device against resolutions and actions that the USSR did not support. In 1949, the North Atlantic Treaty Organization, under American leadership, was created joining most of the noncommunist European states with the United States and Canada in a common military alliance directed against potential Soviet aggression, with the former commander of the Allied invasion of Europe, General Eisenhower, as its first chief. In Greece, the United States was

[9] For a discussion of the origins of the People's Democracies, see H. Gordon Skilling, *The Governments of Communist Europe* (New York: Crowell, 1966), pp. 1–40.

helping the royal Greek government stamp out the revolutionary insurrection of the communists in a full-fledged civil war. President Harry Truman proclaimed the so-called Truman Doctrine in 1947, offering continued support to both Greece and Turkey and, by implication, to others resisting communist pressures from within and without.

The Cold War quickly spread into other parts of the world, militarily, economically, diplomatically: China, Malaya, Philippines, and Indochina, the Middle East, Africa and Latin America, all became foci of the global conflict.

The least popular view in the period 1941–1945, but most popular in the next decade, was that, after all, Stalin really was actuated by the aspiration to world communist revolution and inexorably committed to destroying his once-dear-allies, the Western "imperialist" powers.

Thus, World War II gave rise to the Cold War and the bipolar struggle between the United States and Russia which dominated the next three decades. It also produced new, important entities in the world community of states.

When World War II began, Black Africa was still very much a White Africa. World War I shook but did not destroy Europe's colonial empires. Only Ethiopia and Liberia maintained precarious and primitive existence as independent states in 1914–1918. The outcome of the First World War led *not* to independence for the African peoples, but rather to a reshuffle of influence among European powers. German colonies passed under Franco-British influences in the guise of the League of Nations mandates. The League itself was still a predominantly European organization, even though its theoretical, legal, and organizational aspirations were worldwide. India was still British India, and Indonesia was still a Dutch colonial province.

Economically and militarily, Europe still held the trump cards of power on the eve of the Second World War. In the aftermath of 1945, however, the age of Europe's hegemony came to an end.

In World War I (1914–1918) an unprecedented 8 million men died as casualties of the fighting. In World War II (1939–1945) the total military casualties were easily twice that figure, and the slaughter of civilians was so prodigious in consequence of extermination camps, deportations, mass bombings, and other forms of warfare against noncombatants, that the total casualties may well have been between 30 and 40 million persons.

The war was also much more costly economically than previous conflicts and, above all, disproportionately costly for Europe. One of its consequences was the drastic impoverishment of the great colonial powers of the pre-1939 period, particularly Britain, France, Italy, Holland, Belgium; their overseas investments, productive capacities, manpower, and naval and merchant fleet tonnage were all drastically depleted. In turn, these losses produced their political consequences in Africa and Asia, creating new opportunities for self-assertion to the peoples inhabiting the colonial possessions of these states. In 1919 at the founding of the League of Nations, 16 out of the 41 members were European states. The United Nations, founded in April 1945 at San Francisco, as a successor to the League of Nations counted only 9 European states exclusive of the USSR among its original 46. Crumbling European empires set the stage for the colonies' emergence into independence. Indonesian nationalism, for example, mounting in the 1920's and 1930's, had been precariously "contained" by Dutch administration and police controls in the 1919–1939 interwar period. But following the Japanese conquest of the Indonesians in 1942 and the occupation until 1945, the Dutch found it extremely difficult, both militarily and economically, to reimpose their rule. After four years of intermittent fighting and negotiations, Indonesia emerged independent in December 1949.

The establishment of India and Pakistan as independent states was similarly aided by the lessened ability of the colonial power to assert its control as a consequence of the war. Thus, in 1940 British officials repeatedly promised Indians eventual independence in the form of "full dominion status" inasmuch as Britain was hardly able to face the prospect of an Indian insurrection. In March 1942, alarmed by rapid Japanese advances in Southeast Asia, and heavily committed in the European theaters of war, Prime Minister Churchill dispatched Sir Stafford Cripps to assure the Indians that Britain would move to grant them freedom as soon as the war was concluded.

In Indochina, the French had managed to contain nationalist and communist insurgents for many years prior to 1941 and the Japanese conquest. Following the collapse of Japanese occupation in 1945, the French were unable to resume even nominal control of the area until early in 1946. Between 1947 and 1954 the French struggled vainly to repress nationalist and communist opposition, grown disproportionately powerful and militant since the 1930's. In 1954 they finally left Indochina in the wake of their dramatic defeat at Dienbienphu at the hands of Ho Chi Minh's guerrilla forces.

The war similarly galvanized nationalism and weakened colonialism in Burma, Malaya, Philippines and Algeria.

Western rule and influence helped to produce a momentum toward the development of indigeneous nationalism and aspirations to political independence which eventually made colonialism increasingly untenable. In Asia, Africa and, to some extent, Latin America also, the European influence produced a pattern of change that included: (1) economically

—a shift from a subsistence to a money economy; growth of a wage-labor force; rise of a new middle class; (2) socially—greater urbanization; increased social mobility; spread of Western education and skills; (3) spiritually—spread of Christian religion and other Western values, and a frustrating neglect of native, local elements inculcated with these very values and skills through Western education; (4) politically—the eclipse of traditional authorities and the forging of new symbols of national identity.[10]

The weakening of the colonial regimes began with the crisis of World War I (1914–1918) and was completed and consummated in the course of World War II. Africans and Asians were politicized by service in the colonial armies;[11] by exposure to foreign conquest, particularly in the Middle East and in Asia; they were encouraged and emboldened by the obvious weakening of colonial powers to dominate them because of the scale and intensity of conflict among them; by concessions wrung piecemeal in consequence of this weakness, and lastly also by the slogans of freedom, equality, and self-determination that the winners of these conflicts solemnly proclaimed to all the world. The principles that were enunciated by President Wilson for the League of Nations in 1919, by Churchill and Roosevelt for the Atlantic Charter in 1941, and the United Nations in 1945, were difficult to confine to "Europeans and whites only."

But the increased aspirations to freedom and statehood in the so-called Third World, and the increased capacity for its assertion in the face of imperial decline, went hand in hand with some basic problems that have increasingly plagued and baffled the international community since the 1940's.

Two of these problems have been at the root of modernization and development, both economic and political, in the postcolonial world of the 1950's, 1960's, and clearly the 1970's, too. These were the overriding problems of poverty and lack of social, political, and cultural cohesion among many emergent nation-states of this period. Independence could not quickly cure these problems.

At the end of the 1940's, about two-thirds of the world population lived in the so-called underdeveloped areas. The average per capita income in Asia, Africa, and Latin America was less than one-twentieth that of the United States. In fact, India, Pakistan, China, and Indonesia, ac-

[10] This classification was developed by James S. Coleman in his "Current Political Movements in Africa," *The Annals of the American Academy of Political and Social Science*, CCXCVIII, March 1955, pp. 96–97.

[11] See, e.g., Donald S. Rothchild, *The Effects of Mobilization in British Africa* (Duquesne University: Institute of African Affairs, 1959).

counting for the bulk of world population, were estimated to have per capita incomes of less than one-thirtieth of that of the U.S. Even a more "reasonable" comparison of Ireland with India was 9 to 1; Ireland and China about 16 to 1. Given a world median per capita income of about $250 in 1949 (27 states above the mark and 27 below), India's population averaged one-fifth of that figure; China's one-tenth.[12] Many of the new nations were dependent on just one or two raw material products for their foreign trade sustenance. Illustratively, in 1950–1954, cotton and jute accounted for 85 percent of Pakistan's exports; Burma depended on rice to the extent of 79 percent of her sales abroad; rubber and oil added up to 62 percent of Indonesia's exports; tea and rubber gave Ceylon 74 percent of its trade. In Latin America, around 1950, Cuban dependence on sugar amounted to 77 percent of all exports; tin in Bolivia and bananas in Honduras accounted for 66 and 61 percent of exports, respectively. In five countries (El Salvador, Colombia, Guatemala, Brazil, and Haiti) coffee exports added up to between 87 and 66 percent of total exports.[13] Decline in demand and price levels of these products were likely to have calamitous consequences for all these countries. For the 1.3 billion Asians in 1950, economic primitivism and poverty translated into a vicious cycle of social consequences. Life expectancy was 35 years as compared with 67 in Europe, Russia, and North America; illiteracy was 68 percent as compared with only 5 percent in the more "advanced" regions. Yet, it was precisely here, in Asia, that the pressure of population on resources was greatest.

In fact, most of the underdeveloped nations could not satisfy the ever greater demands for food, shelter, and all the amenities of life that twentieth-century communication media—the proverbial transistor radios in the jungle—brought to public attention. Western rule stimulated nationalist aspirations without developing adequate economic and social infrastructures to support them. Independence frequently became more a prelude to frustration than tranquility. Moreover, among the underdeveloped states, the roots of nationalism were still, in many respects, new and shallow. The nationalist ideal of community, of oneness, in Europe was variously reinforced by common language, religion, culture, dynastic ties, physical proximity, and substantial economic interchange. Present-day ideals and future aspirations rested on commonly perceived legacies of the past. In the African, Asian, and even Latin American states, it was still the task of a small, middle-class intellectual

[12] Data from U. N. *National and Per Capita Incomes*, (New York 1950), Table i, pp. 14–16.

[13] U.S. Department of State Publication 6131, Inter-American Series 51 (November 1955), p. 23.

elite to substitute for the legacy of folklore and tradition some ready-made contrivances of unifying political myths.[14]

The war produced a shift in resources and influence. The power of the United States and the Soviet Union, closely followed by the rise of Communist China, overshadowed the shrunken capabilities of Europe's once powerful states. Unlike the old League, the United Nations became, within a decade of 1945, a genuinely worldwide organization. Political conflicts spilled markedly beyond the confines of Europe. And, since the establishment of Cold War frontiers between states allied with the U.S. in the West, and the USSR in the East of Europe, the battleground of world politics shifted overwhelmingly to Asia, Africa, and Latin America. The destructiveness and range of new weapons for the first time endangered the existence of the whole world, irrespective of the parties to a particular conflict.

The war that began in 1939 in Europe ushered in a period of global ideological conflicts which, in scale and intensity, exceeded all the previous conflicts of history. In some respects, one could justifiably say that the circumstances of political life in mid-twentieth century have been changing in the *same* direction as they had in the Age of the Renaissance, the Reformation and the Enlightenment—only *more* so, or more rapidly than ever. Thus, there have been comparable trends to secularism as opposed to religiosity in people's lives; the remarkable expansion of science and technology; an increased mobility of people, goods, ideas, and communications throughout the world; an accelerated growth of urban life at the expense of the rural; more complex and mobile forms of economic, social, and cultural organization; and in consequence of all of these changes, occurring ever more rapidly, the tendency to obsolescence (or what we now commonly call, irrelevance) among old concepts, values, and formulas also appreciably increased.[15] World changes have shattered or shaken belief-systems. They have dictated ideological changes and adaptations.

[14] See, e.g., Paul M. Linebarger, "Asian Nationalism: Some Psychiatric Aspects of Political Nimesis," *Psychiatry*, XVII, August 1954, p. 262: "Though Asian nationalism functions in the modern world it is derived from an identification on the part of Asians themselves with the image "Asian" projected to Asia by Europeans, whether in person or through mass communications . . . . for (this concept) neologisms have had to be created in most of the Asian languages concerned. The Asian nationalism which confronts the world today is, ideologically and emotionally considered, not an internal dynamic springing from the older pre-modern Asian cultures. It is instead an entirely valid response to massive western emotional and spiritual demands."

[15] On the "roots of secularism," see Jacob Burckhardt, *The Civilization of the Renaissance in Italy*, 8th ed., Trans. by S. G. C. Middlemore (London: Allen and Unwin, 1921).

CHAPTER 8

Postwar Communism

In the aftermath of the war, communism in Europe developed two new tendencies now usually labeled in communist polemics as "revisionism and dogmatism." The first is most often identified with Yugoslavia, the second with China.

In the 1945–1947 period, the "thaw" in relations between Russia and the Western powers was brought to an end. Stalin moved back to a position of isolationism and hostility. Ideologically, this meant renewing the Leninist Doctrine that armed conflict between communist and capitalist forces was sooner or later inevitable. Despite four years of alliance with Britain and America during 1941–1945, the Soviet view was that these states were imperialist wolves, after all. The coincidence of interests between them and the Soviet Union during what communist propaganda called the Great Patriotic War, was merely temporary and superficial. The imperialists helped the USSR grudgingly, out of sinister self-interest. Lasting world peace would only come through the overthrow of world imperialism, the ultimate producer of war. Stalin thus renewed Lenin's teachings and concomittantly the doctrine of Soviet encirclement by hostile capitalist states. Both propositions implied that the USSR had to prepare for all-out war against the imperialists; that victory over the Axis was no time to settle down to genuine peace; and that the Soviet Union needed to maintain the utmost vigilance in her internal security, and in her diplomatic dealings with the external world.[1]

---

[1] See Francis B. Randall, *Stalin's Russia* (New York: Free Press, 1965) p. 64–95, for a brief account of his ideas. See also W. W. Kulski, *Peaceful Coexistence: An Analysis*

In practice, this meant renewed police terror and intimidation of the Rusian people; renewed campaigns against "bourgeois-cosmopolitan", influences in Soviet art, science, and literature; severe restrictions on contacts with foreigners; cutting the flow of trade and tourism; and, very significantly, the renewed commitment of Soviet resources to the industrial-military priorities of the 1930's: heavy industry and weaponry. Given the enormous destruction of the war in Russia with its 20 million casualties and untold number of cities, towns, and villages in rubble, Stalin's policy cast a bleak pall on the reconstruction of Soviet life in the wake of the conflict. The consumers were back to an era of austerity. Once again, steel plants, coal mines, and tank factories would be given priority over the basic amenities of food, clothes, and shelter.

Stalinism connoted fear—in talking to strangers or even one's neighbors, one could never be sure about being reported to the secret police. Even the most innocent contacts with those—particularly foreigners—suspected of espionage or subversion by the NKVD could lead to one's own downfall. The arbitrariness of Beria's police made people feel unsafe anywhere, at any time—day or night, at home or at work; Stalinism also meant crowded, ill-equipped housing with several families sharing a few rooms and little, if any, privacy. It meant spending much of one's waking hours, outside of work, freezing in interminable waiting lines in front of shops and stores. Frequently, the goods that one had patiently waited for would no longer be available; or there would be a lack of selection in the colors and sizes or varieties that the purchaser wanted. Life in postwar Russia was thus singularly drab and barren from the standpoint of an average wage earner. The statistics of Russia's rising industrial and political power bore little relationship to the private affluence and happiness of the man-in-the-street.

In the Soviet Union the years between 1948 and 1953 were the apogee of Stalinism. Andrei Zhdanov, boss of the Party's Leningrad organization, and Lavrenti Beria, leader of the secret police, dominated the political life of the country. Repression and fear ruled Russian society.[2]

All of these trends became substantially modified in the wake of Stalin's death in March 1953. What followed this epochal event was first a period of interregnum. Stalin was succeeded not by one but by a

---

of Soviet Foreign Policy (Chicago: Regnery, 1959), for an excellent analysis of Stalinist and post-Stalinist attitudes to the world.

[2] See Julian Towster, *Political Power in the USSR, 1917–1947* (New York: Oxford University Press, 1948), for an account of Soviet politics in the heyday of Stalin; see also Naum Jasny, *Soviet Industrialization, 1928–1952* (Chicago: University of Chicago Press, 1961).

coalition of leaders. Georgi Malenkov became General Secretary of the CPSU and Prime Minister but within a few months was replaced by Nikita Khrushchev as the Party's General Secretary. Other powerful leaders included the police chief Beria, and several old-time Stalinist stalwarts, among them V. M. Molotov, Nikolai Bulganin, Klimenti Voroshilov, and Lazar Kaganovich. Beria was the first to lose out in the power struggle that took place. He was reported to have been tried and executed in December 1953.[3] Gradually, the other contestants for power were weakened and eliminated by Khrushchev who, by 1957, managed to establish an undisputed primacy over the Soviet state.

One of the principal tactics Khrushchev used in gaining power was de-Stalinization. He had made himself the champion of a cause popular with the masses of the Russian people and many rank-and-file Party members; simultaneously he discredited his principal rivals for power by linking them with the hateful oppression of Stalin's rule.[4] The most dramatic act of de-Stalinization took place at the CPSU's 20th Congress in Moscow in October 1956. Khrushchev delivered a secret report at this meeting. It was a lengthy expose and denunciation of Stalin, the man, his methods of government, and the crimes and follies of his policy. The report did not remain secret very long either in Russia or abroad, and it soon had profound ideological and practical consequences for world communism.

In Russia, Stalinism became known by the name Khrushchev gave it, "the cult of personality." It was blamed for all sorts of disasters that had befallen the Soviet Union in the past, such as wrongful incarceration and execution of men, economic failures, lack of preparedness and consequent losses in the wake of Nazi invasion of 1941, and the defection of Marshal Tito's Yugoslavia from the "communist family of nations," among others. Khrushchev maintained that Stalin was insensitive to human needs and dictatorial in his management of the Party.[5] His anti-Stalinism, or denunciation of the "cult of personality" gave Soviet policy several new directions. First, Khrushchev called for a return to "Leninist norms of party democracy." Thus—typically giving the most sacred communist source as his model—he advocated that the Party become

3 See Myron Rush, *Political Succession in the USSR* (New York: Columbia University Press, 1965), on the disposition of Lavrenti Beria, pp. 58–60.

4 Among many sources, see A. J. Groth, "Krushchev on Stalin," *Problems of Communism*, Vol. XII, No. 1, Winter 1963, pp. 66–70.

5 On Khrushchev's "secret" report to the 20th Party Congress, see *Report to the Central Committee of the Communist Party of the Soviet Union to the 20th Party Congress* (Moscow: Foreign Languages Publishing House, 1956).

more collegial in its decision-making, more open to dissent and debate within its duly constituted organs that was the case under Stalin. He also advocated "satisfying the needs of the people," that is, heeding the plight of the consumer for housing, food, and clothing. And, most characteristically perhaps, he advocated relaxation of police terror and the dreaded extraordinary justice of Stalin's day. These new orientations became linked with certain new policies.

Khrushchev adopted the view that war had ceased to be "fatally inevitable" in the nuclear age and committed the Soviets to the alternative of peaceful coexistence with imperialist states He argued that because thermonuclear weapons had brought on the likelihood of mutual extinction as between the communist and the capitalist states, the latter could be dissuaded from attacking the USSR. Khrushchev never ruled out the possibility of all-out war between East and West. He rather moved from the category of something that was certain sooner or later to something that might well be avoided. In making this argument, Khrushchev assigned great weight to two new factors: the super destructiveness of the atomic weapons, and the shift in the balance of world power. This shift resulted, Khrushchev argued, from the rise of the People's Democracies in Europe and the rise of Mao's People's China in Asia. Because of these new additions to the communist fold, the encirclement of the USSR alleged by Stalin was at an end. In substance, then, according to Khrushchev, the USSR had become too strong and war too terrible in the 1950's for the imperialists to risk war lightly.

In changing Soviet views from those of Lenin and Stalin on the inevitability of war, Khrushchev argued that new circumstances dictated a change in doctrine. Things were clearly different in Lenin's time. Russia stood alone. Weapons were still relatively primitive. As for Stalin, Khrushchev did not mind finding him short of the mark as a Marxist theoretician. Stalin, he argued, was a paranoiac obsessed with external threats and suspicions of their domestic connections and repercussions.

Khrushchev supported the workers' class struggle and the more general struggle against imperialism. But so far as the Soviet role was concerned, it could be conducted peacefully. The USSR could win converts to its cause by example and persuasion; by trade and aid; by negotiation; and finally by putting sufficient pressure short-of-war (political, economic, diplomatic) upon the imperialist mischiefmakers.[6]

6 Krushchev's views on foreign policy are set out in his *Speeches and Interviews on World Problems 1957* (Moscow: Foreign Languages Publishing House, 1958); and *A Peace Treaty with Germany* (New York: Cross-Currents Press, 1961).

In general, Khrushchev's interpretation of Marxist ideology supported a "thaw" both at home and abroad. But it was open to the charge of revisionism, and it produced at least as many problems as it solved.

Mao Tse-tung and the Chinese Party accused the Soviet leader of a sell-out to the imperialists, labeling Khrushchev a right-wing deviationist. The predatory character of imperialism could not be changed by weapons' technology, the Chinese argued. Khrushchev overestimated the significance of nuclear arms, and allowed himself to be intimidated by them. Khrushchev's peaceful coexistence was not a militant enough form of struggle against imperialism. By deprecating violence, co-existence implied accommodation and reconciliation with imperialism, not its extinction. And the Chinese argued (plausibly enough) that Khrushchev could achieve this kind of communist-capitalist cooperation, even partnership, by increasingly making the Soviet Union into a snug, "safe," complacent, bourgeois state. They professed to see an emerging convergence between Russia and the West that would ultimately result in an alliance directed against the true Marxist revolutionaries, the Chinese and their allies.[7]

Thus, one of the adverse consequences of Khrushchev's reinterpretation of Lenin was a split with China. Another was a growing unmanageability of Soviet allies and followers throughout the world.

Khrushchev's anti-Stalin campaign caught Moscow's East European allies, the heretofore docile, pliant, and obedient "satellites," on the horns of a painful dilemma. If they wished to remain true and loyal followers of Moscow, then de-Stalinization had to apply to them as much as to the Russians. This meant "overcoming the cult of personality" in the management of local communist parties and regimes; if one-man rule was bad in the USSR, it was bad elsewhere, too. Collective, collegial, and deliberative proceedings were now called for. Secret police terror, brutal persecution of deviationists, indifference to the privations of consumers, callous exploitation of workers and farmers, all of these were slated for amelioration. The demand for such changes placed the East European leaders in the position of having to be unorthodox in order to be orthodox. Not only were they required to drastically

---

[7] On this subject see Donald W. Treadgold (ed.), *Soviet and Chinese Communism: Similarities and Differences* (Seattle: University of Washington Press, 1967). See also William E. Griffith, *Sino-Soviet Relations 1964–1965* (Cambridge, Mass.: MIT Press, 1967); See also Mao Tse-tung, *On Revolution and War*, ed. by M. Rejai (Garden City, N.Y.: Doubleday, 1969); *Our Study and the Current Situation* (Peking: Foreign Languages Press, 1960); *The Political Thought of Mao Tse-tung*, ed. by Stuart R. Schram (New York: Praeger, 1969); *Selected Works* (New York: International Publishers, 1954–1961); see also Yung Ping Chen, *Chinese Political Thought; Mao Tse-Tung and Liu Shao-chi* (Hague: M. Nijhoff, 1966).

change their whole style of government to please Moscow but, in addition, they were now asked to strike an extremely difficult and delicate balance between the tendency to a presumably more open, democratic, and humane society and the contrived maintenance of communism's monopolistic one-party rule at the same time. This meant making all sorts of reforms and concessions to popular discontent but somehow managing not to whet the appetite of the beneficiaries too much. It soon became obvious that this was indeed difficult, and that Khrushchev himself was not willing to accept some of the more extreme consequences of de-Stalinization in Eastern Europe.

In summarizing institutional changes of the Khrushchev years within the USSR itself, we can say that they were all clearly incremental. None of the basic organs of the party and the state were abolished. The monopolistic role of the CPSU was not only preserved, but actually somewhat strengthened in the period between 1957 and 1964 as opposed to the years 1953–1957. In this earlier period Khrushchev needed to balance the army and the secret police against one another in his own bid for power.

What his regime produced was a relaxation of police controls, a diminution of the dreaded KGB, and an increased recourse to ordinary processes of law; a considerable increase in Russian contacts with foreigners, in terms of trade, tourism, and cultural exchanges; an increased volume of consumer goods and some decentralization in the management of Russian agriculture and industrial economy, and a far greater—even if still modest by Western standards—tolerance of dissent among the country's intellectuals than in Stalin's day.[8]

Between 1955 and 1957 Nikita Khrushchev had eased out his competitors and rivals for power—men like Malenkov, Molotov, Kaganovich, Bulganin, and Zhukov—largely by "packing" the party organs with his personal supporters. By some estimates, he had succeeded in adding as many as 50 men dedicated to his cause, from 1956 to 1957, in the Party's Central Committee. The membership of that body was 133 full members and 112 candidate (nonvoting) members following the 20th CPSU Congress of 1956. In June of 1957, when Khrushchev was about to be ousted by a majority of the 11-man Party Presidium, his Central Committee supporters upheld him, expelling and demoting his opponents instead. In 1958, Khrushchev became simultaneously First Secretary of the Party and Premier. He reached a pinnacle of power unmatched since Stalin ascended to both these offices in 1941!

---

[8] On Krushchev's problems with the Soviet cultural establishment and intellectuals, see Walter Z. Laqueur and George Lichtheim, *The Soviet Cultural Scene, 1956–1957* (New York: Praeger, 1958).

Unlike Stalin, however, Khrushchev did not manage to hold on to power very long. In 1964 he was ousted from all the top offices of the Party and the state, replaced as First Secretary by Leonid Brezhnev and as Premier by Aleksei Kosygin.

Khrushchev was, to all appearances, brought down by a diverse coalition of Party elements. He was blamed for the failure of Russia's agriculture to produce more food; for neglect of the needs of heavy industry and the military in favor of "consumer frivolities"; for championing risky and imprudent disarmament schemes; and mismanagement of de-Stalinization both at home and abroad. His attacks on the legacy of Stalin were regarded by Party stalwarts as undermining their position in the eyes of the Russian people, promoting Sino-Soviet conflict, bringing about the dissolution of the Cominform at Tito's insistence in 1956 (without winning Tito back into the Warsaw Pact bloc), and the "unrest" evidenced by developments in Poland, and above all, Hungary in 1956 (see p. 155). His confrontation with President Kennedy in 1962 over the emplacements of Soviet missiles in Cuba was remembered, too. Khrushchev was publicly denounced by his successors for "adventurism" and fostering his own, Stalin-like cult of personality.

The Khrushchev "thaw" was soon replaced by a cautious and gradual "refreeze," one which, by 1970, included even a partial rehabilitation of Stalin.

It is appropriate to note, however, that the Khrushchev phenomenon was not merely a personal one. The change from Stalin to Khrushchev coincided with profound changes in the whole Soviet system, too. The USSR of the late 1950's and early 1960's was a much more technologically advanced, urban, literate, and bureaucratized society than the impoverished, rural, and underdeveloped Russia of the 1920's, 1930's, and even the 1940's. The transition from police-rule tyranny to more sophisticated managerial manipulation was not simply a Khrushchevian whim. It probably corresponded to the needs and demands of a much more complex and developed economic and social system; thus, the Brezhnev-Kosygin regime, for all its reaction, stopped far short of restoring a 1929–1953 version of Stalinism in the Soviet Union.

As we have already noted in Chapter 6, one of the consequences of the Second World War had been the establishment of several communist regimes outside the USSR. In Eastern Europe, an assortment of techniques, including Soviet military power and diplomacy, internal subversion, guerrilla warfare, propaganda, and astute alliances between communists and noncommunists were variously combined to carve out a large communist-ruled, Soviet-oriented sphere of influence. At its zenith, this sphere included the eastern parts of Germany and Austria, Poland, Czechoslovakia, Hungary, Yugoslavia, Rumania, Bulgaria, and Albania. About 96 million people of diverse cultures and nationalities became part of the Soviet bloc.

So-called People's Democracies were established throughout the region. The People's Democracies were ostensibly coalition regimes in which communists appeared to share power with representatives of other parties, usually peasant, socialist, and urban liberals or democrats. In fact, the key governmental positions, particularly those of police and security, were invariably held by communists. The undisputed leadership of the Party was barely disguised by the coalitional window-dressing. The communists did not hesitate to use terror, and they subjected the societies under their control to massive social and political upheavals.[9]

Political parties and public organizations not specifically subordinated to Party control were dissolved and prohibited. Trade unions became agencies of the Party for the fulfillment of its economic and political programs instead of defending the interests of the workers; strikes were prohibited. All mass media became vehicles for the dissemination of Party ideology and propaganda. The churches, particularly the Catholic Church, were subjected to persecution. Social autonomy, whether expressed in ethnic demands for self-rule or in the traditional independence of the universities, were subordinated to the overriding demands of the Party. The tasks of the judiciary—like those of the secret police—were defined in terms of the ideological-political needs and objectives of the Party, not in terms of universal, neutral, legal-rational norms. Law or no law, the enemies of the regime had to be rooted out and destroyed.

Salinist patterns of economic development were imposed throughout Eastern Europe. Redistribution of land from large to small holders was followed by massive collectivization drives, and preponderant emphasis on industrial development, the production of minerals, semifinished products, energy sources, and capital goods. Moreover, the economies of Eastern Europe, which had long maintained trading links with the West, were reoriented to an increasing dependence on the Soviet Union.

The emphasis on capital goods as opposed to consumer goods was coupled with disproportionate underinvestment in agriculture as compared with industry. The effect of this on the consumer was made worse by (1) the establishment of an extremely rigid, central planning

[9] See Francis J. Kase, *People's Democracy: A Contribution to the Study of the Communist Theory of State and Revolution* (Leyden: Sijthoff, 1968); and A. I. Sobolev, *People's Democracy; A New Form of Political Organization* (Moscow: Foreign Languages Publishing House, 1954).

system by the Party in each country; (2) the demoralizing effects of collectivization on peasant productivity; and (3) the callous indifference of the Party-run bureaucracy to the demands, tastes, and preferences of ordinary people.

All these policies had their ideological-political justifications. Industrialization fulfilled Marxist-Leninist requirements for the development of the preponderant power of the proletariat over the peasantry and other "reactionary" or "backward" classes. It provided the material basis for the eventual achievement, presumably, of the highest phase of communism—a classless society. Collectivization of land and central planning were seen by the Party as instruments of control enabling it to keep a tight grip on power and to promote its cherished social revolution.

The neglect of agriculture and the emphasis on industrialization brought large numbers of people from the countryside into urban areas. There they were caught in still another "squeeze," inasmuch as the communists channeled scarce resources away from housing construction to "more important" industrial, military, and export purposes. The Soviet Union—seen as bastion and beacon of world revolution—reaped the harvest of products and services at below world market prices from the East European "satellites." Polish coal, Rumanian oil, Czechoslovakian uranium ore, all flowed into the USSR.

Communist policies of the 1940's and 1950's had many positive effects, too. Industrial output in terms of products such as steel, iron ore, coal, natural gas, cement, machine tools, and chemicals rose to unprecedented high levels. The communist regimes also extended the range of certain public benefits such as education, medical care, recreation and cultural facilities, and social security and pension coverage.

But in terms of food, housing, clothing, and assorted goods of private consumption including appliances, cosmetics, and automobiles, there was considerable undersupply and privation. In Czechoslovakia, which was economically the most highly developed communist state in the 1950's, the average worker's pay could buy only half the amount of clothing that its 1937 precommunist counterpart did! With one of the world's highest *per capita* indices of industrial output (e.g., more steel than the U.S.), the average Czechoslovak worker in 1957 needed to work twice as long to buy the same quantity of bread, rice, butter, ham, eggs, or apples as a worker in "capitalist" Belgium. Illustrative of other communist regimes as well, Czechoslovakia increased her steel output from 2.2 million tons in 1937 to 5.5 in 1958; cement from 1.3 to 4.1 million tons; coal from 16.7 to 25.8 million tons; electric power from 4.1 billion to 19.6 billion kilowatt-hours. But the output of textiles, clothing, and shoes rose by just a few percentage points. As of 1957

Czechoslovakia registered an absolute decline in four of seven major crops as compared with the 1937–38 period.[10]

The suppression of dissent and discontent throughout Eastern Europe involved party purges in the 1950's that were reminiscent of the Moscow purge trials of the 1930's. Party leaders were accused of "national deviationism" and "cosmopolitan" or Zionist influences. Many of these were Jews. In Czechoslovakia, Party Secretary Rudolf Slansky was executed in 1952 along with 10 other leaders. In Hungary and Bulgaria, party bureaucrats Laszlo Rajk and Traicho Kostov met the same fate. In Poland, Wladyslaw Gomulka was expelled as Party leader, denounced and kept under house arrest for several years until 1955.

The only East European state that escaped Stalinization while becoming "communist" was Marshal Tito's Yugoslavia. Its break with Moscow in 1948 was, in fact, one of the reasons for the purges carried out elsewhere in Eastern Europe, inasmuch as Stalin feared that Titoism would prove contagious.

Actually, Tito's communist regime in the 1940's was not much different internally from the other People's Democracies. The communists of Yugoslavia managed to gain as firm a grip on their countrymen as any of the other East European parties. They operated under the same dual structure of power—state and party—with the former serving as coalitional "window-dressing" of all so-called "progressive," "democratic," "antifascist" elements and the latter as the de facto core of power. Their persecution of political opponents and dissenters, including the churches, was no less thorough and ruthless than in Poland, Rumania, or Bulgaria. They differed mainly in the fact that they did not want to subordinate their policies, present and future, to Russian scrutiny and control. Tito wanted to develop Yugoslav communism in his own way, subject to what he regarded as Yugoslav rather than Soviet needs and realities. In Tito's bold attempt to assert his independence of Stalin, he was aided by two factors that made his position analogous to Mao's China and Hoxha's Albania, and different from all the other communist states of the late 1940's.

Yugoslavia was neither occupied nor encircled by Soviet troops in 1948. Her territory, though not large, was mountainous, well suited to guerilla warfare, and likely to prove difficult for an invading army marching from, say, Hungary, Rumania, or Bulgaria. She possessed ample land and water access to Western nations—Italy, Austria, Greece

[10] See Edward Taborsky, *Communism in Czechoslavakia 1948–1960* (Princeton N.J.: Princeton University Press, 1961); he presents detailed information and an analysis of economic policy that is applicable to the other communist states of Eastern Europe as well, pp. 361–467.

and, above all, the Adriatic Sea. Most importantly, Tito, like Mao Tse-tung, was not a foreign puppet. Unlike East German, Rumanian, Polish, or even Hungarian communists, Tito's followers had very considerable local, popular support. They did not depend, even initially, on Soviet troops to put them into or keep them in power in 1944–1946, anymore than Mao Tse-tung did in 1947–1949.

Initially, the principal domestic difference between Tito's and other East European regimes was that Tito did not proceed from radical land redistribution to collectivization. It was only in the mid-1950's that certain reforms, emphasizing decentralized management of the economy, representation of employees in worker councils, easements on consumers and police rule gave Yugoslavia a more liberal image than that of her East European neighbors.[11] But so long as Stalin ruled in the Kremlin, and Russian forces held sway over the whole region from East Germany to Bulgaria, the example of Tito could not be imitated among the so-called satellites. It was, however, as Moscow well knew, a tempting example to local communists. Tito traded with the West, received substantial aid from the United States, both economic and military, and was relatively free to adapt his domestic policies to the needs and demands of his immediate environment. His independence of Moscow proved a great source of strength to his regime; even those Yugoslavs who hated communism were willing to support Tito's defiance of Moscow. He was thus able to capitalize on the feelings of nationalism as much as socialism or communism. Thus, Communist party leaders outside Yugoslavia saw in Tito's example not only a chance to do what they wanted, or improve the position of their economies but, above all, the chance to develop sources of local, indigenous support on the analogous platform of their particular national sentiments.

Stalin's death in March 1953 ushered in an era of opportunity for these leaders. At last, the Russians themselves were *asking* them to "liberalize" communist rule. However, it also began a period of intense ferment in Eastern Europe, where many people hoped and expected that the death of Stalin would bring about an end to the communist system itself.

---

[11] On the Yugoslav brand of communism, see Milovan Djilas, *The New Class* (New York: Praeger, 1957); *Land Without Justice* (New York: Harcourt, Brace, 1958), and his *The Unperfect Society: Beyond the New Class* (New York: Harcourt, Brace and World, 1969); see also Charles P. McVicker, *Titoism: Pattern for International Communism* (New York: H. Martin's Press, 1957); F. W. Neal, *Titoism in Action* (Berkeley: University of California Press, 1958); N. D. Popovic, *Yugoslavia: The New Class in Crisis* (Syracuse: Syracuse University Press, 1968); W. S. Vucinich (ed.), *Contemporary Yugoslavia* (Berkeley: Univ. of California Press, 1969).

In 1953, widespread riots in East Germany signaled the beginning. But more serious troubles still lay ahead for Moscow and the communists in Eastern Europe. Illustratively, the gradual liberalization of the Party regime in Hungary in 1955 led to public denunciations of Matyas Rakosi and other old-time Stalinist leaders by those Party members whom they had just "magnanimously" let out of jails. Criticism and denunciation grew and multiplied. In 1955 Rakosi was forced out and by 1956 leadership of the Communist party and government in Hungary passed precisely to those elements that Stalin and his henchmen had dubbed as deviationist and unreliable or even treasonable. The more open the Party became to the expression of different points of view from within and without, the more vulnerable it seemed. In Hungary the process of erosion culminated in the October 1956 Revolution, led by Imre Nagy, a communist once expelled and now reinstated by the Party. The Hungarian Revolution resulted for a period of a few weeks in the de facto removal of the country from the Soviet bloc. Nagy committed Hungary to abandonment of the Warsaw Pact military alliance with the USSR and other communist states. He constituted a government inclusive of genuine noncommunists for the first time in nearly a decade, and called for free elections. One-party rule was thus all but doomed in Hungary. The Soviet response was massive military intervention. It quickly overcame the heroic but hopeless resistance of Hungary's soldiers and Freedom Fighters. Heavy damage and many thousands of casualties constituted the price of reestablishing a reliably pro-Moscow, one-party regime in Hungary.[12] Although full-scale war was avoided in the case of Poland, here, too, de-Stalinization coincided with challenges to Soviet control and influence. And here also the liberalization of the regime under the leadership of Wladyslaw Gomulka led to periodic outbursts of unrest.[13] The disaffection and the growing spirit of independence throughout Eastern Europe were sanctioned, if not promoted, by another feature of de-Stalinization: the doctrine of polycentrism.

Stalin had always insisted not only on monolithic unity in the communist movement but also on Soviet primacy. In practice, this

[12] See accounts by Paul Kecskemeti, *The Unexpected Revolution* (Stanford: Stanford University Press, 1961); Paul E. Zinner, *Revolution in Hungary* (New York: Columbia University Press, 1962); and Ferenc A. Vali, *Rift and Revolt in Hungary: Nationalism versus Communism* (Cambridge: Harvard University Press, 1961).

[13] On the Polish model, see Adam Bromke, *Poland's Politics: Idealism vs. Realism* (Cambridge: Harvard University Press, 1967); Konrad Syrop, *Spring in October: The Polish Revolution of 1956* (London: Weidenfeld and Nicolson, 1957); Richard Hiscocks, *Poland, Bridge to the Abyss?* (London: Oxford University Press, 1963); Hansjakob Stehle, *The Independent Satellite* (New York: Praeger, 1965), and an early account by Czeslaw Milosz, *The Captive Mind* (New York: A. A. Knopf, 1953).

meant that whether one was a communist in Russia—or somewhere in Asia or Latin America or Europe—to be out of step with the USSR was tantamount to treason. Obedience to Moscow was presumably the acid test of Party loyalty anywhere.

Stalin's successors, new in their jobs, found it difficult to command the obedience that Stalin had exacted. They also hoped that they could achieve better results by cooperation and consultation with foreign communist parties than by crude coercion. In his famous speech in 1956, Khrushchev cited Stalin's failure to coerce Tito into subservience to Moscow after the 1948 break as evidence of Stalin's shortsightedness and characteristic meanness. Under the guise of "return to Leninist principles," Khrushchev openly advocated a policy of polycentrism. Each communist party was presumably the equal of every other; each had to adapt its particular policies to its own environment, its own problems and, ultimately, the wishes of its own leadership. Soviet primacy was seen as simply stemming from the longer experience and revoultionary success of the CPSU. It no longer connoted the right to issue orders to other parties. If the Soviets had subscribed to this policy fully and completely, international communism would have been transformed from a hierarchic organizational alliance of parties into a loose association of like-minded people. It would have been a transition from a political catholicism to a political protestantism. Only the holy writ of Marx, Engels, Lenin, and possibly others at the discretion of each party, would unite them all. What it all meant, how it should be interpreted, and what policies should be followed at any moment would be up to each party to decide for itself. However, neither Khrushchev nor the other Kremlin leaders since his time have been willing to accept polycentrism in such pristine form.[14]

A recent confirmation of the Kremlin's intolerance was the doctrine enunciated by Leonid Brezhnev, Khrushchev's successor as CPSU's First Secretary. In October 1968, Brezhnev declared that the USSR would, in fact, construe it a duty to defend socialist regimes from subversion as it did in August 1968 in Czechoslovakia. In December 1970, Soviet troops again appeared ready for intervention in Poland as Edward Gierek replaced Wladyslaw Gomulka.

Like the Universal Church in the period of the Reformation, Stalin's

---

14 On polycentrism, see Walter Laqueur and Leopold Labedz, *Polycentrism, the New Factor in International Communism* (New York: Praeger, 1962); Peter Mayer, *Cohesion and Conflict in International Communism* (The Hague: Nijhoff, 1968); J. D. B. Miller and T. H. Rigby (eds.), *The Disintegrating Monolith: Pluralist Trends in the Communist World* (New York: M. Kelley, 1968); Adam Bromke (ed.), *The Communist States at the Crossroads: Between Moscow and Peking* (New York: Praeger, 1965).

monolith was plunged into a ferment of doctrinal disputes. We can identify here at least two major cleavages within the movement, with some subvariations in each. The first of these has been the schism between Red China and the Soviet Union.

The Chinese received Khrushchev's de-Stalinization campaign with mixed feelings. What they liked about it was, in their own language, an end to "great power chauvinism." Mao Tse-tung and his cohorts had long privately resented Soviet paternalism, and Moscow's attempts to dictate or interfere in their affairs. They recalled that Stalin was in the habit of sacrificing the fledgling Chinese Communist party in the early 1930's for the sake of good relations with its enemies, such as Chiang Kai-shek in the 1930's. They remembered also that until they had won power in all of China in 1949, Stalin treated them as if they were scarcely noticeable "poor relations." Material Soviet support for them was very scant until at least 1945. Mao's contributions to Marxist ideology, strategy, and tactics went unnoticed, while the adulation of Stalin as the all-wise, all-knowing leader of world communism was being daily disseminated by Soviet propaganda. Mao lived in Stalin's shadow even after he had won power in the most populous country in the world; latent feelings of Chinese nationalism were thus bruised by the whole panorama of Soviet-Chinese relations. Moreover, specific but still publicly concealed policy differences between the two countries in the period between 1949 and 1953 exacerbated the tensions in Sino-Soviet relations.

Thus, the Chinese communists welcomed both the Khrushchev idea that Stalin was far from faultless and, more importantly still, that there ought to be greater autonomy and independence for member parties in the world communist movement.

But there was even more in Khrushchev's "revisionism," as they called it, that they thoroughly disapproved. Despite their differences, Mao and Stalin were analogously authoritarian leaders of their respective parties; moreover, they shared militantly antiimperialist, anti-Western, and anti-American orientations. Stalin and Mao had been the foremost champions of the Cold War against the West. In casting opprobrium on Stalin's political style and on his ruthless, uncompromising militancy, Khrushchev was really being as anti-Maoist as he was anti-Stalinist. And although China had received considerable amounts of Soviet aid during the Korean War (1950–1953), Mao was not in the uncomfortable position of East Germany's Walter Ulbricht. He was strong enough both within the Party and the country to sustain his own leadership without any Soviet aid, if necessary.

Mao viewed Khrushchev's "peaceful coexistence" line, the "avoidability of war" thesis, and his arduous pursuit of "summitry"—or negoti-ations with the West—as concessions to imperialism and as abandonment of the cause of world revolution. Soviet party overtures to Tito, who had declared himself a neutral in the Cold War, and had accepted American military aid, impressed the Chinese as proof positive of Khrushchev's "right-wing deviationism," or "capitulationism" vis-á-vis the imperialist states. As the Chinese saw it, if it was no longer necessary to fight imperialism in order to be a good communist, the Marxist-Leninist legacy was a shambles![15] Among the issues that brought about the Sino-Soviet rift was China's establishment of the people's communes in 1958. Mao Tse-tung launched what the Chinese called a "Great Leap For-ward" in the path to full-fledged communism. The communes were suppose to integrate and increase agricultural and industrial production by resort to farm work units larger and more versatile than Russia's col-lective farms. Khrushchev, however, declared in 1959 that it was impos-sible to proceed to the building of communism by any new stages, unknown to the Soviet Union, thus branding the Chinese as Marxist-Leninist mavericks and upstarts.

Khrushchev, in turn, scandalized the Chinese, and fanned their suspicions of a Russian "embourgeoisement," by the announced con-version of the USSR into a "People's State." This move, undertaken at the Twenty-Second Party Congress, indicated a transition from the dicta-torship of the proletariat to a "higher phase" of social development on the road to pure communism. Allegedly, the workers and their party vanguard no longer needed to rule dictatorially. A higher state of social homogeneity and security had been reached. The Party and the working class, in the official Soviet view, would still be needed as leaders. But their coercive, suppressive roles could now be deemphasized. This principle complemented the Khrushchev ideas that the encirclement of the USSR was ended; that the balance of power had shifted toward the Soviet Union; that "socialist legality" should replace police terror; and that the USSR, after nearly fifty years of existence, was beginning to reap the fruits of "socialist construction." To the Chinese, however, it appeared a highly suspect renunciation of a fundamental Marxist-Leninist concept. Khrushchev's journey to the United States in 1959, with visits spanning Hollywood and the White House, only served to deepen the impression in Peiping that the new Soviet leadership was in fact, scuttling the revolutionary legacy of the CPSU.

We may note that the Chinese were never averse to peaceful co-

15 On the Maoist response to changes in Soviet world policy, see Benjamin I. Schwartz, *Communism and China: Ideology in Flux* (Cambridge: Harvard University Press, 1968), pp. 149–161.

existence as a tactic to gain greater advantage over an adversary. They, in fact, subscribed to such a policy in the Conference of the so-called nonaligned nations at Bandung, Indonesia in 1955.[16] What they did not accept, however, was peaceful coexistence as an immutable party principle. Where Khrushchev argued that a new world war was well-nigh inconceivable and unacceptable because it would destroy humanity, the Chinese believed that if it occurred, the war would see the end of capitalism and the triumph of communism rather than the doom of mankind. Khrushchev's refusal to share nuclear weapons, delivery systems, and knowhow provoked Chinese resentment and suspicion. In 1959, when China claimed certain border areas from India, Moscow avowed its neutrality and deplored the violence between the two Asian nations. The Chinese viewed Moscow's detachment as a betrayal of one Marxist-Leninist state by, ostensibly, another. The Moscow Conference of 81 Communist Parties in 1960 was the last attempt to "paper over" the ideological rift between the two great communist powers. Soviet experts and technicians left China; Soviet aid and development projects were halted. In 1962 the renewal of Indian-Chinese border conflicts again worsened Soviet-Chinese relations, with the Chinese accusing the Russians of giving arms and munitions to the Indians. As the Vietnam War intensified, the Chinese accused the Soviets of collusion with the United States while the Russians alleged that China was deliberately holding up overland deliveries of Soviet material to the North Vietnamese and the Viet Cong.

In 1966, Mao launched the Great Cultural Revolution in China and Sino-Soviet relations soon reached an all-time nadir. The Red Guard units of students, workers, and young peasants, with whom Mao hoped to infuse new revolutionary militancy into an ossifying Party, Army, and state bureaucracy, regarded Russians as "revisionists"—hypocritical pseudobourgeois "running dogs of U. S. imperialism"—if we may borrow their vocabulary. Soviet diplomatic personnel in China were attacked by Red Guard mobs; Chinese students in Moscow demonstrated against the Soviet authorities. In the aftermath of Russian counterdemonstrations, both sides withdrew their diplomatic representatives. When in August 1968 the Soviets invaded Czechoslovakia, China condemned this as an act of "Russian imperialism." Military preparations began on both sides of the Sino-Soviet frontier. In March 1969, an armed skirmish was fought by the Russians and the Chinese on the Ussuri River. In May, June, and August, clashes occurred in China's western province, Sin Kiang. The tensions were intensified when, in May 1969, the Chinese

---

[16] On the Bandung Conference of Asian and African states in 1955 and other efforts for regional cooperation in Asia, see J. Leo Cefkin, *The Background of Current World Problems* (New York: McKay, 1967), pp. 312–340.

publicly accused Russia of holding some 600,000 square miles of Chinese territory and, in effect, continuing Tsarist imperialism toward them. Threats of nuclear attacks and all-out war were exchanged by the two sides until late 1969 when, following a visit by Soviet Premier Kosygin, the two Red giants agreed to negotiate their border disputes.

In any case, since the late 1950's, Mao has seen an opportunity of making himself the worldwide spokesman of the Marxist militants. To this task he brought formidable skills and credentials. He was the twentieth century's foremost exponent of successful guerrilla warfare, tenaciously waged from the countryside against isolated and vulnerable urban centers.[17] Just as Lenin had adapted the teaching of Marx in the direction of a more inclusive and compelling revolutionary doctrine, Mao adapted those of Lenin. He asserted the need for a very broad coalition of social forces to unite in the struggle against imperialism. Nearly anyone who wanted to do so, could find room under the spacious Maoist umbrella of antiimperialism. In one of his basic works, *On The People's Democratic Dictatorship*, Mao spelled out the unity of workers, peasants, petite bourgeoisie, and even so-called national bourgeoisie of China, against the imperialist enemy. Internationally, Mao identified as allies all "those nations of the world who treat us on the basis of equality" and "the proletariat and the broad masses of the people of (all) countries." He identified his enemies in China as the landlord class, the bureaucratic capitalist class, and sundry reactionaries siding with the Chiang Kai-shek regime. The Maoist scheme attached special significance in achieving a revolutionary victory to the alliance of workers and peasants. In common with other communists, the Chinese also used the Marxian concept of the "proletariat" to legitimize the special status of their Party, often applying the terms interchangeably. Like Lenin, Mao bestowed a special place for the workers:

"The people's democratic dictatorship needs the leadership of the working class, because only the working class is most far-sighted, just and unselfish and endowed with revolutionary thoroughness. The history of the entire revolution proves that without the leadership of the working class, the revolution is bound to fail, and with the leadership of the working class, the revolution is victorious. In the era of imperialism no other class in any country can lead any genuine revolution to victory.

[17] In Mao's celebrated summary of his strategy of persistence: "Enemy advances; we retreat; enemy halts, we harass; enemy tires, we attack; enemy retreats, we pursue." Cited by Robert Strausz-Hupe et al., *Protracted Conflict* (New York: Harper & Row, 1959), p. 33.

This is clearly proved by the fact that the Chinese national bourgeoisie has led the revolution many times and each time it has failed."[18]

But, while thus preserving the traditional formula of Marxism and stressing revolutionary militancy, Mao also emphasized a very important national, and essentially subjective aspect of revolution. The struggle that Mao envisioned and promoted, first in China and then internationally, was a struggle of all the oppressed and impoverished peoples against the Western super capitalists and their—in his language—particular domestic lackeys. In China, those lackeys and henchmen were identified as Chiang Kai-shek's Kuo Min Tang. With the exception of landlords and state bureaucrats, and partly even to them, Mao offered possibilities of "reeducation"—the door to participation in the people's revolution and people's dictatorship was wide open. Even the bourgeoisie were asked to join in the struggle for China's national liberation against colonial exploitation, against forced underdevelopment and national humiliation at the hands of foreign capitalists and their domestic agents.

In Mao's version, "communism" was thus a doctrine of all the world's poor peoples, set against the rule of the rich, determined to control their destiny, and develop society toward the general vision of Karl Marx's paradise of abundance, equality, and freedom throughout the whole world.

Thus, Maoism equipped the Chinese in the late 1950's and 1960's to seek the leadership of the so-called Third World (see Chapter 10). Since the Western imperialists could be obviously identified with predominantly urban, racially "white" cultures, the Marxism of Mao coincided with the claims of the countryside against the city, and of a great non-white majority against a minority of white imperialist oppressors of European and North American origin. In the Maoist guise, communism had become, as John H. Kautsky noted, a doctrine of national development.[19] The appeals of Maoism in the direction of the Third World

[18] See William T. Liu, *Chinese Society Under Communism: A Reader* (New York: John Wiley, 1967), pp. 105–106.

[19] As Professor John H. Kausky says: "We can be fairly sure . . . that . . . modernizing intellectuals will pursue certain policies growing out of their anti-traditional and anti-colonial attitudes, regardless of whether they think of themselves and are thought of by others as Communists or not. Always allowing for the self-fulfilling element of myths which *can* make Communists behave differently because they think they are Communists, one may say that in policy terms it makes little difference whether the modernizers coming to power are Communists or not, simply because the policies pursued by Communist and non-Communist modernizers are not necessarily different." *Communism and the Politics of Development* (New York: John Wiley, 1968), pp. 213–214.

were, if anything, strengthened by the Sino-Soviet split of the 1950's. For while Mao continued to be vociferously anti-American in his orientation, he now took up a "plague on both your houses" position vis-á-vis Russia and the United States. Africans and Asians could now see themselves as neutral toward both of these powers while following the line set by Mao. Moreover, whether Marxist or not, they no longer needed to follow the leadership of whites, Russians or Americans. China's posture appealed to the militant nationalism of poor and backward peoples in terms that were only remotely linked to the industrial-urban-Western context of nineteenth-century Marxism.

We may note, however, that by preserving his Marxian lineage, Mao continued to maintain the universalism, potentially significant, of his doctrine, and a certain revolutionary clientele in the industrialized West, too. It was the revisionists of Yugoslavia and Russia who had gone astray in interpreting Marxism-Leninism, Mao argued. The retention of a large body of communist doctrine enabled the Maoists not only to claim the universal legacy for themselves, but also, as in the case of the other ruling communist parties, to protect their claim to direct the domestic development of their nation's economy and society in an authoritarian, omniscient manner.

In the latter respect, China differed strikingly from other post-World War II communist regimes. In virtually all of these (China's allies, Albania and North Korea conspicuously excluded), the 1950's and 1960's brought about either a decline or at least a stabilization in the tendency of the Party to revolutionize the society around it. Mao's China followed the opposite course. Instead of "settling down" to piecemeal, bureaucratic adaptations in the wake of their power seizure, the Chinese communists set out to extend the revolution. The Great Leap Forward of 1958 and The Great Cultural Revolution of the 1960's expressed the continuing revolutionism of Mao's communism. The mass militancy of the Revolution's Red Guards in the late 1960's plunged Chinese society, economy, and government into a crisis bordering on chaos. As youths scuffled and fought with Party officialdom, books and other relics of pre-revolutionary Chinese culture were burned. Production and transport broke down. By 1970, the Revolution's chief result seemed to be the strengthened influence of the Chinese Army under the leadership of Mao's heir-apparent, Lin Piao.

Notwithstanding frequent rumors of reconciliation, the rift between Moscow and Peking transcended personal differences among leaders. In the early 1970's, Red China continued to be one of the world's least affluent nations. Mao's revolution had not yet transformed a backward agrarian economy into a modern industrial one. The capacity for meeting even the most basic wants of China's millions has yet to be created. By comparison, the Soviet economy has become modern, rich, and diversified. Mao's China in the 1970's is more like Stalin's Russia of the 1930's than Brezhnev's Russia of 1971. The Soviet Communist party had become the party of the rich; its bureaucrats could contemplate the status quo with considerable, some would say smug, satisfaction. They have much to lose, and they no longer need desperate gambles or heroic militancy to preserve their positions. They can cherish prudence and make incremental improvements in managerial efficiency. For the Chinese communists, economic and social conditions are still characterized by an acute crisis, requiring great outpourings of energy from the people and the leaders.

Still another schism in the world communist movement began with Yugoslavia in the period between 1946–1948. The reasons for the split between Stalin and Tito were more than ideological but the conflict gave rise to certain well-defined ideological differences. Having escaped the clutches of Stalin's control over his domestic and foreign policy, Tito began to rationalize his position ideologically to espouse the view that (a) communist parties ought to be equal and independent in relation to one another and that (b) neutrality in the conflict between the USSR and its allies on the one hand, and the United States and its allies on the other was not only ideologically permissible but even desirable in view of the paramount dangers to humanity of another world war. A related aspect of Titoism has been a much more tolerant view on the crucial question of achieving the goals of communism in any given society. Unlike Lenin and Stalin, Tito espoused a very advanced pluralistic view of many roads leading to these Marxist goals. The gist of Tito's position, developed in the 1950's and 1960's, was that neither the dictatorship of the proletariat nor the leadership of the Party vanguard was really a universal necessity. Nor was violent revolution everywhere necessary. Thus, far from holding foreign social-democratic parties in disdain as betrayers of the working class, Titoism conceded the possibility of a peaceful evolution through political democracy and gradual reforms to full-blown socialism and ultimately even communism. The Yugoslavs regarded the Scandinavian socialist regimes, for example, in this favorable category, and they professed the same optimism about sundry anti-colonialist, vaguely socialistic regimes of Asia and Africa. This position made it at once unnecessary for them to worry greatly about "exporting the revolution," and it made it perfectly respectable for Tito to keep his independence of Russia with U. S. military aid, and maintain neutrality between the Warsaw Pact nations and NATO.[20] The Yugoslav brand of communism has been less liberal in its domestic applications than in foreign affairs. The so-called League of Yugoslav Communists has been markedly reluctant to give up the monopoly of political power it had acquired in the 1940's. Thus, no rival socialist, peasant, or other parties are allowed to challenge the LYC for control of the country. But *within* the limits of one-party rule, the Titoist model has allowed extensive private land ownership, decentralization of the economy, and a relaxation of police controls which, during the past 10 to 20 years, have certainly exceeded such bounds in virtually all other communist countries.

Titoism—sometimes identified as "right-wing nationalist deviationism" in the Soviet press of Stalin's time—has always been a more or less natural ideological development in Eastern Europe. Stalinism simply repressed and delayed its expressions wherever it could. The lands conquered by the Red Army in the 1940's were not conspicuously hospitable to their native communist movements. In the interwar period of 1919–1939, no communist party ever polled as much as 15 percent of the vote in any national election in this region of the world.[21] In several countries, the influences of anti-Marxist religious traditions among the people, the peasants, the middle classes, and even workers were very strong. In some countries, as in Poland, Rumania, and Hungary, communists were additionally handicapped by their identification with the Soviet Union. To these nations, Russia was the historic, traditional enemy. The local parties drew their followings very heavily, even predominantly in some cases, from among the ethnic minorities in each of these countries.[22] Thus, the regimes established in Eastern Europe between 1944 and 1948 were, to a large degree imported from the USSR—in terms of the Party personnel that assumed the positions of power.[23] Gradually, of course, this situation changed. More and more local, native persons were recruited into the parties and they progressed on the ladder

---

[20] On Tito's foreign policy, Charles P. McVicker, op. cit., p. 306, says, ". . . Titoism is national communism as opposed to international communism. It proves that Marxists given the opportunity to choose between patriotism and socialism under foreign domination are likely to choose patriotism." Tito, balancing between blocs of states, operates in the "primeval forest of normal international relations."

[21] See R. V. Burks, *The Dynamics of Communism in Eastern Europe* (Princeton, N.J.: Princeton University Press, 1961), pp. 19–87, on sources of communist support before World War II.

[22] On the role of ethnic minority groups in communist movements, Ibid., pp. 188–190.

[23] See, e.g., Ithiel de Sola Pool, *Satellite Generals: A Study of Military Elites in the Soviet Sphere* (Stanford: Stanford University Press, 1955), on the ubiquitous presence of Russian personnel among the armies of Eastern European states.

of office and influence. The older, Muscovite elements died, retired, or were purged, particularly under the impact of Khrushchev's de-Stalinization. Despite all of the vigilance, repression, and reeducation of cadres to which the Party leaders had resorted, the local communist movements were bound to reflect their particular social-cultural contexts. Therefore, the desire to *adapt* the framework of Marxism-Leninism, and the more general slogans of the Party to local traditions, aspirations, and values was not only always very strong but it also worked against the maintenance of Russian hegemony in the area.

Substantial elements in the local parties tended to cherish their national individuality, were suspicious of the Russians, reflected old nationalist quarrels and prejudices of Balkan politics in relation to one another, and generally wanted to reestablish profitable economic relations with the West-European nations, particularly West Germany, with whom Eastern Europe—communist or not—had always traded. Thus, they remained suspicious of Soviet schemes to integrate and subordinate their economic development to the USSR through the so-called COMECON[24] or their military and diplomatic options through adherence to the Warsaw Pact. They were always loath to subject their societies to traumatic internal changes in response to a Moscow pushbutton. Since, for many of them, membership in the Party was simply the only outlet for political activity that the Russians would tolerate, the object of politics was not to cultivate communism as a means of revolutionizing the world but rather its opposite: infuse it with a locally acceptable, eclectic, popular, or bureaucratic content.

The problem for the Soviets in the 1950's and 1960's became how much polycentrism could they tolerate on their doorstep. Some of it seemed desirable because it made communist rule more acceptable locally, and therefore easier and more stable. On the other hand, too much polycentrism meant a potential loss of allies, resources, and trade; it even presented the danger of a hostile military presence on the Soviet's doorstep and also some potentially corrosive political influences spilling from Eastern Europe into the USSR itself.[25] To a marked degree, the turbulent changes in Poland, Hungary, Rumania, and Czechoslovakia

[24] See Nicholas Spulber, *The Economics of Communist Eastern Europe* (Cambridge: Technology Press of MIT, 1957), and his *The State and Economic Development in Eastern Europe* (New York: Random House, 1966).

[25] See Colin Chapman, *August 21: The Rape of Czechoslovakia* (Philadelphia: Lippincott 1968); Harry Schwartz *Prague's 200 Days: The Struggle For Democracy in Czechoslovakia* (New York: Praeger, 1969); and A. J. Groth, *Eastern Europe After Czechoslovakia* (New York: Foreign Policy Association 1969), on Soviet fears that the Czechoslovak experiments would prove "contagious."

were, from the Soviet point of view, Titoist deviations. They were all marked by the pursuit of autonomy, if not yet complete independence of the USSR. They were characterized by attempts, not always successful, to resume more friendly and essentially more independent relations with Russia's enemies in the West. In the case of Poland, the national communism of Gomulka did not attempt to go nearly as far as Tito, partly at least because of Gomulka's recognition of Poland's geographic-military vulnerability. Gomulka did secure for Poland some internal autonomy with respect to land policy, for example; he succeeded in halting and reversing collectivization measures of the early 1950's imposed by Moscow's essentially "one-way-to-communism."[26] In the case of Hungary, Imre Nagy's attempt to emulate Tito's neutrality vis-à-vis the USSR, and even exceed him in allowing several political parties to operate freely, was defeated by Russian intervention. The successor regime of Janos Kadar, however, also proved more nationalist or autonomous in its economic and domestic policies than the pre-1955 Stalinist regimes. In Czechoslovakia, the followers of Dubcek in the late 1960's attempted to nationalize communism even more than Tito did in internal politics. They moved to allow a great deal of freedom within the framework of the ruling communist party. In the international sphere, they solemnly protested their loyalty to the Warsaw Pact. But all their protestations proved to no avail. Suspicious of Dubcek's liberalism, allowance of opposition, and trade relations between Czechoslovakia and West Germany, the USSR and its Warsaw Pact Allies invaded Czechoslovakia in August 1968. The Dubcek regime was destroyed much as the Nagy regime had been in 1956.

The boldest experimenter within the bloc in the 1970's remained Rumania. The Rumanians were Titoist more in their foreign rather than domestic orientation. They carried out a thorough collectivization of the land, and permitted very little overt dissent, cultural freedom, or economic autonomy. The rule of the Party was firmly maintained since the 1940's. There were no efforts made under Gheorzhiu-Dej or his current successor, Ceausesecu, to liberalize the regime by allowing political opposition to manifest itself either as Hungary had done in 1956 under Imre Nagy—by allowing noncommunist parties to emerge, or as Czechoslovakia had done under Alexander Dubcek—through trade unions, professional associations, and the party itself; or even as Mao Tse-tung briefly allowed it in the cultural and intellectual sphere during the "Hundred Flowers Campaign" of 1958.

[26] It remains to be seen whether the substitution of Gierek for Gomulka will significantly alter Poland's "correct" relationship with Moscow.

On the other hand, the Rumanian Communist party reasserted a vigorous, and frankly anti-Russian nationalism in its educational, cultural and propaganda media. Above all, it challenged Soviet hegemony by its refusal to subordinate Rumania's economic development to Soviet wishes, by the rapid expansion of trade with West Germany at the expense of Russia, and its emphatic support of poycentrism.[27]

Another consequence of the 1956 de-Stalinization was the growth of polycentrism among the nongoverning communist parties, too, particularly in Western Europe. The parties in France and Italy especially had developed large followings after World War II. Their members, militants, and even voters were predominantly drawn from the ranks of urban workers but they also attracted a substantial following among the peasants, intellectuals, and the lower middle class. In both countries, the communists drew a smattering of protest voters who, more than anything else, saw in the communists their chance to say "no" to the prevailing political-social and economic status quo. In many national and statewide local elections, these parties drew between a quarter and a third of the total electorate. They thus entertained hopes of someday winning power by the ballot, particularly in alliance with at least one or two kindred political groupings. During Stalin's rule, these communist parties were handicapped in their popular appeals by the charge of subservience to Moscow. Possible allies in other parties simply saw them as Stalin's stooges or, as philosopher Sidney Hook called them, foreign nationalist parties. Every time the Soviet Union changed its policy, the local communists meekly followed suit. Many people felt the communists could not be trusted with power inasmuch as their loyalties appeared to rest not at home but abroad. These perceptions affected the parties' possibilities of coalition-building with various other leftist or left-of-center political groupings. Thus, when Khrushchev attacked Stalinism, Western communist leaders seized on the opportunity to espouse polycentrism. One of Moscow's ablest and staunchest foreign followers, Palmiro Togliatti of Italy, became the leading Western spokesman for the new line.

Togliatti espoused the view that only the leadership of each party could decide, in the light of its own peculiar circumstances and experience, what its strategy and tactics must be, and that all communist parties should be regarded as fundamentally equal. Thus the question of whether violence or peaceful methods would win power in country X could not be answered by the communists of country Y or Z; each party should

---

27 On Rumania's recent developments, see Stephen A. Fischer-Galati, *The Socialist Republic of Rumania* (Baltimore: Johns Hopkins Press, 1969).

remain free to judge particular actions or policies according to its own lights. For the first time, this included a right of publicly criticizing the Russian comrades and dissenting from their policies. The new Togliatti line still emphasized a general unity of outlook among the parties, traditional, sentimental ties to Moscow, and the important role of the USSR in the worldwide struggle for socialism and communism, but it enabled the parties outside the USSR to repudiate specific policies with which they disagreed. The parties could thus seek a more attractive image: Communists were no longer "stooges"; they were just another variety of local left-wingers or progressives if one preferred. Thus, the invasion of Czechoslovakia by the Russians in 1968 brought criticism from the French and Italian, as well as many other world communist parties, all seeking to escape the censure of public opinion and retain their own followings. To the extent that communist prospects for power "within-the-system", that is, by peaceful, parliamentary means were being enhanced, the incentives to foreign communist leaders to keep independent of Moscow were great. Some of these communist leaders, however, worried about the consequences of becoming "too much like everyone else." The rise of the as yet minuscule Maoist factions within the Western parties indicated that the communists might well lose some of their most dedicated clientele among the alienated political irreconcilables, who resent the communists' growing "embourgeoisment."[28]

The last of communism's postwar adaptations came in 1959, with the assumption of power by Fidel Castro in Cuba. In its origins, Castroism was an ad hoc, eclectic movement. Until Castro's own declaration in 1961, the very idea of it being communist was hotly disputed by proponents and observers of the new Cuban regime. The Fidelista guerrilla movement that Castro had assembled in the early 1950's was not originally committed to Marxism-Leninism. Its public aims and slogans could be much better described as loosely democratic and populist. Castro pledged himself to fight for the restoration of Cuba's ultra-liberal Constitution of 1940, for freedom, democracy, and social justice. Certainly, several of his co-leaders, like Che Guevara, were old communist activists; Castro was not. His intentions in the 1940's and 1950's are still subject to speculation. According to some observers, his conversion to Marxism-Leninism was dictated by necessity—the refusal of the United States to countenance the survival of his regime and the availability of Soviet aid indispensable to its survival.

Nevertheless, the regime that Castro established in Cuba in the 1960's

---

[28] See William E. Griffith (ed.), *Communism in Europe Continuity, Change and the Sino-Soviet Dispute* (Cambridge, Mass.: MIT Press, 1964).

synthesized many of the Maoist as well as Soviet communist characteristics. Castro, like Mao, strove to link the nationalist aspirations of the
people with the quest for drastic social change on the Marxian model.
To many Cubans and many other Latin Americans, Castro's antiimperialism and anti-Americanism was as much nationalism as communism. The Castro-Guevara approach to organizing the revolution was,
like Mao's, broadly coalitional. It emphasized the participation of the
peasant and the rural hinterlands against the isolated urban enclaves
much more than it did the role of an urban proletariat. It emphasized
revolutionary militancy symbolized in unceasing guerrilla warfare. On
the Maoist model, there would be no respite or let-up in the struggle in
the countryside. The success of such activities would wax and wane, to
be sure, but hopefully, the tenacity of the rural revolutionaries, their
numerical and land-mass reservoirs of power, and the inevitable long-
term decline of the imperialist economic, political, and social structure
would yield an ultimate victory for the side of the revolution.

Castro and Guevara eagerly supported the export of Cuba's successful
revolution to the rest of Latin America in the mid-1960's.[29] Both the
Soviets and the Chinese had given doctrinal blessings to "just wars of
national liberation," which Cuba exemplified and advocated. But while
outwardly Cuban militancy was equally sanctioned by Peiping and
Moscow, the latter was much more cautious and wary. Castro was being
restrained by Moscow, fearful of another confrontation with the United
States such as the one occasioned by the 1962 missile crisis. And if Castro's—and Guevara's—hearts were with the Chinese firebrands of revolution, their stomachs and pockets depended overwhelmingly on Soviet aid
for which the relatively poor Chinese could not hope to offer a substitute.

For several years, during the 1960's the Russians sought a world conference of communist parties to gain support against the Chinese, possibly
have them branded as traitors to the cause of Marxism-Leninism, and
to reunify the communist movement on the lines of the old Communist
International of 1919–1943. When the Conference finally gathered in
Moscow in June 1969, it proved a great disappointment to the Russians.
It also demonstrated the depth of schism in the world communist movement. Only 75 of the 95 parties attended. The defections were most
serious in Asia. The Communist parties of China, Burma, Cambodia,
Indonesia, Japan, Laos, Malaysia, New Zealand, North Korea, North

---

[29] On Cuban communism, see Theodore Draper, *Castroism, Theory and Practice*
(New York: Praeger, 1965) and his *Castro's Revolution, Myths and Realities* (New
York: Praeger, 1962).

Vietnam, the Philippines, Singapore, South Vietnam, and Thailand did not send their representatives. Among the absentees were also five European parties—Abanian, Dutch, Icelandic, West German, and Yugoslav.

Those who attended did not subscribe to various Soviet positions. The Italians and the Rumanians publicly opposed expulsion of the Chinese; the representatives of Australia, Austria, Belgium, Great Britain, Denmark, France, Italy, Norway, Spain, Sweden, and Switzerland criticized the Soviet invasion of Czechoslovakia in 1968. The Conference concluded by affirming the independence of all parties; did not endorse the Brezhnev doctrine justifying Russian intervention to restore or save communist rule outside the USSR; it failed to condemn Red China, and it made no provision for a new international organization of the parties which Moscow had hoped it could dominate once again.

The Soviets experienced similar difficulties elsewhere; their Warsaw Pact allies in Europe—once docile satellites of Stalin's time—refused to involve themselves in the Sino-Soviet conflict, either by sending token troop contingents to the Far East or even by any declarations against China. True to the pattern of the last several years, Soviet leadership in Eastern Europe was opposed most actively by the Rumanians. Rumanian defiance of Moscow expressed itself in several ways; denial of access to the Warsaw Pact forces for maneuvers on Rumanian soil; support of China's rights to differ with Russia; public opposition to the principles of the Brezhnev doctrine;[30] appeals for withdrawal of *all* foreign troops from Europe; vigorous diplomatic and trade contacts with the West; opposition to economic control of the Rumanian economy by the Soviet-led Council of Mutual Economic Assistance (CEMA or COMECON); and even token participation—through "observers"—at the 1969 Congress of the League of Yugoslav Communists, a meeting boycotted by Moscow and its more pliant allies.

Finally, we may note that in the postwar era "communism," as a structural-ideological universal from Cuba to North Vietnam, connoted certain kinds of domestic resource allocations that gave it a distinct, common meaning—despite all the interbloc disputes on strategy, tactics, and allegiance.[31] According to data compiled by the United Nations in 1968, the accomplishments of the several communist regimes[32] in many

[30] I.e. Russia's alleged right to intervene abroad to "save socialism".

[31] On the subject of a distinctively "communist" cluster of public policies, after all (cf. J. H. Kautsky, footnote 19), see A. J. Groth *Comparative Politics: A Distributive Approach* (New York: Macmillan, 1971); and A. J. Groth and L. L. Wade, "Educational Policy Outcomes in Communist, Democratic and Autocratic Political Systems," *American Political Science Association Paper*, September 1970.

[32] East Germany, Czechoslovakia, USSR, Poland, Hungary, Rumania, Bulgaria,

aspects of education and culture were exceeded, if at all, only by a few of the wealthiest members of the community of nations. Communist regimes ranked first in the provision of mass education at the primary level, exceeding the average enrolments of the 15 richest democracies.[33] They also averaged first in the student-teacher ratios for the whole educational system. They ranked a close second to the affluent democracies in university enrolments. Moreover, whether one averaged the communist states vis-á-vis the wealthiest democracies by total populations or by individual countries, the former provided more libraries, about as many volumes per inhabitant, and achieved higher averages in cinema attendance and in library borrowers than the former. At the university level, the communist systems averaged the highest percentage of students enrolled in scientific and technological subjects—about 59 percent as compared with only 40.3 percent in the affluent democracies. Many other examples to the same effect could be readily cited.

Yugoslavia, Cuba, Albania, and China, in order of estimated per capita income. The data on Mongolia, North Korea, and North Vietnam are generally fragmentary.

[33] United States, Sweden, Switzerland, Canada, Iceland, Denmark, Australia, France, New Zealand, Luxembourg, Belgium, Britain, West Germany, Finland, and the Netherlands, in order of estimated per capita income.

CHAPTER **9**

Democracy, Socialism, and the New Left

In the aftermath of the Second World War, particularly during the 1940's and the 1950's, a remarkable convergence took place between proponents of socialism and pragmatic political democracy. From the perspective of the nineteenth century, this development could be seen as a movement toward the "center." On the one hand, many of those who had identified themselves with the claims, goals, and rhetoric of revolutionary socialism increasingly accepted democracy for the realization of their aspirations; on the other hand, those who once regarded the leveling claims of socialism as anathema were increasingly disposed to "live with" and accept more or less moderate doses of these very claims. In essence, the strength of democratic liberalism in its free-trade, laissez-faire forms seriously declined. On the other extreme, the support for intransigent socialism, brooking no compromise with the bourgeoisie, profoundly suspicious of bourgeois institutions, clamoring for direct action on the model of the syndicalists, also subsided. This was particularly evident in such economically advanced countries as Great Britain, the United States, West Germany, Scandinavia, the Low Countries, and members of the Old British Commonwealth. To some extent, but only partially, this moderation on the political left was compensated by the emergence of communist parties as spokesmen of the most radically discontented. However, with the exceptions of France and Italy, the communists did not manage to attract a large following in the so-called advanced, industrialized states: either in Western Europe, North America or the Commonwealth. Thus, not a mere change of labels but a genuine "deradicalization" occurred in much of the western world.[1] The causes, though complex, were rooted in the new socioeconomic and political environment. Partly in continuance of measures begun before World War II, partly because of the experience of the war, with all its attendant human privations, the still vivid recollections of the Great Depression, and the specter of Stalin's Russian communism advancing through Europe in the period from 1944 through 1948, a certain coalescence in the politics of many states outside the Soviet domain became desirable. Relatively conservative, basically middle class political groupings were increasingly prepared to make concessions toward a "welfare-state" concept of politics. In a sense, they were now willing to shoulder some additional social costs as a price for avoiding greater, more traumatic costs of domestic upheaval and, in some cases, possible Soviet subversion and intervention.

The welfare state concept meant an acceptance of responsibility by governments for certain minimal standards of life and opportunity in terms of housing, employment, education, and medical care for all the people in the society. It connoted, first, increased public subsidies for these purposes out of the proceeds of taxation and, second, various controls by governments over the working of the economy. These controls involved, in some cases, direct government ownership of key industrial and commercial facilities—including banks, transportation networks, mining deposits, and power-generating plants. In some instances, the controls were indirect and quasi-voluntary. Governments were expected to manipulate the allocation of resources and the distribution of incomes through tax and fiscal reforms and the establishment of planning agencies to coordinate and influence the work of both private and public sectors of the economy.[2] The old notion of government, as mere "nightwatchman of society," keeping a minimum of law and order in the streets, and letting citizens fend for themselves as best they could, was being increasingly abandoned. The agreement on the proposition that every person, by his mere humanity or existence in society, was entitled to a minimally decent level of housing, to the dignity of work, to leisure, and to the provision of adequate health care and educational opportunity spread far and wide through the spectrum of political movements. For those who opposed such ideas before the war, humanitarian as well as prudential considerations combined to bring about a significant change of heart.[3]

[1] Compare William Ebenstein, *Today's Isms*, 3rd ed. (Englewood Cliffs, N.J.: Prentice-Hall, 1961), p. 205.

[2] On procedures of nationalization in Britain—under the auspices of democratic socialism—see, e.g., William N. Loucks, *Comparative Economic Systems*, 6th ed. (New York: Harper, 1961), pp. 263–346.

[3] In the postwar period, as James P. Young notes, liberals have "characteristically

In Britain, Winston Churchill's Conservative party turned to a broadly welfare state orientation even during the war. Its milestone was the so-called Beveridge Report of 1942. In France, the large Catholic Republican party (MRP) of the 1940's also espoused it. In Germany, the dominant Christian Democrats led by Konrad Adenauer and Ludwig Erhard accepted the notion of a so-called "social market economy."[4] In the United States, the conclusion of the war saw the continuation and extension of the Depression Era "New Deal" in the guise of President Harry S. Truman's "Fair Deal," while Republicans led by Wendell Willkie and Thomas Dewey were being accused by conservative die-hards of "me-too-ism."

On the political Left, the zeal for intransigence was generally on the decline. Just as many conservatives felt that glaring want and inequality had to be remedied if communism was to be arrested at the doorstep, many erstwhile radicals feared to jeopardize their political, cultural, and individual freedoms to the advantage of Stalinist communism by division and chaos at home. Between 1945 and 1951, no American ally was more staunchly anticommunist, and in this sense "loyal," than Britain's Labour party government led by Clement Attlee and his formidable Foreign Secretary and trade union leader, Ernest Bevin.[5] Similarly in France, the socialists led by men like Leon Blum, Guy Mollett, and Jules Moch were willing to moderate the pace and scale of socioeconomic reforms at home to the exigency of saving France and Europe from the clutches of Soviet totalitarianism. The moderation of each side reinforced the orientation of the other. Each side could see the other as increasingly more "reasonable."

Both the "leftbound" conservatives and the "rightbound" radicals could find adequate support for their actions on ideological grounds. Reputable sanctions and precedents among democratic theorists have long existed. The nineteenth century ideals of such famed spokesmen of liberalism as Thomas Hill Green and John Stuart Mill, for example, readily lent them-

adhered to the belief that private persons cannot or will not solve (their) problems with the result that government must assume this role. Thus health, housing, education. . . . The functioning of the economy—in brief most matters of social welfare—are causes of governmental concern." *The Politics of Affluence* (San Francisco: Chandler, 1968), p. 6.

[4] Compare Young on West German resort to practices of "creeping socialism" combined with professions of laissez-faire. Ibid, p. 58.

[5] See biographies of Ernest Bevin by Trevor Evans, *Bevin* (London: Allen and Unwin, 1946); Francis Williams, *Ernest Bevin* (London: Hutchinson 1952); and Alan Bullock *The Life and Times of Ernest Bevin* (London: Heineman, 1960). As Labour's Foreign Secretary, Bevin was one of Russian Communism's most formidable enemies both in Britain and abroad. See also Clement R. Attlee, *As It Happened* (New York: Viking, 1954) and Francis Williams, *A Prime Minister Remembers* (London: Heineman, 1961).

selves to what might be termed socialist experiments.[6] Thus, T. H. Green, a liberal theorist influenced by the writings of Hegel, had redefined the notion of freedom to mean not merely, or even primarily, the absence of restraints upon the individual but rather as a positive capacity for making rational, self-fulfilling choices. Impressed by the widespread misery and social degradation of nineteenth-century workingmen, Green argued that individual freedom was virtually meaningless without the means needed to make choices. In his view, the freedom of a man stranded on a barren island was but a freedom to die; similarly, the freedom to move about as and when one might want was an illusion for those who did not have the use of their limbs. And drawing upon the actual experience of English factory towns of his time, Green believed that a worker's freedom to choose what we might call a life-style was severely limited. Monopolistic control of all the possible sources of employment, housing, or types of schooling and recreation gave millions of people no options as to what they might do with their lives. Thus, Green argued, a man who emerged from a mineshaft after many hours of labor to find no leisure facilities in his town other than liquor stores or pubs was not really free to drink or not to drink. His choices were socially prestructured for him and beyond his power to change or control.

In common with John Stuart Mill in the latter's later years, Green did not think that the unaided workings of free economic competition could really alter such situations. He appealed to society at large to intervene so as to provide more meaningful choices and opportunities for men.

Such ideological formulas made it possible for those who did *not* consider themselves socialists, and in fact were not principally interested in achieving some general ideal of economic equality, to appreciate, sympathize with, and perhaps support many socialist policies on other grounds.

Among the parties of the Left, there were corresponding ideological formulas that sanctioned consensual, relatively conservative orientations. Marxist revisionists of the nineteenth century like Eduard Bernstein, and democratic-gradualist interpreters of Karl Marx like Karl Kautsky, and the Fabians, and the representatives of Christian socialism, had all pre-

---

[6] On T. H. Green, (1836–1882), see John R. Rodman (ed.), *The Political Theory of T. H. Green* (New York: Appleton-Century-Crofts, 1964). Green's liberalism was influenced by the philosophy of Hegel. His efforts to make liberalism more humanistic and meaningful are embodied particularly in *The Principles of Political Obligation* (1884); and in the *Principles of State Interference* and *Darwinism and Politics*. See *Works*, 3 vols. ed. by R. L. Nettleship (London: Longmans, Green, 1885–1891). John Stuart Mill's socialist views are reflected in the last edition of his *Principles of Political Economy* (1874) (Toronto: University of Toronto Press, 1965). See Book II especially.

pared socialist and working class opinion for the desirability of a peaceable and constitutional struggle.[7] Having long advocated the idea that moral suasion was preferable to force and violence, and that progress in behalf of workers' claims could, in fact, be made through the ballot box, socialists drew understandable encouragement from the accomplishments of the postwar years.

Thus the moderate socialists and the relatively radical democrats might agree that the state should control and restrain business competition, even if the socialists saw this as a step on the way to replacing private enterprise altogether, while the democrats simply wished to provide a minimal range of choices to employees and to protect some indispensable mimima of human dignity.

The experiences of the Great Depression in the 1930's, the war, and the fear of communist inroads furthered the acceptance of such ideas for both sides and the emergence of consensus on many welfare state issues. Illustratively, in the 1940's, 1950's, and 1960's, the differences between most Conservatives and Labourites in Britain were to all appearances not of principle but of detail.[8] The major parties were agreed that the state had an obligation to prevent mass unemployment, provide jobs, care for the indigent and the aged, institute publicly supported health care, and to assure a suitable physical and cultural environment for all the people in the country. The real question seemed to be not whether governments had a role to perform in all this, but how it ought to be done; whether more or less money would suffice; whether tax burdens in specific cases would not be too great; or whether particular types of bureaucratic controls would be effective in guaranteeing desirable standards of employment, health care, education, and the like.

One consequence of this convergence from Left to Right and Right to Left appeared to be, in the 1950's at least, an end of ideology in the politics of Europe and America. General principles, grandiose ideals,

---

[7] On the contributions of Eduard Bernstein and Karl Kautsky to socialist thought, see Peter Gay, *The Dilemma of Democratic Socialism: Eduard Bernstein's Challenge to Marx* (New York: Collier, 1962); Eduard Bernstein, *Evolutionary Socialism*, trans. by Edith C. Harvey (New York: B. W. Huebsch, 1909); Karl Kautsky, *The Social Revolution*, trans. by A. M. and Mary W. Simons (Chicago: Charles H. Kerr, 1903). See also Kautsky's *Communism and Socialism* (New York: American League for Democratic Socialism, 1932); and *The Dictatorship of the Proletariat* (Ann Arbor: University of Michigan Press, 1964). Both of these socialists consistently opposed Lenin on the issue of democracy versus dictatorship as a road to socialism.

[8] The British equivalent of political "tweedledee-tweedledum" was embodied in the phrase popular in the 1950's, "Buttskellism," from the combined names of R. A. Butler, Conservative Chancellor of the Exchequer in the Macmillan cabinet, and Hugh Gaitskell, leader of the opposition Labour party in the House of Commons.

and great slogans seemed to be out of place in the relatively consensual, pragmatically oriented politics of the "developed" Western world. Choices between parties often seemed no more than between "tweedle-dee" and "tweedledum." Programs based on ideological postulates of nineteenth-century liberalism or socialism, Marxian or otherwise, seemed to many people to be merely ancient rhetoric; ritualistic "baggage" that testified not to what people really did and believed in the here-and-now but rather to the particular origins of parties and movements.[9] Occasionally, such ideological baggage was viewed with embarrassment, as in the case of West Germany's Social Democratic party which, in a 1959 convention, decided to rid itself of its old Marxist image. After all, students of public-opinion claimed that archaic radicalism was a distinct disadvantage with the voters.[10]

In terms of institutions, democracy in the postwar world may be described as busy with essentially marginal, incremental improvements. The big issues of universal suffrage, secret ballot, honest elections, organizational rights of political parties and trade unions, parliamentary representation and procedures, the legal protections of individual rights had all found sundry, institutional expressions in the period before 1939.

In the 1940's came refinement and improvements. Thus, for example, in Western Europe the recent experience of totalitarian abuses produced an increased emphasis on the power of courts to protect basic rights.[11] Adaptations of the American practice of judicial review were made in West Germany and in Italy.[12] For the first time courts were given power to set aside legislative and executive decrees if these were believed by the judges to conflict with the respective German and Italian constitutions. In the new constitutions of Europe, fundamental rights were framed in

---

[9] See Daniel Bell, *The End of Ideology: On the Exhaustion of Political Ideas in the Fifties*, rev. ed. (New York: Free Press, 1962), particularly pp. 392–407. Clifford Geertz, "Ideology as a Cultural System" in David Apter (ed.), *Ideology and Discontent* (New York: Free Press, 1964), pp. 47–76; and James P. Young *The Politics of Affluence* (San Francisco: Chandler, 1968), pp. 201–208.

[10] On the German Social Democrats, Bad Godesberg program of November 1959, renouncing the old Marxist slogans, see Steven Muller (ed.), *Documents on European Government* (New York: Macmillan, 1963), pp. 148–164.

[11] See Arnold Zurcher, *Constitutions and Constitutional Trends Since World War II* (New York: New York University Press, 1951), pp. 21–22, 78–79, 216–217, and Appendixes, pp. 225–324 on the increased roles of the judiciary.

[12] On the role of constitutional courts in Germany and Italy see, e.g., Michael L. Balfour, *West Germany* (New York: Praeger, 1968), pp. 192–199, and John C. Adams and Paolo Barile, *The Government of Republican Italy* (Boston: Houghton Mifflin, 1961), pp. 127–132.

such a way as to add social and economic guarantees of state protection for individuals to the more traditional, purely political ones.[13] The powers of governments to invoke emergency measures, such as those Hindenburg and Hitler invoked under Article 48 of the Weimar Constitution, were subjected to greater legislative and or judicial controls. In France, the immediate postwar period brought attempts to make parliamentary democracy more sensitive to popular opinion. Proportional representation replaced the two-ballot plurality prewar system.[14] Italy, too, opted for proportional representation. Female suffrage was extended in both countries. Interestingly, West Germany, aware of the harm produced in her parliamentary system by the dramatic upsurge of nazism between 1930 and 1933, moved in the opposite direction from that of France and Italy. The sensitivity of the electoral system was dampened here by a balancing of proportional representation, and plurality single member constituencies in the lower house (Bundestag) and, in effect, indirect election in the upper house (Bundesrat).[15] Attempts were made to establish and stimulate better regional and local government mechanisms. In Britain, the veto power of the House of Lords was cut down; the "one-man-one-vote" principle was at last fully realized in a 1949 act that eliminated the double vote of some business proprietors and university graduates. Minimum age requirements for voting were reduced. In the United States, the issue of legislative reapportionment received wide attention. The principle of "one-man-one-vote" found its logical expression in the drive for equal weighting of legislative districts. Reformers hoped to end predominance of sparsely populated rural districts in Congress and state legislatures and thereby increase government sensitivity to the needs and problems of an increasingly and overwhelmingly urban na-

[13] On the expanded Bills of Rights in the new European constitutions, emphasizing social and economic rights see Zurcher, op. cit., pp. 67, 218 and Appendixes, pp. 225–324.

[14] See Gordon Wright, *The Reshaping of French Democracy* (New York: Reynal and Hitchcock, 1948), pp. 112–230, on the attitudes of the French Left and Right with respect to proportional representation and other political mechanisms at the founding of the Fourth Republic.

[15] On proportional representation, see the classic work of Thomas Hare, *The Election of Representatives* (London: Longman, Green, 1865); Enid Lakeman and James D. Lambert, *Voting in Democracies; A Study in Majority and Proportional Electoral Systems* (London: Faber and Faber, 1959); John R. Commons, *Proportional Representation* (New York: A. M. Kelley, 1967). See also F. A. Hermens, *The Representative Republic* (Notre Dame: University of Notre Dame Press, 1958); Hermens was influential in persuading West Germans to modify the proportionality of their proportional representation system, which he linked with the multiparty cleavages of pre-Hitler days.

tion.[16] There was interest in the reform of the electoral college to insure against the election of a president not supported by a majority of voters.

Appropriately enough, in the controversies surrounding such proposals in the United States and elsewhere, the conflicts faithfully reflected traditional problems of the democratic creed. Where some wanted to maximize the impact of public opinion on government, others feared the instability or division that more inclusive and wider representation might induce. The assurance to individuals of their basic rights clashed with majoritarianism on such issues as judicial review versus legislative supremacy.[17] Cohesion and effectiveness of government on the one hand and accuracy of representation clashed on such issues as proportional representation versus single-ballot plurality systems or electoral college reform.

The contributions of European social democracy also built incrementally on established systems. Nationalization and planning all had their "respectable," that is, nonsocialist, forerunners. Public enterprise had been organized, often in state-owned monopolies, long before the advent of political democracy in much of the Western world. State bureaucracies supervised the running of railroads, public utilities, occasionally armament industries, harbor facilities, salt and tobacco monopolies, and sundry economic enterprises for centuries. In Europe, mercantilism preceded socialism everywhere.[18] The Social Democratic and Labour parties of the moderate Left generally adapted the approach of representative political democracy to the takeover and management of the economy.

In Britain, independent management boards were set up for the nationalized industries under parlimentary auspices and subject to periodic scrutiny by and accountable to parliament. In France, mixed, tripartite boards of state bureaucrats, labor, and consumer representatives were convoked to run these enterprises, again with ultimate—at least periodic—accountability to parliament.

Representation of conflicting interests, due process of law, compensa-

---

16 Robert B. McKay, *Reapportionment: Law and Politics of Equal Representation* (New York: Twentieth Century Fund, 1965), and Glendon A. Schubert, *Reapportionment* (New York: Scribner, 1965).

17 On these issues, see Charles G. Post, *The Supreme Court and Political Questions* (Baltimore: Johns Hopkins Press, 1936); Charles H. Beard, *The Supreme Court and the Constitution* (Englewood Cliffs, N.J.: Prentice-Hall, 1962); James E. Clayton, *The Making of Justice* (New York: Dutton, 1964); and Carl B. Swisher, *The Supreme Court in Modern Role*, rev. ed. (New York: New York University Press, 1965).

18 See, e.g., Eli F. Heckscher, *Mercantilism*, rev. ed. (London: Allen and Unwin, 1955), and also Shepard B. Clough, *European Economic History*, 2nd ed. (New York: McGraw-Hill, 1968).

tion of former owners, administrative and political recourse to all segments of the economy—all of these rather unspectacular features characterized the approach of democratic socialism to economic management. Outright confiscation, the threat to life and limb of former owners and, above all, dictatorial management procedures of the communist parties in Eastern Europe and the USSR stood in sharp contrast to all this.

Nevertheless, the usefulness and relevance of the changing mechanisms of Western democracy did not long remain immune to attacks from within.

Actually, the death of ideological cleavages in the 1950's could be attributed, in part at least, to the successful solution of problems that once sharply divided people, and also to the fact that in the context of democratic politics, the parties often competed for the same electoral clientele. Thus, German or British socialists knew that without the support of many middle class voters they could hardly secure control of parliament and power. On the other hand, the incentive to "cry wolf," that is, to invoke revolutionary rhetoric against the bourgeoisie, the landlords, or other privileged segments of society, was minimized by the affluence and security that workers had achieved in the largely consensual welfare state. Mass unemployment was, happily, a fading memory in the 1950's, not a live political issue.

American liberals such as A. A. Berle, Jr. or John Kenneth Galbraith found themselves ideologically reconciled to big business, finding virtues and compensations where they once feared the concentration of corporate power.[19] Those of relatively more conservative persuasion in Europe and America were less prone to accept the gloomy prognosis of Frederick A. Hayek, whose attitude toward economic planning was epitomized by the title of his book published in 1944, *The Road to Serfdom*.

But in the West even the relatively quiescent and consensual 1950's were not without serious ideological dissent. From the standpoint of our interest—in those who believed that the Right went too far to the Left, and those who believed that the Left all but sold out to the Right— there were portents of fissure. Apart from the communists, there were men like the eminent American sociologist, C. Wright Mills, who suspected that business tycoons were really running American society, all pretense notwithstanding.[20] There were also conservative critics, like

[19] On this theme, see A. A. Berle, Jr., *The 20th Century Capitalist Revolution* (New York: Harcourt, Harvest Books, 1960); and John K. Galbraith, *American Capitalism: The Concept of Countervailing Power* (Boston: Houghton Mifflin, 1956).

[20] Among outstanding works that have served to stimulate and justify the ideological discontent on the New Left are C. Wright Mills, *The Power Elite* (New York: Oxford

Russell Kirk, Willmore Kendall, or Peter Viereck, among others, who deplored and feared the aimless drift of a hedonistic mass society in which no traditions, values, or institutions were either sacred or safe.[21]

Some people attributed the decline of controversy-over-principle to the temporary, soothing effects of postwar recovery and prosperity. Perhaps as soon as prosperity was jeopardized, many old wounds might be reopened. Nationalism, class conflict, and extremism of every sort, were likely to feed on adversity. Perhaps the fissures of fundamental conflict were therefore not healed but simply hidden. There were also other reasons for unease, and some nagging doubts that ideological differences could be permanently submerged, dissolved, and forgotten.

Some of the reforms of the postwar years turned out to be disappointments for those who initiated them and, more important still, for the intended beneficiaries. One example of this was nationalization of industry. Much of the drive behind nationalization in Europe was the hope of socialist reformers that it would change workers' lives. It was believed that if men worked for the state rather than for private, self-seeking capitalists, this would give them a more wholesome, different sense of involvement, participation, and individual dignity. It was hoped that state ownership and control of industry would contribute to better industrial relations; that it would lessen man's alienation both from his work and his employers. It was also a prevalent hope among socialists that productivity and wealth would be generally increased by the substitution of a more intelligent and altruistic management in place of the old "anarchistic" profit seekers. Most of these hopes were disappointed. Neither productivity, industrial peace, nor worker happiness seemed significantly aided by nationalization. There were even indications that in some ways the state was a worse manager than the private employer.[22] To some people, this record of failure simply furnished support for an "I told you so" attitude. They had always thought socialism was a folly. Now that these socialist measures had been tried with such poor results, they believed that socialism's critics were right all along. Tacitly, even many

University Press, 1956); Gabriel Kolko, *Wealth and Power in America* (New York: Praeger, 1962); and Herbert Marcuse's *One Dimensional Man: Studies in the Ideology of Advanced Industrial Society* (Boston: Beacon Press, 1968).

[21] For outstanding works by American conservatives, see Clinton Rossiter, *Conservatism in America*, 2nd rev. ed. (New York: Random House, 1962); Russell Kirk, *The Conservative Mind* (Chicago: Regnery, 1960), and *A Program for Conservatives* (Chicago: Regnery, 1954); Willmore Kendall, *The Conservative Affirmation* (Chicago: Regnery, 1963) and Frank Meyer (ed.), *What is Conservatism?* (New York: Holt, 1964).

[22] On disenchantment with nationalization, see Reuben Kelf-Cohen, *Nationalization in Britain; The End of A Dogma* (London: Macmillan, 1958); Eldon Barry, *Nationalization in British Politics* (Stanford: Stanford University Press, 1965).

socialists seemed to believe this, too. Others, of course, continued either to cling to their old beliefs or identify socialism with other, more successful programs and achievements.

To the extent that consensual reforms of the 1940's and 1950's failed, they drew attention to the many as yet unsolved problems of Western societies, and also to the emergence of some new problems that did not fit the patterns of the old ideologies. The regimes of the 1940's and 1950's had succeeded in three very important tasks. They carried out the physical and social reconstruction in the aftermath of the Second World War. They cooperated to bring about a containment of Soviet expansion into Western Europe. They acted to prevent a recurrence of the economic horrors of the Great Depression, with its bread lines and its mass unemployment. In all these endeavors they were remarkably successful or, to put it more accurately, their efforts coincided with successes. Stalin's rule did not spill over the frontiers of Czechoslovakia where it had been established at its 1948 apogee. The recovery and affluence of Europe in the 1950's was all but indisputably evident. The United States shared in these accomplishments. Here, too, recovery and reconversion from war were brought about without a lapse into depression. Record levels of employment were continually being attained. The framework of the North Atlantic Treaty Organization seemed to have served its principal purpose with great success, whether judged from Washington, D. C., Bonn, or Paris. But certain problems persisted and new ones emerged. Among the so-called old problems was the multifaceted issue of peace.

The policies pursued by the United States and its allies could be credited—they certainly coincided—with "stopping communism" in Europe, and with the maintenance of peace on that continent. But such success could not be claimed even during the 1940's and 1950's for many other parts of the world, particularly in Asia. China, Korea, Malaya, the Philippines and, above all, Indochina were all targets of varyingly successful communist insurrections. In fact, outside of the sanctuaries of Western Europe and North America, the world at large was in ferment. Although no shots were—directly—exchanged for decades, American policy toward Russia and Russian policy toward America were both based on the recognition of a deep and irreconcilable mutual conflict. The containment of communism, for better or worse, implied a warlike existence, with warlike tensions, for millions of people around the world.

Great material resources of the world's richest states were committed to armaments. The destructiveness of weapons grew from "simple" A-bombs carried in 1945 to Hiroshima and Nagasaki by piston-engine B-24's to gruesome H-bombs, orbital missiles, nuclear submarines, ultrasonic jets, and spy satellites. It became plausible to believe that any resort to war would be eventually suicidal. All the traditional protections of oceans and landscape collapsed. Defensive and offensive military installations maintained by the great powers on foreign soil grew rather than diminished in the two decades following World War II. Trade, travel, and cultural relations between peoples were disrupted by Cold War barriers. Yet, the remarkable interdependence, and insecurity, of the world in this new age was perhaps best illustrated by the contamination resultant from H-bomb tests. Experiments carried out within the legal frontiers of several nation-states now threatened the atmosphere, air, and nutrition of virtually all other states. The conflict between the West and East—the Cold War—not only served to maintain divisions and tensions in the world along with high costs of military expenditure. It served to draw attention away from other critical problems of world social and economic development—overpopulation, depletion of resources, pollution, and famine—among them.

Even the so-called developed nations, the relatively rich, industrialized, and literate polities, were experiencing traumatic changes. Thus, rising urbanization and the progress of automation not only made the rich richer but also tended to continually raise the levels of expectations among people with respect to the quality of life and the amenities and services available in society. Social change created new conflicts while rendering some old ones "obsolete." It played havoc with traditional values and orientations. The rapidity and the discontinuity of change in the human environment made it difficult for established political institutions and ideals to command support, deference, or even attention.

The Cold War illustrates the dilemmas of consensual politics of this period, and the problem of "issue obsolesscence." In the 1940's, actual war, invasion, and conquest were vivid concepts to *all* participants in politics. One did not need to read history books to find out about them. The question of a communist conquest of Western Europe was dramatized with the progress of Stalin's army toward the Vistula, the Oder, the Elbe, and the Danube. It was dramatized in the frightening occupation of East Germany, Hungary, and Czechoslovakia, by the atrocities of a none-too-humane Red Army. Similarly, the grim political consequences of this occupation under Stalin were readily evident. By the 1950's and 1960's, however, all of these developments became rather distant memories for some people and but faint historical echoes for the young. Communist regimes in Russia and Europe had also sufficiently reformed and "humanized" in the years after Stalin, so as to create a much more mellow and innocent image for themselves abroad.[23] In the 1960's industrial air pollution (including radiation fallout) seemed more tangibly important to many people than "the threat of communist aggression." Increasingly, the appreciation of such a threat was *not* being shared between government intelligence experts and the ordinary man-in-the-street. To many people, and the young particularly, it seemed that even the most conscientious and energetic politicans adopted postures, spoke words, and engaged in actions that somehow fit the needs of the past rather than of the present. Traditional political symbols and styles began to experience a crisis of relevance.

In the United States, particularly, the increasing accumulation of unprecedented wealth contrasted starkly with the plight of millions of blacks and with the urban blight of ghettoes. The continuing war in Indochina, demanding the sacrifice of many young lives on behalf of a dimly perceived communist menace, also acted as a strong "destabilizer" in the political system. So did widespread sympathy for millions of Asian victims of that war. Involvement in the struggle for civil rights at home and against the war in Vietnam abroad mobilized the disenchanted. To many, wealth itself became synonymous with the evils of exploitation, oppression, war, and bureaucracy.

Thus, in the 1960's a wave of new radicalism swept the world. One of its singular features was the widespread support of youth, particularly among university students. Soon the new radicals had earned themselves a general appellation of the "New Left," and a number of intellectuals and political spokesmen became identified under this label.[24] Certainly, the problems that brought about this new ideological orientation were in degree, at least, without precedent, and its clientele also represented a new departure. Hitherto, left-wing political movements drew their mass support primarily from workers and peasants. The New Left, however, depended much more heavily on the sons and daughters of a relatively affluent middle class than upon either of these traditional elements. Yet,

[23] On the argument that "war and death are worse than communism" in their various ramifications, see particularly H. Stuart Hughes, *An Approach To Peace* (New York: Atheneum, 1962).

[24] Among some recent examples of literature of protest and dissent identified with the New Left, see Staughton Lynd and Thomas Hayden, *The Other Side* (New York: New American Library 1967); Thomas Hayden, *Rebellion and Repression* (New York: World Publishing Co., 1969) and *Rebellion in Newark: Official Violence and Ghetto Response* (New York: Vintage Books, 1967); Robert P. Wolff, Barrington Moore, Jr., and Herbert Marcuse, *A Critique of Pure Tolerance* (Boston: Beacon Press, 1965); *Eros and Civilization* (Boston: Beacon Press, (1966); *An Essay on Liberation* (Boston: Beacon Press, 1969); *Negations: Essays in Critical Theory* (Boston: Beacon Press, 1968).

both the radicalism of the New Left and its political pedigree were not wholly new.[25] What the radicals of the New Left brought back into the focus of world attention was ideas and claims that derive from both democratic and socialist political traditions.

The New Left grew in response to social problems that were both old and new. Among the new ones were the consequences of the industrial, or even postindustrial age. With the inexorable advances of machinery and computers, human life in most industrialized nations tended to become increasingly mechanistic, bureaucratic, and unfeeling. To use a clumsy word, it had grown more and more depersonalized. Large organizations, with rigid hierarchic structures and coldly rational achievement criteria, had replaced the intimacy and easygoing ways of earlier days. Personal relationships had been replaced by dials, numbers, automatic record retrievers, and the like. If these tendencies were evident and implicit in earlier times, they now grew more rapidly than ever, perhaps uncontrollably. Quantitative changes seemed to become qualitative.

The little red schoolhouse and the cloistered ivy-covered college became a "multiversity," where no one knew anyone else and no one seemed to care. The cozy corner grocery yielded its place to a chain store whose personnel came and went with the regularity of the seasons. The family physician gave way to a specialist whose examinations were conducted by technicians in a laboratory. Urban life, with its crowding, pollution, decay, crime, and breakdowns in all sorts of public services imposed tremendous hardships on people and great anxieties about the future. People increasingly asked themselves whether the emergent world was one that they could confidently anticipate for themselves and for their children.

Moreover, the new problems were complicated by the legacy of the old. A quarter-century after Hiroshima and Nagasaki, the world seemed not less but more endangered by nuclear holocaust. The tensions and enmities dividing East and West, though somewhat transmuted, were still very much in evidence. Despite the United Nations, despite all the security treaties and all the negotiations that had taken place during the years since 1945, the world seemed more of a powder keg than ever. The aspirations of the poor and exploited seemed strangely unfulfilled despite all the great progress in technology, science and the increase in national income figures around the world. In fact, increasing population— in large measure attributable to better public health technology of the

---

[25] See Richard F. Hamilton, *Affluence and the French Worker in the Fourth Republic* (Princeton: Princeton University Press, 1967), p. 5, for a definition of radicalism stressing changes in social stratification, economy and political controls.

last century—threatened to make the poor even poorer, and to overwhelm all the material gains of the age of industrialism.[26]

It is in this setting of unprecedented new problems and the conspicuous failure to resolve some of the old ones, that the New Left emerged to pose its characteristic challenge to established political patterns. It called for a new politics, against and outside the "system." It attacked the conventional, customary, legal, and established procedures of political life as the root cause of the world's problems and as the requisite of their solutions.

Viewed in the light of its own rhetoric and ideals, the New Left could be described, in all its various branches, as committed to the creation of a more humane social and political order through direct participation of the masses in the making of decisions.

The mixture of elements underlying this formula combines democracy and Marxian socialism with strong overtones of the traditional tenets of anarchism.

To begin with, the New Left is strongly anti-elitist in its critique of present-day society. Its faith is, like Rousseau's, in the efficacy of self-government. It sees oppression and evil in the world—not only in politics but in every branch of human activity, in science, religion, education, law, and the arts—because the masses of people are powerless and simply allow themselves to be led and exploited by a relative handful of selfish, indifferent leaders. In common with Marxism and also with the legacy of Rousseau, the New Left does not believe either in the intrinsic inevitability of elites in human society, or in the pluralistic theories which claim that elites, by competing with one another, moderate each other's power and strive to fulfill the aspirations of their rank and file. Thus, they reject the purely technocratic model of elites according to which the very complexity and sophistication of human organization imposes an indispensable need for expertise and the primacy of the few over the many who, by special ability, skills, and experience must, in one way or another, "run things" as the only alternative to loss of efficiency, chaos, and paralysis. They also reject the political pragmatic-bargaining model of elites which, granting the existence and inevitability of elites in every field of human endeavor, attempts to square the "fact" and the "need" with the desiderata of democratic theory.[27] In this latter view, elites, at

26 On the problems of population and pollution crises see, e.g., Philip Appleman, *The Silent Explosion* (Boston: Beacon Press, 1965); Colin Clark, *Population Growth and Land Use* (London: Macmillan, 1967); John Perry, *Our Polluted World: Can Man Survive?* (New York: F. Watts, 1967); John Rose, *Technological Injury* (London: Gordon and Breach Science, 1969).

27 See Peter Bachrach, *The Theory of Democratic Elitism* (Boston: Little, Brown,

least in the constitutional-liberal or democratic states, are always seen as dependent on other elites for support and consent, always required to compete with at least some other elites. The requirements of competition among various pressure-group elites, buttressed by recourse to periodic election, have the effect of keeping the society open—never a monopoly preserve of any single interest or group—and of assuring responsiveness of elites to nonelites. For as long as there is competition, the leaders cannot afford to take their followers completely for granted. Presumably choices, and defections, are possible and therefore it is in the interest of elites to forestall these.

The New Left critique of modern society, even the liberal-democratic, minimizes the degree of competition among elites, and in common with the Marxian tradition, believes in the fused or interlocking character of the ruling class. Like the Marxians, it sees society's rulers as all of a piece, or part of an integrated pattern. The men who run the principal business enterprises are also seen as the political, cultural, and social leaders of the system. What unites them is much more important than what divides them. The spokesmen of the New Left see a Ruling Class that is basically homogeneous on what might be termed the "big issues," those that touch on its power and perquisites, and divided only on nonessential, trivial, peripheral matters.

What liberal democratic theorists see as a mosaic of genuinely competing, interdependent decision-makers, appears to the New Left theorists in much the same light as it did to Marx and Lenin. Bourgeois liberal politics serves as a camouflage for bourgeois bankers, industrialists, and financiers. Its apparent openness and competitiveness are but a smokescreen for the more effective rule by the "establishment." Elections and pressure group squabbles give people an illusion of participation, and competition in the system. The illusion keeps them satisfied and quiescent. In fact, however, the processes of competition and participation are usually so structured (or "rigged") that the range of outcomes is always kept within limits that are regarded as safe and permissible by the rulers. Generally, only people with substantial means at their disposal can afford to take an active part in politics, run for office, or publicize political causes. The hierarchic and elite-ridden political parties "screen" candidates who would upset the elite consensus or the tacit understanding about the kind of public policies that governments should follow. Control of indispensable news media and educational institutions

1967) on the idea that in modern-day democracies, the American particularly, competing elites are neither sufficiently representative of the masses nor, indeed, sufficiently competitive and, hence, mutually restraining (pp. 36–37).

by the rich, and those subservient to them, reinforces the exclusion of radicals from the system. If true dissenters—that is, those who dissent on really fundamental issues—are thus not *wholly* kept out of political offices or other positions of power, they are at least made into innocuous rarities. By their very existence they "prove" that the system is open— as it claims in order to establish its legitimacy—but by their powerlessness they make the claim virtually meaningless.[28]

In its negative and suspicious attitude toward bourgeois society, the New Left had much in common with at least one branch of the Old Left —Marxist socialism. But in some respects it went much beyond the confines of Marxist-Leninist orthodoxy, veering closer to the positions of anarchism.

For in its *ultimate* objectives, Marxism in Lenin's, and even Stalin's and Mao's versions, has always been antiauthoritarian. The ideal society that was to follow the conflict of classes, the era of scarcity and oppression, would be libertarian. Men would be free to do as they liked and no institutional authorities would compel A to obey B. But in this Marxist vision, the era of optimum individual liberty and spontaniety lay far ahead. In order to achieve it, years of iron discipline would be required. The proletraiat would lead all mankind to its liberation, but on the way the Party would lead the proletariat, and wise and experienced Marxist-Leninists would (authoritatively) lead the Party. Marx himself quarreled with the anarchists on what was to him, their illusion that all that divided man from the blessed conditions of freedom, peace, and plenty was the act of revolution—the breaking of the chains. For Lenin, Stalin, and Mao, quite explicitly, man emergent from the contemporary, corrupt capitalist society is not yet ready to live according to the ideal "from each according to his ability; to each according to his need." He needs be educated and reeducated first. The material conditions, too, must first be created.

In the New Left, however, the pristine faith of nineteenth-century anarchism, and of Rousseau's faith in the uncorruptibility of the General Will, have found a modern echo. All authority and all authoritarianism, however allegedly transient, have become targets. Disdainful of the skills of experts or the alleged need for forbearance and self-restraint on the part of the ignorant masses, the New Left has staked out the claim to freedom, peace, and justice through participation.[29]

---

[28] On "repressive tolerance" see Wolff, Moore, Marcuse, op. cit. In the 1960's, Herbert Marcuse, Professor Emeritus of Philosophy at University of California, San Diego (b. 1898), became the widely acknowledged spokesman of the revived Marxian-Leninist view that bourgeois democracy is essentially "hypocritical", its tolerance favoring the position of the "strong and the wrong."

[29] See the Port Huron Statement by one of the founders of the Students for a

Interestingly also, in doing this the New Left has transcended an important distinction between most versions of democracy and socialism. It has proclaimed the distinction between "private" and "public" spheres of decision-making, and specifically between public and private property, to be spurious. With considerable plausibility, New Left political theorists have argued that if people must have control over all those decisions that seriously affect their lives, then the activities of giant private corporations, for example, are no less in need of popular control than the actions of the openly/legally public agencies of government.

In the United States, for example, the choices and life styles of workers and consumers are clearly and heavily influenced by the decisions of several large corporations, such as General Motors, Ford, or Chrysler in one field, International Telephone and Telegraph in another, and General Electric or Westinghouse in still others.

Without taking the position that private property ought to be abolished or confiscated, New Left theorists have demanded worker and consumer decision-making to make these and other institutions of private property more responsive and accountable to their employees, their customers, and to the public at large. Indeed, the threats to individual freedom, democracy, welfare, health, and public security posed by corporate wealth have been among the principal themes of the New Left. Similarly, the New Left has concentrated attention and effort on popular rule of educational institutions, arguing that the recipients or consumers of education and the numerically largest component within the educational system—the students—ought to share in the decision-making powers of these institutions. Thus, the roles of private proprietors and administrators have been implicitly devalued; in some cases denied all legitimacy; in some ignored; in still others simply consigned to a smaller sphere— in a much larger total pool of decision-makers.

The significance of this orientation is partly in establishing a link between the Old and the New Left. For now, instead of "socialist," "communist," or "syndicalist," other more culturally accepted words are used such as "participation," "sharing the decision-making," and "responsiveness," and much of the same objectives are pursued, though under different labels.[30]

Another significance of the New Left orientation is as political as it is broadly cultural. It relates to boundary maintenance. The New Left

Democratic Society, Tom Hayden, in Kenneth M. Dolbeare (ed.), *Directions in American Political Thought* (New York: Wiley, 1969), pp. 468–476. "Our work is guided by the sense that we may be the last generation in the experiment with living . . ." (p. 469).

[30] See Bachrach op. cit., on the need to control corporations as government is (or ought to be) controlled (pp. 78–82).

sees modern society as so interdependent that, broadly speaking, everyone is affected by everything; hence, everyone ought to have a voice in everything. Granted the fact of interdependence, the problems of organizing mass decision-making on the principle of "nothing about me without me" are formidable. Judging by past experience, the problem of how to organize voting and maintain the participatory interest of the rank and file in every field of endeavor so as to prevent slippage back into "elitism" is a difficult task. One New Left argument for it is that if people are given meaningful participatory rights—that is, over questions that really, directly touch their lives, they will not allow self-selected elites to usurp the decision-making, as they presumably do on the more remote, so-called, irrelevant issues. There is also the possibility, so characteristically accepted in the anarchist tradition, that "if the system changes so will human nature." Finally, and concomitantly, the proposition may be buttressed by ambiguity and antihistoricism.

The distinction between "important" and "unimportant" issues is most appealing in explaining away voter apathy until we try to define what the distinction is and then relate this definition to past experience. Would inquiry into past voting patterns on such issues as municipal bonds, tax levies, public improvements, and the like reassure us that people do indeed vote on those things that are "relevant" or "important"?

If we assume that somehow past experience is not relevant to what may happen in the future (1) because the world has changed so much, and/or (2) because the oppressive total political-social system has warped human attitudes, and/or (3) any other reason(s), much less justification is required to support the rhetoric of the participatory revolution.

One of the hallmarks of the New Left has been its militant antinationalism. Many New Left advocates have characteristically tended to denigrate, ridicule, and bring into ill repute various symbols of national identity and national power. These have conspicuously included flags and other national insignia; military or patriotic demonstrations; virtually all objects, symbols, and properties identified with the armed forces or with local or municipal police agencies. Such institutions as Congress, the Presidency, the courts, and state and local governments have all come under particularly heavy attack, partly verbal and partly physical. In Europe, Asia, and Latin America, there have been corresponding assaults on analogous national symbols and institutions.

The New Left has, in fact, developed its own worldwide countertradition as an integral part of a more general counterculture. This countertradition is in a sense paradoxical because many of the New Left are averse to historicism as simply trivial and irrelevant antiquarianism.

They avow instead a kind of here-and-now orientation; the attitudes of many of the New Left proponents are analogous to Jeremy Bentham's: history deserves to be remembered only to be condemned. Yet, part of the ideology or outlook of the New Left militants is grounded in a very special interpretation of history that emphasizes and condemns acts of violence, lawlessness, treachery, and other assorted evils attributed to the national government, its organs and agents. In the United States, it implicitly and explicitly evokes guilt on such questions: How did we *really* win the West? How and why have we treated Indians, Blacks, Mexicans, or Asians in the country? Have we always sought peace, justice, and democracy in our dealings with other nations? The historicism of the New Left is overtly political and remedial. That is, the study of the past is consciously subordinated to the task of undoing evil and of promoting salutary political, social, cultural, and economic changes in present-day society. Much of its concern is with a reinterpretation of certain standard, widely disseminated versions of history and supportive of particular political objectives.

For example, one of the fundamental assumptions of the New Left is that the status quo political-economic system is incapable of successful adaptations. It can never bring about or sanction fundamental reforms by its very nature, by its basic rigidity and inflexibility. If the argument is advanced that the "system" has, in fact, witnessed *some* specific salutary changes, the historical ideologues of the New Left appropriately discount them. Thus, if it is argued that slavery was abolished in the course of the Civil War, and that this was a progressive step, New Left historicism retorts by discounting the magnanimity of reformers like Lincoln, emphasizing their opportunistic motives and, above all, stressing the limited practical impact of abolition both in the South and in the North in the years following the Civil War.[31]

The view of the past is a buttress to the view of the present. In the American experience, New Left ideologues see Congress as a hopeless captive of rural-reactionary and moneyed interests. Their grip on the legislative power structure—through malapportionment, the seniority system in both houses, the subservience of the two major parties to the economic, corporate power structure, and the conditioned apathy of the voters, is all but unshakable. Hope for reform "within the system," that is, according to the rules and procedures of the ongoing constitutional structure, are represented as a hoax and an illusion. In common with the

31 On some reinterpretations of Civil War North-South conflicts see, e.g., Lorman Ratner, *Powder Keg; Northern Opposition to the Anti-Slavery Movement* (New York: Basic Books, 1968); and Arthur Zilversmit, *The First Emancipation; The Abolition of Slavery in the North* (Chicago: University of Chicago Press, 1967).

communist Left, particularly the Maoist, the New Left sees social democratic aspirations for "change from within" as naïve and untenable. Consequently, it also sees the proponents of such change, assorted liberals, moderates, socialists, or social-democrats of the Old Left, as dangerous deceivers of the people. Such liberals and socialists are pictured by the New Left of the 1960's and 1970's in the same light as they once were in Germany and France by the communists in the early 1930's: as valuable allies to the bourgeoisie and, willy-nilly, traitors to the masses. Again, in common with the militant Marxian view, whose intellectual pedigree goes back at least to the 1848 Manifesto, the prevailing bourgeois economic-political order is seen as willing and capable of responding with but crumbs and sops (sometimes called "tokenism") to the demands of the masses or, even more characteristically, with verbal deception and repressive violence.

The American involvement in the war in Indochina, grown large-scale and intense in the 1960's, has confirmed for the New Left, both in the United States and abroad, the traditional Marxian-Leninist stereotypes about imperialism. It has been interpreted as a confirmation of the predatory, ruthless, and inhuman character of monopoly capitalism. In this view, the war has served to maintain domestic profits and prosperity at the cost of lives—American and Vietnamese—and to stifle a just struggle for popular liberation from the oppressive rule of the imperialists and their "stooges" (successively, such Vietnamese rulers as Bao Dai, Ngo Dingh Diem, Kao Ky, and Van Thieu).

The New Left has reinterpreted the whole history of the Cold War from the versions popular in the United States and Western Europe in the 1940's and 1950's.[32] Its reinterpretation has again brought it closer to the official Soviet and most other communist parties' positions about these events. The aspirations and machinations of American imperialism, not Stalin's expansionist policies, are thought to be at the root of the Cold War. The general line of the New Left has been that resistance to communist aggression has been an artificial contrivance of Western, and particularly American imperialism. It has served as a smoke screen for the domination and exploitation of the masses at home and abroad, a device for deflecting popular attention from the real and urgent griev-

---

[32] Among works that interpret American foreign policy vis-à-vis Russia since 1945 as a colossal mistake, see William A. Williams, *The Tragedy of American Diplomacy* (Cleveland: World Publishing Co., 1959); Denna F. Fleming, *The Cold War and Its Origins 1917–1960* (Garden City, N.Y.: Doubleday, 1961); and Gar Alperovitz, *Atomic Diplomacy: Hiroshima and Potsdam* (New York: Simon and Schuster, 1965). See also his *Cold War Essays* (Garden City, N.Y., Doubleday, 1970).

ances and needs of the masses—for freedom, equality, economic well-being and, above all, world peace.

The ideas of the New Left presented an attractive image of compassion for the poor and oppressed, of concern for the ghetto dweller, for the migrant farm worker, the racial minorities, and the disenfranchised youth. In an era when America's population increasingly consisted of those under the age of 30, these orientations grew increasingly important for the political system as a whole. On the American scene, problems of urban squalor, hunger, racial oppression, and the appalling waste of man's environment had assumed an immediacy—to the eye, ear, and nose—that was hard to match on behalf of such remote Cold War issues as say, maintaining parity with Russia in thermonuclear missiles or keeping a balance of conventional forces in Europe. Indeed, did these issues continue to have any reality and urgency at all? Much of the concern and moral indignation manifested by the New Left was hard to discount. And much of its reinterpretation of the past and present served to balance and deflate once smugly accepted notions about various facets of man's social history, politics, and economic life. It produced a new social awareness and dampened the once predominant exuberant faith that the continuing progress of science and accumulation of wealth would somehow cure all social ills—without disturbing even slightly what was so widely assumed to be a basically just, if not near-perfect, political order. The attraction of the New Left also consisted in its emphasis of a subjective humanism, with maximum freedom for the individual to pursue his own distinctive life style unhampered by punitive-legal restraints imposed by the state.

Persistent criticisms of the New Left centered partly around the vagueness or lack of its positive programs, and even more so around the seeming extremism in its critical role. To many people, young and old, the New Left seemed intent on throwing out the baby with the bath. The language of its social critique seemed singularly inflated and exaggerated. If the traditions of Western societies, particularly the American, had overemphasized and sugarcoated the accomplishments of the status quo, did not the New Left substitute grotesquely simple caricatures of evil for some complex realities? The rhetoric and militancy of extremism were not without their dangers. For indeed if people began to believe that a Willy Brandt was no different from a Hitler, or Attorney General Mitchell from a Heinrich Himmler, bombings and armed confrontations could eventually lead to civil war. If—regardless of the facts—people became convinced that the "system" was completely unresponsive, there could indeed be no alternative but violent revolution for those seeking change.

And this would surely increase the violence from the military and police forces confronted by insurrection, and guerrilla warfare. Actually, some on the New Left followed the pattern of communist anticipations of the 1930's. They welcomed the prospect of repression because they thought it would help to "open the eyes of the masses as to the true character of their rulers." Political mobilization against the old order would thus be speeded up, presumably, and revolutionary objectives would be more easily achieved. Others, however, were less optimistic and feared the possibility of widespread civil conflict and its long-term consequences of repression and reaction.

The institutional expressions of the New Left are still fragmentary and largely confined to the one area where the new movement has at least occasionally managed to assert its power: universities and institutions of learning. As portents of changes to come, these examples set a pattern of participatory decision-making. The subordination of expert to nonexpert, of technicians to consumers, implicit in the management of a professional minority by a student majority await to be extended not only throughout educational systems but to other—economic, political, social, and cultural—decision-making structures of society as well.

In identifying itself with all-pervasive slogans of participatory democracy, the New Left of the 1960's and 1970's veered away from the individualistic liberalism of men like John Locke and John Stuart Mill toward a populist type of democracy often attributed to Jean Jacques Rousseau.[33]

If the popular will was to prevail in all endeavors, if not only government but also economy and culture were to be drawn into the vortex of popular power, wouldn't the imperfect competition of various elites be replaced by a mobocracy? Would a "private sphere," opposition, or dissent be tolerated? And if a mobocracy proved to be practically unworkable, wouldn't some powerful leader of the people, a Hitler or Mao, speak in the name of what the people *truly* needed and wanted? In the early 1970's, it seemed clear that for many leaders of the New Left there were scarcely any limits to what they might do, on behalf of the people's "just and true needs" in the time-honored formula.

Thus, democratic and socialist politics traveled full-circle, as it were: from ideology to pragmatism, and back to new ideology. In the process, the old adage that "politics makes strange bedfellows" was once again illustrated. For in consequence of the realignments of the 1960's, some

---

[33] See J. L. Talmon, *The Origins of Totalitarian Democracy* (New York: Praeger, 1960); see also his *Romanticism and Revolt; Europe 1815–1848* (New York: Harcourt, Brace and World, 1967).

who were once identified with the Left, or "Old Left," now became identified with the Right.

Many liberals, democrats, and socialists sympathized with the general New Left goals of humanizing society but feared that its excesses might bring about a calamitous collapse of economy, science, culture, and technology. To many people who could see that efficiency, discipline, and authority could all be abused, it also seemed that massive breakdowns in essential social services could follow from their abandonment.

Marxian socialists and communists were willing to accept authority, discipline, and long-term privations in the belief that the Party, or the movement, would lead them to a brighter tomorrow of a classless society. Nationalist conservatives accepted still other notions that justified authority, discipline, and the bureaucratic-industrial order. Some found it to be a natural principle—some men were simply better, wiser, and stronger, or more efficient than others. Still others believed that "holding people in check"—through force, law, or the manipulation of material and symbolic rewards—was required by the inherent faults of human nature.

What the New Left sought, from its own perspective, was a more humane society. It rebelled against the rigid disciplines, hierarchies, and penalties imposed on man by his industrial civilization. It rebelled against technocratic bureaucracy, against the soulless efficiency experts, against the preoccupation with production, material achievement, and wealth as society's dominant values. In an age of great and increasing productivity, it demanded the subordination of technology to the needs of the idiosyncratic individual. At a time of ever-increasing numbers of men and machines, it demanded that no individual be treated as a mere number or a tool. It refused to countenance the continuation of discrimination, subjection, or the economic or social inferiority of any group in society. For the most part, the New Left rejected those rationalizations of inequality or want to which some of its "Old Left" counterparts at least transitionally resigned themselves.

If the New Left shared some common assumptions about man and society with eighteenth-century democracy, its tactics were heavily influenced by the legacy of Marxism-Leninism. To the extent that in politics the means to particular ends often overshadow the ends themselves, the mix of democracy and Marxism on the New Left was often heavily tilted toward the latter.

In common with anarchist and socialist revolutionaries of the past two centuries, the new extremist groups deprecated persuasion and valued violence. For the American leaders of the Students for a Democratic Society and similar radical student groups in the United States and elsewhere, propaganda remained an important focus of political activity. But belief in the persuadability of *all* men—at least in this, contemporary, "corrupt" society—was distinctly lacking. Like Lenin, Mao, and Guevara, the revolutionaries of the New Left viewed their adversaries as "hopeless." Only force could move them, and only sweeping changes in society could be genuinely effective against the "Establishment," or the bourgeoisie, as the case might be. People in the "nonenemy" category—whether students, workers, peasants, employees, etc.—could not be trusted to sort things out for themselves. They could do so only if led by those with superior political, moral, and strategic-tactical insights—the new elite of the non-elite, as it were. The resort to violent confrontations and, above all, conspiratorial and terrorist techniques of politics in preference to the established, constitutional-electoral channels, reflected the movement's deep pessimism about its human environment.

In the late 1960's, the significance of the new radicalism on the Left was in its demonstrated capacity for disruption of established institutions—political, legal, economic, and cultural. But beyond some impressive assaults on law and order, the New Left had yet to establish itself as a major spokesman for the masses—either on the barricades or at the ballot box. It was still a highly vocal, visible, yet esoteric political movement.

CHAPTER 10

Nationalism, Democracy, and Socialism in the Third World

Among the poorest and least industrialized members of the world community of states are to be found the most varied transmutations of all the old ideologies of Europe. In part, this has resulted from the colonial heritage of Africa, Asia, and Latin America. The colonizing powers exported not only goods and personnel but belief-systems as well. They generally attempted to insure the supremacy of their own ideals and values by destroying or preventing the further development of native, local educational systems. For most Asians or Africans of the nineteenth and twentieth centuries, schooling, and particularly higher education, was synonymous with Europeanization. Men like Nkrumah, Ho Chi Minh, and Chou En-lai studied in Western universities; most of their countrymen who received any education at all did so in institutions whose sourcebooks, programs, administrators, and teachers were either European in origin or outlook or both.[1]

The domination of the poor by the rich, and of the weak by the powerful, was extended from the realm of politics, economics, and arms to most branches of mass popular culture. Newspapers, books, and films emphasized and disseminated the ideals, styles, interests, and values of the rulers rather than the ruled. Transplanted European institutions

[1] See particularly Rupert Emerson, *From Empire to Nation* (Cambridge: Harvard University Press, 1960) Chapter 10, "The West and Non-Western Nationalism."

relating to government, law, and the economy all tended to reinforce these orientations. Finally, the sequence of development—the lateness and the special problems of independence among these new states—has also contributed to an ideological mosaic.

Obviously, generalizations about ideologies of so many different societies—spanning the enormous cultural-physical-economic geographic divergences of, say Jamaica in the Caribbean, Indonesia in the Pacific, or Ceylon in the Indian Ocean—are extremely difficult. For purposes of an introductory survey, we can at best single out certain trends that can serve as starting points of further analysis and comparisons.

First, what is distinctive about the ideologies of the states often referred to as the Third World is the degree to which, in terms of European ideology, they have synthesized the belief-systems of "Right" with "Left."[2] Thus we find, above all, nationalism a dominant theme in their ideological orientations. In order to overcome the legacy of colonial tutelage, of habitual subservience to others and tribal disunity among themselves, the ideologues of Africa, Asia, and even Latin America have all sought to instill a new pride, a new sense of identity and belonging. Only through these could the people of any given region muster the strength required to win and maintain independence of their old colonial masters, to support an autonomous statehood, and to contribute the resources, labor, and loyalties necessary for building a common future.[3] To the extent that nationalism has served the functions of integration and cohesion among individuals, localities, and some larger—actual or merely projected—political units, it has followed the pattern of European nationalism of yesterday. In Europe, however, nationalism became largely transmuted in the course of the nineteenth century into an ideology of the "Right." Integration and cohesion became instruments for suppressing socio-economic discontent, ferment, and consequent "differentiation" at home. It frequently served to buttress the status quo for the upper classes, while

[2] The term "Third World" as used in this chapter generally refers to countries of Asia, Africa, and Latin America, exclusive of those run by one-party professedly Marxist-Leninist regimes, and the several predominantly "white" states of the British Commonwealth.

[3] See Gabriel A. Almond and James S. Coleman (eds.), *The Politics of the Developing Areas* (Princeton, N.J.: Princeton University Press, 1960), pp. 548–550, on nationalism's impact on interest articulation. See also Paul E. Sigmund (ed.), *The Ideologies of the Developing Nations* (New York: Praeger, 1967), and Clifford Geertz (ed.), *Old Societies and New States: Quest for Modernity in Asia and Africa* (New York: Free Press, 1963). Geertz describes the institutional experiments of the new states in terms of an "integrative revolution" in which relatively more narrow "primordial" loyalties and the new, more inclusive "civic" loyalties are being, hopefully, reconciled (p. 156). This revolution does not destroy ethnocentrism; it attempts to modernize it (p. 154).

supporting compensatory conquests and expansion at the cost of others abroad. Conceivably, nationalism in the new states of Africa, Asia, and Latin America could yet follow the same course. But in the period of the 1940's, 1950's, and 1960's, the context of politics in virtually all of these areas contributed to the rise of a different, characteristically left-of-center type of nationalism. This nationalism was more akin to the young European nationalisms in the era of 1789–1848 than to the more recent mature varieties. It typically combined the notion of a separate national identity for the new states with the ideal of liberation for all the hitherto oppressed peoples. It did not embrace imperialism; it condemned it.

In fact, antiimperialism and anticapitalism have been the most characteristic features in the nationalist ideologies of the Third World.[4] Understandably, one of the consequences of the colonial experience there has been the creation of certain common communist-nationalist stereotypes with respect to the rich industrial nations of the world. The Marxist-Leninist view of the bloated international financier lording it over the poor and downtrodden of the world has had strong parallels in the experience and ideology of the Third World. It has also produced an analogous tendency in Third World nationalism to advocate the solidarity of the poor and oppressed against the exploiting rich. Moreover, certain typical virtues of socialism, such as emphasis on equality and on a compassionate concern for the welfare of all members of society have been characteristic. Local aristocrats, landlords, and great merchants have been looked upon as allies of international capitalism and of the particular colonial rulers—British, French, Dutch, or American.[5] Capitalism is decried as insensitive to human want and suffering. Collective action, under state auspices, and planning toward equality are often regarded as ethically superior.

There are important mobilizational parallels here to the circumstances of nineteenth- and even twentieth-century Europe. We may recall that in Europe the most self-conscious, virulently xenophobic forms of nationalism arose precisely in those countries that had inherited the least impressive backgrounds of national unity. Italy and Germany, where fascism and nazism appeared, were both countries whose unifications, out of a

---

[4] On this theme see, e.g., Fenner Brockway, *African Socialism: A Background Book* (Chester Springs, Pa.: Dufour Editions, 1963); William H. Friedland and Carl G. Rosberg (eds.), *African Socialism* (Stanford: Stanford University Press, 1964); Leopold Senghor, *On African Socialism* (New York: Praeger, 1964).

[5] The subject of communist Third World "ideological convergence" is ably explored by John H. Kautsky in *Political Change in Underdeveloped Countries: Nationalism and Communism* (New York: John Wiley, 1962), pp. 79–89. Hugh Seton-Watson, *Nationalism and Communism, Essays, 1946–1963* (New York: Praeger, 1964).

welter of small principalities, occurred late in the nineteenth century and where regional and cultural differences continued to be serious, long after formal unification. Similarly, nationalism in Eastern Europe was most salient precisely where the demarcations and identities of particular ethnic groups were most fluid, and most subject to doubt. In these coun-tries, as in Africa and Asia many years later, a very ardent nationalism was developed by some elements in the body politic to provide unity and cohesion in the face of actual disunity and disarray. Where colonialism had all but destroyed and uprooted traditional identifications and had prepared people for new identifications, nationalism sought to provide these.

India's Mahatma Gandhi (1869–1948) and Jawahrlal Nehru (1889–1964) both exemplified Third World leaders who had synthesized important ideals of nationalism, socialism, and democracy. In some respects, their ideologies were modern, post-Marxian; yet both were throwbacks to the progressive, democratically oriented nationalists of pre-1848 Europe.

Gandhi was a modern nationalist in his goal of independence and common statehood for a nation of diverse languages, traditions, and creeds. The sense of national identity and unity that would actually support an Indian state was more a vision that Gandhi helped to bring into life than a reality when he started out on his political struggle in the first decade of the twentieth century.

Like other nationalists, Gandhi, too, rejected the notion of class strug-gle as being either inevitable or salutary for human development. He also rejected the extreme fragmentation and social alienation produced by an unbridled liberalism, with its economic and political "catch-as-catch-can" overtones.

To a large extent, Gandhi's writings and, above all, his actions sought to provide unifying national values and symbols for his countrymen. They were also attempts to overcome the disruptive effects of economic and social modernization that would undermine any kind of social co-hesion and stability. In the face of onrushing industrialization and tech-nological progress, Gandhi sought a substitute for the "corrective" of class-conscious socialism with all its antagonisms and violence. Thus he developed a view of social justice that he hoped would be harmonious, cooperative, and communal. He sought a revival of the spirit of India's ancient village life, accentuating handicrafts, simplicity, autarchy, face-to-face relationships and, above all, the feeling of human cooperation and kinship. He feared and opposed Western centralization and deper-sonalization of man's economic and social life. His political creed, too, rested on a cooperative decentralization of national power. He sought a society based on mutual cooperation of all classes rather than the forceful leveling of some by others.

Gandhi sought to alleviate India's rural poverty and remove the sting of discrimination attaching to caste distinctions—by appealing to human compassion. He idealized the work of the peasant, his closeness to the soil, and he deprecated the insatiable materialism associated with industrial and urban life. His great collaborator, Nehru, believed Gandhi to be a dynamic peasant leader rather than a pragmatic, broker-politician in the western tradition.[6]

In his views toward Marxism-Leninism, Gandhi characteristically called himself a "nonviolent communist." In fact, he attempted to be a humanist without being an individualist in the tradition of Western Enlightenment. He also sought to achieve at least some of the objectives of modern socialism without resorting either to a divisive class struggle or to industrialization. In the latter respect, Gandhi was atypical of modern anti-colonialism.

His links with progressive nationalism rested on his acceptance—albeit qualified and less than enthusiastic—of the representatice mechanisms of Western democracy and in his profound regard for the value and sanctity of individual human life. Above all, Gandhi's attitude toward war and conquest, his repugnance toward violence, and his belief that the community of nations could coexist in permanent peace and harmony sharply differentiate him from the predatory nationalists of Europe. In this respect, above all, he was a "throwback" to the earlier nationalists of the 1789–1848 era. He even nourished the hope at one time that Hitler and Mussolini could be persuaded to the ways of peace, inasmuch as all men were, he believed, open to the persuasion of love.[7]

Like other nationalists, Gandhi sought and developed native embodiments for his most characteristic general principles. His denial of violence, for example, embodied in the concept of *ahisma* had traditional forerunners in Indian religion history, and culture as did the pacific-communalist ideal of *swadeshi*. Both had their counterparts in the traditions and religions of the West, too, but Gandhi skillfully emphasized the distinctive and uniquely Indian contributions to these concepts. As one of his intellectual biographers noted:

"(Gandhi) contended that India's village society expressed the pacific ideal before the West introduced centralizing and depersonalizing forces.

[6] See Paul F. Power, *Gandhi on World Affairs* (Washington D.C.: Public Affairs Press, 1960), p. 32.

[7] Ibid., p. 49.

His social thought drew from Hindu cosmogony ideas analogous to the Golden Age in Greek mythology and to the Judeo-Christian concept about man's innocence before the Fall . . . . Apart from myths, Gandhi found a basis for his communal ideas in the history of the autonomous, village-based republics during the Indian Buddhist age, 557–477 B.C.

Despite Western encrustations, Gandhi claimed that the Indian village had retained its ancient characteristics of social cohesion, economic simplicity and political autonomy. But it is especially significant that his interpretation of traditional Indian village life did not mean that he advocated its literal revival. The spirit, not the historic form of an institution was vital to him."[8]

Thus, characteristically, Gandhi reinforced the sense of national identity and tradition at least as much as he depended on them. Among other Third World leaders particularly adept at "nationalizing" the more general Western-derived concepts of socialism, democracy, and even nationalism itself, have been Indonesia's Sukarno and Ghana's Nkrumah. Each was influential not merely by adapting Western notions but by arguing that African and Indonesian combinations of these creeds were actually even more "natural" and "effective" than their foreign counterparts.

The acceptance of the political method of parliamentary democracy, and the combination of nationalism with internationalism also characterized Gandhi's successor, Jawahrlal Nehru. Educated in Britain, Nehru absorbed the traditions of English liberal democracy, unlike Gandhi, from book learning as well as from personal exposure. Much more than Gandhi—and in common with many of the contemporary leaders of Asian and African nationalist movements—Nehru became strongly influenced by Marxism. Its characteristic general concepts and ideas permeated his whole outlook. In this ideological orientation, Nehru was a modern "nationalist-of-the left," akin to many of the current leaders of Asia and Africa. In 1933 he wrote:

"I dislike fascism intensely and indeed I do not think it is anything more than a crude and brutal effort of the present capitalist order to

---

[8] Ibid., p. 24. Other interesting works on Gandhi include his *Autobiography: The Story of My Experiments with Truth* (Washington D.C.: Public Affairs Press, 1960) and *All Men are Brothers: Life and Thoughts of Mahatma Gandhi As Told in His Own Words*, (Paris: Unesco, 1958); Bondurant, *Conquest of Violence: The Gandhian Philosophy of Conflict* (Berkeley: University of California Press, 1965); and Louis Fisher, *The Life of Mahatma Gandhi* (New York: Harper, 1950); B. R. Nanda, *Mahatma Gandhi* (London: Allen and Unwin, 1958); and particularly Lloyd I. Rudolph, *The Modernity of Tradition: Political Development in India*, (Chicago: University of Chicago Press, 1967).

preserve itself at any cost. There is no middle road between fascism and communism. One has to choose between the two and I choose the communist ideal. In regard to the methods and approach to this ideal, I may not agree with everything that the orthodox Communists have done. I think that these methods will have to adapt themselves to changing conditions and may vary in different countries. But I do not think that the basic ideology of communism and its scientific interpretation of history is sound."[9]

In 1937, he expressed his internationalism in this way:

"Nationalist as I am in regard to Indian freedom, I do not look upon contacts with other peoples from a narrow nationalist viewpoint. My very nationalism is based on internationalism, and I am very conscious of the fact that the modern world, with its science and world trade and swift methods of transport, is based on internationalism. The country or people can isolate themselves from the rest of the world, and if they attempt it, they do so at their peril and the attempt is bound to fail in the end."[10]

Once in office, when Nehru led India as Prime Minister in the late 1940's, the 1950's, and 1960's, his socialism was of a fairly tepid variety. He believed that India's basic problem was not redistribution from rich to poor, but rather an increase in the nation's abysmally low level of economic development. Nehru contributed much more to the perpetuation of British-style parliamentarism in India than to the maintenance of revolutionary ideals. As one of his biographers wrote, "In the broadest sense Parliament in India is a symbol of the method of government which Nehru is trying to establish and an instrument to educate those who will wield power in the future."[11] Nehru's democratism proved stronger than his socialism.

[9] Cited by M. N. Das, *The Political Philosophy of Jawaharlal Nehru* (New York: John Day, 1961), pp. 133–134. Similarly, in March 1933, on the fiftieth anniversary of the death of Karl Marx, Indonesia's Sukarno wrote that "Nationalism in the Eastern world has been wed to Marxism; it has become a new nationalism. . . ." As Bernhard Dahm observes, "Marxism, for Sukarno, gave not only proof of the depravity of capitalism and of imperialism but also hope for their defeat. . . . Marxism was the assurance of victory." *Sukarno and the Struggle for Indonesian Independence* (Ithaca: Cornell University Press, 1969), pp. 153–154. Appropriately, Sukarno's diagnosis of fascism was akin to Nehru's. It was "the logical consequence of a mature capitalism which could no longer tolerate the free competition secured by parliamentary democracy but required a police state for the protection of its interests." Dahm, Ibid., p. 201.

[10] See M. N. Das, op. cit., p. 198.

[11] Michael Brecher, *Nehru: A Political Biography* (Boston: Beacon Press, 1959), p. 178. Cf. W. H. Morris-Jones, *Parliament in India* (London: 1957).

Indian participation in the United Nations, her efforts to bridge the gap between East and West, and in 1955 her participation—with Red China—in the Bandung Conference, were all reflections of the internationalism of Nehru's outlook and policy.

But India's quest for social justice with national unity at home, and for peace and international cooperation throughout the world illustrates the uncertain relationship between ideological aspirations, institutionalized attempts to carry them out, and the concomitant realities.

Thus, linguistic differences in independent India proved so serious that in 1956 the several Indian states had to be realigned from the constitutional pattern of 1947. Intense conflict led to repeated outbursts of mass violence and in 1960, hundreds of people died in widespread rioting between the Marathi and Gujarati-speaking inhabitants in Bombay, bringing about new administrative divisions. The leaders' aspirations to national unity and nonviolence were unavailing. In the southern Indian province of Kerala, communists dislodged Nehru's Congress party from power. Indian voters manifested resentment at the failure of the regime to make the aspirations of socialism meaningful to them.

The disappointments in the field of world politics were no less serious. In 1955, India joined with some thirty Asian and African states in a declaration in which all the signatories—Red China included—pledged themselves to (1) mutual respect for each other's territorial integrity and sovereignty; (2) nonaggression; (3) noninterference in each other's affairs; (4) equality and mutual advantage; (5) peaceful coexistence and cooperation.[12]

Yet, between 1959 and 1962, China invaded and occupied portions of Indian territory with intermittent fighting and casualties on both sides. In 1961, the Indians themselves resorted to arms in the takeover of small Portuguese colonies on the Indian peninsula. In 1965, full-scale war broke out between India and Pakistan, ending in an armistice negotiated under Soviet auspices in Tashkent.

Analogous disappointments and failures have plagued other Asian and African regimes ideologically committed to the objectives of national cohesion, economic development, and international harmony.

We have noted in our previous discussion of European nationalism that in several of its forms, during the nineteenth and twentieth centuries, it has been racist. The most overt example of this was Hitler's National Socialism with its explicit doctrine of world mastery for the Germanic "master race" and the subjugation and extermination of all the inferior races. But even in several of the more moderate, conservative,

[12] See J. Leo Cefkin, *The Background of Current World Problems* (New York: David McKay, 1967), p. 335.

and reactionary forms of European nationalism, racism has been, at least implicitly, very important. Much of the emphasis on the "duty to conquer" rested on the assumption of the intrinsic superiority of one's own people, its peculiar genius and civilization. Race consciousness has been an important element in the nationalisms of the Third World, too. But initially, at least, its orientation has been *compensatory* rather than *aggressive*. As one African scholar expressed it:

". . . whereas . . . Americans proclaimed 'equality' in pursuit of independence, the African nationalists have now sought independence in pursuit of equality . . . . the development of African nationalism is a progressive metamorphosis of what would be acceptable as an adequate expression of racial equality."[13]

Much of the force behind the opposition to "neocolonialism," so favorable to Moscow and Peiping, derives from the still considerable imbalance of European influence in the economies of new African states —even after independence.

Illustratively, a recent survey in Kenya disclosed that in jobs requiring university or higher education, 50 percent were held by Europeans, 27 percent by Asians, and only 23 percent by Africans. Among professionals such as lawyers, physicians, engineers, and surveyors less than 6 percent were Africans. In 1966, the nominal capital of companies owned by Europeans was more than twice as large as that of Africans. The combined wealth of non-African corporations (European and Asian) was five times larger than the African.[14] Imbalances of this kind reflect a lingering colonial heritage which independence has not yet undone. They are a carryover from a period when, as Professor Donald S. Rothchild observes:

"Housing, medical facilities, pensions, and schools were all separate and very unequal. . . . Except in a few unusual cases . . . Africans, Asians and Europeans were educated in separate racial schools. . . . African opportunity was thwarted by colonial budgets which spent more money on European and Asian than on African education, although the latter community represented 97 percent of the population."[15]

These legacies have contributed to the maintenance of a high level of

[13] Ali A. Mazrui, "On the Concept of 'We Are All Africans'," *The American Political Science Review*, Vol. LVII, No. 1 (March 1963), p. 96.

[14] Donald S. Rothchild, "Ethnic Inequalities in Kenya," *The Journal of Modern African Studies*, Vol. 7, No. 4 (December 1969), p. 695.

[15] Ibid., pp. 695–696. Compare David C. Gordon, *The Passing of French Algeria* (New York: Praeger, 1966), p. 56, for comparable data on Algeria.

racial hostility which African political parties and systems understandably project both into their domestic and foreign policies.[16]

Postcolonial domestic policies of the countries of the Third World frequently reflect efforts to overcome the racist tutelage to which they had been long subjected.

A crucial aspect of African nationalism is the aspiration to black freedom for the remainder of the continent. Still held down by all-white regimes are South Africa, Portuguese Angola and Mozambique and, since 1965, Ian Smith's Rhodesia. In all these cases, preponderant black majorities are ruled by small white minorities, and the results in terms of the economic, social, and cultural inequality and bondage for the African are strikingly wide. (See Table 1.)

TABLE 1. South Africa[a]

	White (European)	Black (African)
Population (millions)	3	11
Per capita income (1959)	$1,819	$109
Average wage in mining (1962)	$3,587	$216
Ages subject to tax	21–60	18–65
Income exempt from tax	$ 840	None
Education expenditure per pupil (1962)	$ 182	$ 18
Infant mortality per 1000 births	27	200
Percentage of population (balance: Asian and mixed)	19	68
Percentage of land reserved	87	13
Persons in registered trade unions	340,000	None
Persons convicted of pass offenses (1962)	None	384,000

a *Report of the Special Committee on the Policies of Apartheid of the Government of the Republic of South Africa*, United Nations General Assembly, September 16, 1963; State of South Africa: *Economic, Financial and Statistical Yearbook for the Republic of South Africa*, Johannesburg, 1962.

Although the African states are generally still far too poor and weak, militarily and economically, to adopt a policy of liberation toward remaining white dominions the aspiration to freedom for their African brethren is an important rallying point—a common denominator—of African nationalism. It finds expression in the anticolonialist diplomacy of the African states in the United Nations, in the sympathy with the militant antiimperialism of China, Russia, and other communist states,

16 For some pioneering surveys of African attitudes toward non-Africans in Kenya, see Donald S. Rothchild's "Kenya's Minorities and the African Crisis over Citizenship," *Race*, Vol. IX, No. 4 (December 1968), pp. 421–437.

as well as a natural receptivity to aid and support from them. It also finds expression in periodic attempts—thus far more symbolic than substantively fruitful—to forge regional unity among the African states, so as to give them greater political, economic, and military leverage against the colonial powers.[17]

The existence and the threat of a foreign foe, sometimes within the body politic and sometimes without, have their particular forms in Africa. But they are characteristic aids in the development of integrative nationalism anywhere. The growth of the late Gamal Abdul Nasser's Arab socialism, with its focus on the alien presence and threat of Israel has had similar objectives—and to some extent, results also.[18] Analogously, the internal cohesion of Nasserism's archenemy, Israel, has been undoubtedly bolstered by the need of "all those within to unite against the real—or greater—danger without." In nineteenth-century Europe, the Germans provided unifying symbols for French nationalists, as indeed the fear of French revenge bolstered Bismarck's appeals for national unity in Germany.

The ideological devices of nationalism have not always proved successful or adequate, of course, either to the accomplishment of their immediate outward objectives (i.e., the subjugation of a particular enemy) or their derivative advantage of unifying political communities. The example of the Arab quest against Israel or the African quest against the remaining colonial powers are amply illustrative of both these problems.

The predominant vehicle of modern African nationalism has been an integrative one-party state. Given an underlying legacy of disunity carried over from colonial times, most African nationalists have felt that they could not "afford" pluralistic, multiparty systems of power. The tribal, ethnic, geographic, cultural, and economic divisions in these new states have been sharp and long standing. Many nationalists regard open, unbridled political competition as simply untenable. It would either plunge the state into chaos, civil war, and secession, and/or it would be used by foreigners—most likely former colonial masters trying to reestablish their

[17] See Zdenek Cervenka, *The Organization of African Unity and Its Charter* (New York: Praeger, 1969). See also Mamadou Dia, *The African Nations and World Solidarity* (New York: Praeger, 1961); Ali A. Mazrui, *Towards a Pax Africana: A Study of Ideology and Ambition* (Chicago: University of Chicago Press, 1967); and Ndabaningi Sithole, *African Nationalism* (London: Oxford University Press, 1968).

[18] On Arab nationalism, see Arnold Hottinger, *The Arabs* (London: Thames and Hudson, 1963), and Hans E. Tutsch, *Facets of Arab Nationalism* (Detroit: Wayne State University Press, 1965). Walter Laqueur, *Communism and Nationalism in the Middle East* (New York: Praeger, 1956); John Marlowe, *Arab Nationalism and British Imperialism* (London: Cresset Press, 1961). On Zionism see Ben Halpern, *The Idea of the Jewish State* (Cambridge: Harvard University Press, 1961).

influence. The tragic civil wars in the Congo, in Nigeria, have all been indicative of the new nations' potential for internal disruption.

The one-party systems are efforts to strengthen the control of nationalist leaders over their countries. They are also vehicles for social, cultural, political, and economic changes needed to create the very "nations" to which the ruling, nationalistically minded elites aspire.

A current example of this kind of party system is provided by Guinea's PDG under Sekou Toure's leadership. The PDG is a broadly based political movement with an ideology and structure fitted to its several missions.

Above all, it desires to maintain Guinea's national unity; it also seeks to promote social and economic development to raise living standards and increase national power both economically and politically. It also strives to further the liberation of all Africa from colonialism (South Africa and Portugal are seen as the prime examples of colonial rule still in existence) and neocolonialism, that is, the more subtle, covert economic-political influence of former colonial powers. The PDG acts as a mobilizer, propagandizer, and disciplinarian of the masses. It reaches into the grass roots seeking to infuse people with the political ideas of the leaders. It promotes new modes of identification, new forms of behavior, new loyalties and, above all, a willingness to forsake traditions, particularistic orientations in support of the goals of the whole nation as laid down by the leadership.

Although the parallel could be easily overdone, Guinea's PDG is in many respects analogous to the Soviet CPSU. The Party is based on rank-and-file election of officials and is formally ruled by a congress that meets every three years. The congress elects a Political Bureau and a Party chief, or secretary. The PDG is like the CPSU in that its leaders are also the de facto leaders of the state; it is different in that it is a more open party in terms of its membership. Thus, where in Russia CPSU membership is and has been traditionally selective and confined to an elite of persons accepted only after a lengthy probationary period, in Guinea the PDG is open to virtually everybody. On the other hand, the elections of the PDG, like those of the CPSU, tend to co-optation by the elite at the top. The role of the rank and file tends to be a generally passive one. Leaders submit proposals; followers hail them with enthusiasm. Democratic centralism prevails. The Guinean monoparty, though claiming to speak for all the people of the country is, in fact, organized very tightly, cohesively and hierarchically. Party leaders—like Politburo members in the USSR—oversee various fields of political, social, and cultural life of the state. They supervise the execution of specific economic objectives, social reforms, and political demonstrations as the case may be. The Party is regarded as supreme in the state over all other types of association. Doctrinally the PDG has adapted much of the ideology of Marxism-Leninism but with additions and modifications. Its Marxist-style anti-imperialism is fully as strong as its Soviet or Chinese counterparts. But the Party claims to be a movement of the whole people, not just of the proletarians or any one or two social classes. According to Toure, African society has been traditionally based on the family; and the village community. The concept of class conflict does not apply to Africa, although it has and does apply to European societies. The distinctive characteristic of *negritude*, the African personality, with its ingrained collectivism and communal solidarity, transcends class identification prevalent in other societies, Toure argues.

The Guinean PDG may thus be described as a depluralizer of the society that it claims to represent and rule. It represses and inhibits private, corporate and "factional" interests which—like trade unions or business firms—attempt to assert claims that conflict with PDG goals of national development. The Party has on occasion resorted to mass violence in order to secure its rule and it tolerates opposition or criticism —in its own ranks—only within relatively narrow bounds allowed by the leaders. The overriding importance of cohesion and solidarity are reflected in this statement by President Felix Houphouet-Boigny, leader of the Parti Democratique de la Cote d'Ivoire (PDCI) of the Ivory Coast:

"It was the colonialists who divided us, playing off one against the other. . . . Now we have no reason to be divided, so it is desirable that all of us should be members of the sole party, just like an African family . . . . We are not going to pay for an opposition just to please the Occident . . . ."[19]

And in Guinea, President Sekou Toure, leader of the Parti Democratique de Guinee (PDG) expressed it this way:

"We formally reject the principle of the class struggle less by philosophic conviction than by the desire to save at all costs African solidarity . . . . We seek the independence of our society; the prisoner does not consider the liberty he enjoys inside the walls of his jail but only his liberty in relation to the outside world. Socially we consider ourselves prisoners in relationship to the developed nations, and it is this liberation we seek. In such a perspective individual liberty loses a good deal of its savor and attractiveness."[20]

[19] Cited by Virginia Thompson, "The Ivory Coast," in Gwendolen Carter (ed.), *African One-Party States* (Ithaca: Cornell University Press, 1964), p. 275.
[20] Cited by L. Gray Cowan, "Guinea," Ibid., pp. 188, 189.

Undoubtedly the example of Kwame Nkrumah's Convention People's Party (CPP) in Ghana during the 1950's and early 1960's was even more "totalitarian." Organized groups outside the Party, such as the trade unions, the press, cultural and educational institutions, businesses, all possessed even less autonomy vis-à-vis the Party in Ghana than in Guinea. Police terror and intimidation of opposition were generally much more pronounced. On the other hand, the single-party regime of Tunisia, Habib Bourgiba's neo-Destour Party, is illustrative of a more pluralistic nationalist movement. In Tunisia, objectives of cohesion and unification have been brought about not by force and threats but primarily by the more familiar democratic processes of persuasion, negotiation, bargaining, and compromise.

The principal differences between Tunisia and prevailing Western systems have been the adjustment of conflicts within one party rather than *between* two or more parties, and the singular significance of Bourgiba's charismatic leadership in cementing the unity of his new nation through his own party organization. From Bourgiba to Nkrumah, African nationalism has run the gamut of relatively more open and closed one-party systems.

It is significant that even Ghana, which became independent in 1957, began its political existence with a modified application of the British, so-called Westminister model of parliamentary democracy. In these early days, Dr. Nkrumah proclaimed faith in the virtues of two-party democracy and even attempted to make the leader of the parliamentary opposition a paid public functionary, on the British model. But the stresses of tribal, ethnic, religious, and economic conflicts were compounded by a dearth of a democratic political culture among the people. The scale of violence after independence continued ominously high. Many moderate critics of Nkrumah conceded that his gradual curtailment of civil liberties and increasingly authoritarian "charismatic" methods of rule were initially, at least, grounded on a reasonable concern for the stability and cohesion of the new state.[21]

In terms of world outlook, the nationalists of the underdeveloped countries are committed to the general principle of the desirability and urgency of maintaining world peace. There they sharply diverge from the conservative-reactionary nationalists of Europe, who glorified war and regarded it as both inevitable and ennobling. On the other hand— like the communists also—the Afro-Asian nationalists are not pacificists.

21 See Donald S. Rothchild, "On the Application of the Westminister Model to Ghana," *The Centennial Review*, Vol. IV, No. 4 (Fall 1960), pp. 465–483. Compare David E. Apter, *The Gold Coast in Transition* (Princeton, N.J.: Princeton University Press, 1955), pp. 303–308.

They endorse and support so-called Wars of Liberation in which oppressed colonial peoples fight to free themselves from the yoke of their
colonial masters or reactionary local rulers. Examples of such conflicts are
provided by the 1954–1960 Algerian war of independence against France;
Kenya's Mau Mau; India's "liberation" of Goa; Indonesia's struggle
against Malaysia; the struggle of the several Arab states and guerilla
movements against Israeli "colonialists"; Nasser's war effort in Yemen;
and, indeed, to many Third World nationalists, the Viet Cong struggle
against the United States and the Thieu–Ky regime.

Even the most moderate Nationalists of the developing nations usually
accept an ideology of global neutralism. They regard the Cold War as a
conflict between the superpowers that is dangerous to world survival
and deplorable. They do not see it as a struggle between good and evil,
freedom and slavery, right and wrong. They see their duty, above all,
in preventing the spread of the Cold War and shunning involvement in
it. This attitude appears, in part, indicated by pragmatic considerations.
It enables the new states to accept substantial amounts of economic and
even military aid from both sides. It leaves open maximum possibilities
of trade and cultural exchange with both sides. It also has great advantages in terms of domestic public opinion. Nonalignment obviates the
need of foreign military bases, troops, and installations on one's own soil;
and these are often resented among peoples whose newly won sense of
national independence is easily bruised even by token appearances of
subservience to foreign domination.

Actually, the posture of "neutralism" has generally accorded more with
the Sino-Soviet position than the American. Since early in the Cold War,
the foreign policy of the Kremlin and communist states allied with it has
been *not* one of securing military alliances with noncommunist states;
instead, it has sought to detach them from the United States and from
various American alliances like NATO, SEATO, CENTO. It has aimed
at the more pragmatic objective of erosion rather than the more formidable one of conversion among enemies or potential enemies. Thus,
Soviet-sponsored and Soviet-backed peace campaigns have successively
emphasized banning all nuclear weapons, particularly when the USSR
and its allies did not yet possess them in the 1940's; the liquidation of all
military bases on foreign soil; and the dissolution of all military blocs
and alliances.

Denunciations of imperialism, militarism, and colonialism have always
been mixed by Moscow and its allies with pleas for peace, and the promotion of various peace-oriented activities. However self-serving such policies
might be, they always possessed considerable appeal to non-Western
nationalists, suspicious of nations identified with the old colonial masters,

and understandably anxious about the calamitous risks of nuclear war into which they might be drawn through alliances controlled by other powers.

Even in the Third World there have always been some, of course, who argued that it was in the interests of all peoples to resist communist encroachments; that anticommunist alliances would guarantee each nation the right to a truly indigeneous development. But, outside of Europe, this has rarely been a popular position. Anticommunism has been associated with colonialism, with white, rich nations; the financial and psychological attractions of neutralism all combined to render Cold War noninvolvement more appealing throughout the non-Western world.

We may also note here that "neutralism" should not be confused with "neutrality" because it has a very different connotation to its exponents. "Neutrality" is identified by them as aloofness and as a morally damnable indifference to the ills of the world. To most Asians and Africans, however, "neutralism" connotes vigorous involvement and concern on behalf of world peace, elimination of colonialism, racism, and other social and political ills afflicting the world. Although it means nonalignment with either East or West in the Cold War struggle, it also means an active role in promoting reconciliation and disarmament in the world community of states. The latter purpose may best be described as a very general one, and always subject to two qualifications that render its practical applications uncertain: (1) the struggle against all remaining vestiges of imperialism, which for many Asians and Africans is represented by the very existence of such states as the Union of South Africa, Israel, and the Portuguese possessions of Angola and Mozambique; (2) national self-interest and the consequent claim to the rights of self-defense, such as those exercised between India and Pakistan; UAR and Yemen; Indonesia and Malaysia, and recently also within a number of African states, particularly in Biafra and the Congo.[22]

Thus, in terms of foreign policy orientations, we can discern tendencies toward regional unity, an international or multilateral approach to world peace, and neutralism in the East-West struggle. Ideological internationalism is not always consistent with the actual practices of Asian and African states, but as an aspiration it is closer to the traditions of European liberalism and socialism than to those of European nationalism or fascism.

---

[22] See Laurence W. Martin (ed.), *Neutralism and Nonalignment: The New States in World Affairs* (New York: Praeger, 1962), and G. H. Jansen, *Nonalignment and the Afro-Asian States* (New York: Praeger, 1966). Peter H. Lyon, *Neutralism* (Leicester: University Press, 1963); Cyril E. Black et al., *Neutralization and World Politics* (Princeton N.J.: Princeton University Press, 1968).

Domestically, the ideological orientations are often (though not always) authoritarian and even more often conspicuously redistributive-egalitarian, and, in this sense, socialist. These ideologies are also generally developmental in a sense that links them both with traditional nationalism and with Marxian socialism. Thus, autarky or the achievement of national self-sufficiency, independence, or economic power are posited as goals of the states. In this respect, many of the developing nations exhibit aspirations no different from those of mercantilist kings in Renaissance Europe. They are also akin to the aspirations of Marxism-Leninism, however, in their mythology of industrial power. Drawing upon past experience, and frequently viewing technology and power as interchangeable terms, the ideologists of the Third World pursue industrialization as the inescapable path, not only to improved conditions of life for their people, but to independence itself. Many of them believe, with Lenin and Stalin, that only the technologically strong can survive in a world dominated by ruthless economic competition and exploitation of the weak by the strong. Countries with one- or two-crop economies, incapable of producing anything but raw materials, are unlikely to remain independent of their economically superior, versatile trading partners. Given similar assumptions about the economic development as prerequisite to political independence and about the nature and identity of modern imperialism, the nationalisms of the Third World have much in common with Marxism-Leninism.

In fact, as John H. Kautsky argues, "Communism" in all the underdeveloped countries is linked to and indistinguishable from local nationalisms in its three common, characteristic attitudes: (1) hatred of Western imperialism; (2) opposition to traditional, local, aristocratic feudal oligarchies as agents/collaborators of imperialism; and (3) the aspiration to transform their societies from backward-rural economic conditions to advanced, technological industrial ones.[23] These negative and positive aspirations, involving the expulsion of foreign imperialists and their allies as preconditions of intensive industrial development, are to be carried out by local intellectuals, who constitute themselves into a nationalist, development-oriented elite. And, with their disciplined dedication, they hope to bring deliverance to the masses—from want and suffering, from internal and external oppression. These intellectuals are ready to act on behalf of the people, trusting to their own superior understanding of the needs of society. If necessary, they may act in spite of or even against the preferences of the inert and ignorant masses. They accept the

23 See John H. Kautsky, loc. cit.

need for "guiding the people" rather than simply responding to their wishes and traditional preferences. The Rousseauist paradox of forcing men to be free abounds here.

We can thus demonstrate many links between the new ideologies of the Asians and Africans and the older democratic, socialist, and nationalist ideologies of Europe.

In analyzing the sources of support for these new belief-systems, we may also make the claim that many of the developing states are practically indistinguishable from those of the communist states. Is communism, as John H. Kautsky maintains, merely a form of nationalism in the developing societies?[24] On this point, it would be prudent to remember the coalitional, step-by-step character of communist ideology. There can be no doubt of many doctrinal similarities between propositions that are part of the Marxist-Leninist legacy, and the de facto orientations of many who consider themselves "merely" nationalists and local patriots. In a particular period of time, and with respect to specific issues of domestic and foreign policy, communists and noncommunists may be truly indistinguishable. They may see eye-to-eye on questions ranging from an immediate land reform to the expulsion of South Africa from the United Nations.

There may be communist activists, and even whole communist parties, which have become sincerely "nationalist" in the sense that the sum total of their beliefs and aspirations does not *exceed* the beliefs and aspirations of most other indigeneous movements. But for some of the communist leaders and activists this may not be the case.

A radical land reform may be seen as the first step to collectivization. The liquidation of foreign alliances may be but a necessary prelude to a successful communist insurrection. The destruction of reactionary elements at home may be a first step in the establishment of a one-party dictatorship and alliances with Russia or China. Certainly, Marxist-Leninist ideology does provide a basis for much more radical aspirations than those of *many* middle-class Asian or African nationalists. Whether such aspirations and the concepts associated with them, are believed in, or acted upon in country X, Y, or Z, is an empirical fact-finding problem.

Occasionally, some groups or leaders who do *not* call themselves com-

---

[24] See John H. Kautsky's essay on the "Future of Communism" in *Communism and the Politics of Development* (New York: Wiley, 1968), pp. 207–216. "In underdeveloped countries that are not under Communist party rule, Communist and non-Communist modernizing movements tend to converge in terms of policies, ideology and even organization" (p. 213). . . . Modernizing intellectuals will pursue certain policies growing out of their antitraditional and anticolonial attitudes regardless of whether they think of themselves and are thought of by others as Communists or not."

munists may adopt communist ideological positions as advocated by Peking or Moscow; others may evolve from orthodox communist labels in the precisely opposite direction. From the Chinese point of view, Algeria's Ben Bella, who does not call himself a communist, but a nationalist, is ideologically far "sounder" than Tito.

When Red China launched its attack in 1962 upon Indian-held positions in the Himalayas, many Indians found themselves suddenly divided from the pro-Peking Communist party by questions of national loyalty. Pro-Moscow communists condemned China's aggression.

In summary, we can say that while the nationalist ideologies of Asia, Africa and Latin America have some common orientations, they cannot be subsumed under any one ideological label. First, there are many important local variations on the same general themes. Second, there are many countries whose official policies and even prevalent popular attitudes are barely touched by some of the more common ideological currents. The regimes in countries like Afghanistan, Nepal, or Taiwan in Asia, Haiti or Argentina in Latin America, Ethiopia or Liberia in Africa, do not readily fit the pattern of official ideologies developed in the UAR, Syria, Iraq, Ghana, Kenya, India, or Indonesia. Thus, even if the appreciation of ideological common denominators helps us to simplify the diversity of the world around us, it does so only within modest geographic and functional limits.

CHAPTER **11**

Conclusion

Democracy emerged in Europe as the ideology of secular individualism. It became a means for translating the aspirations of a multitude of idiosyncratic individuals into public policy. It sought to reconcile pragmatic, self-seeking diversity of human wants with the common good: stability, order and efficient rule for a whole society. It sought to subordinate the state to individual needs; it focused attention on individual rights, on the accurate and complete representation of what people want, and on the means whereby they might effectively achieve consensus —this highest sanction of an individualistic creed.

Both socialism and nationalism, in their several varieties, historically developed partly as responses to the growing division or atomization of society, and partly in consequence of the increased politicization of the masses. Socialism has sought to reintegrate society essentially from the premise of material well-being, seeking to free the masses from exploitation, and substituting cooperation and equality for competition and domination of the poor by the rich. Nationalism has sought to reintegrate society in a spiritual-psychological way, providing new tenable symbols of unity and faith in place of old, discarded (and on longer tenable) ones. It sought to subordinate, rather than eliminate, social conflict, competition, and strife to the unifying "higher truths" of its creed. From the nineteenth century onward, all these ideologies have borrowed and adapted from one another.

Nevertheless democracy has been, above all, representational. Its chief concern has been with articulation and protection of the claims and

216

rights of individuals. Both socialism and nationalism may be regarded as integrative but socialism has been, above all, redistributive in its concerns; it usually has sought justice before unity; its revolution would precede community; nationalism generally regards unity as the foundation of all public good. Nationalism is integrative, first and foremost.

How does Nationalism fit into the five evaluative criteria of Chapter 1? First, we must realize that its ideology is, by definition, as well as in terms of concrete historical experience, the most varied of our three mainstreams.

1. Nationalism universalizes the particular. Insofar as it has a general view of man and society, it sees these as peculiarly conditioned by the heritage, the experiences, and the circumstances of the given core community. Although nationalists believe that men usually do and ought to identify with national groups, they see actual human behavior and its potential in terms of the nature of each core group. Just as there are different individual characters, there are different national characters, too. Each has its unique genius and distinctive qualities, strengths, and weaknesses. It is also true of all nationalisms, whether Spanish, German, or Indonesian, that one's own "national personality" is regarded as extremely valuable and important. Where nationalist ideologies differ is in the degree of their indifference or hostility toward those outside the core group. In the era between the French Revolution of 1789 and the revolts of 1848, nationalism was outwardly frequently benevolent. Its attitude was that each and every national personality deserved to be preserved, developed, and cultivated; that all could contribute to one another and coexist in harmony. The nationalism of much of Asia and Africa today is still to some extent permeated by such attitudes.

    On the other hand, conservative, reactionary and nazi-fascist types of nationalism view the world external to the core group with neither benevolence nor neutrality. Much of nationalism since the nineteenth century sees humanity in terms of a stark struggle for existence in which the strong devour the weak. The alternatives are simply kill or be killed. The very conception of a "nation" implies to them an organic, given urge for expansion, aggrandizement, and agression. Its view of human nature is tinged heavily with pessimism. Those outside the core group are seen as generally hostile and/or inferior. When the "nation" loses its instinct for self-preservation and expansion against these outside elements, it faces corrosion, slavery, and ultimately demise. It becomes an amorphous mass to be ingested by the organism of some stronger national entity. The concepts of human nature, human culture, or human values, apart from the civilizing agency of the "nation," are seen as meaningless and deceptive Freedom, and most social values, are identified here with the national core group, not with the individual.

2. The implicit premise of the democratic nationalist generally is that the core group should steadfastly cooperate with other national groups—toward world peace, toward greater exchange of cultural and scientific information, toward higher living standards by more international trade. His reactionary-fascist counterpart, may see the premise in terms of killing those outside the core group and promoting conquest for the achievement of material as well as spiritual objectives, its unique personality, eliminating the traits that are harmful and extraneous to it, saving and strengthening the rest.

One who combines nationalist with radically socialist values may also regard foreigners—particularly if they are capitalist—with suspicion, and prefer autarky, economic self-reliance, to generally unrestricted, free and easy contacts with members of the international community of states. Trading with anyone who would sell or buy at an advantageous price, may well be "beneath him." He is likely to think in terms of a priori economic planning for his country. He is probably suspicious of neocolonialism—that is, of attempts to perpetuate or even establish anew the dominance by some overseas power through essentially economic means. In this connection, he is more likely to be suspicious of nonsocialist regimes. Having differentiated the world into "we" and "everyone else," the nationalist of the radical Left subdivides "everyone else" into the more dangerous colonial imperialist category and the more benevolent, progressive, socialist kinds. Toward the former, identified with historic oppression, he may more readily countenance the use of war and violence than toward the latter. He may also be more receptive to contacts with the latter.

3. In terms of characteristic tools or controls, nationalism historically offers a wide mix of symbols and institutions. The common aspect among them is their integrative character; that is, they are generally designed and intended to promote the cohesion of the core group.

Characteristic among these are the single-party systems or movements of Africa and Asia but also, in modern times, monarchies and the armed forces. Whether the institution is King, Army, Movement or Party, the effort in each case is to focus authority. Nationalists want people to look foreward to the "things that unite us rather than dispersing about those (far less important ones) that divide us." The institutions are appropriately envalued for this role either by their long, indigeneous traditions, or some central concept of mission safeguarding the whole society, and indeed often by both.

Thus, the unifying power of the monarchy may be presented as rooted in the very foundations of national life. Its existence is said to transcend the ephemeral comings and goings of politicians, cliques, and individual interests. Its stability is equated with the stability of the nation. Similarly, the armed forces are portrayed as champions of national independence. Their particular histories represent, to the nationalists, long and heroic traditions of sacrifice, skill, and courage in behalf of the very survival of the nation. Their responsibilities for the security and integrity of the nation's life and frontiers are portrayed as vastly more important and demanding than the mundane and selfish concerns of, say, tradesmen or workers, whose horizons are occupied by "petty" concerns about prices, wages, and the like.

The symbols of flag and country, the national anthems, the observances of great patriotic achievements of the past, the belief in a "national" church, and very significantly the military trappings of national grandeur, are all instruments of promoting national consciousness, cohesion, and the subordination of "lesser" to "greater" causes.

This use of symbols in which the German nationalists, both Nazi and pre-Nazi, had reached such fantastic levels of cultivation and adulation is not only a means of legitimizing power and stabilizing the system but also becomes part of the ideology itself. Thus, we can at once appreciate the utilitarian political value to the German Kaiser or his generals of the people's reverence for the military. The Army was the pillar of the regime and it could do no wrong. But we must also appreciate the fact that the consciousness of such symbols often transcended calculated purpose among its proponents. It evoked emotions, loyalties, and quasi-reflex actions that could take precedence over all rational formulas and consciously conceived purposes.

4. Nationalism, of course, is not unique in the use of legitimizing symbols, nor is it alone in promoting core-group cohesion. Other ideologies also resort to the affective and utilitarian aids of symbols and they also show concern with problems of integrating particular communities.

We find that symbols frequently overlap for several political faiths.

Just as Jerusalem is a holy place for three different religious faiths—Christian, Jewish, and Moslem—so also certain events and institutions are revered in the ideologies of different movements. The French Revolution of 1789, for example, is regarded as a great and inspiring landmark of human progress by most liberal democrats and Marxian socialists as well. A measure of reverence for the *same* institutions and the same experiences of a particular core group are usually characteristic of at least several political competitors. Interestingly, for example, the attack of Pierre Poujade's quasi-fascists on the French Fourth Republic in the 1950's was coupled with a call for a reconvening of the People's Estates presumably on the model of the French Revolution. Because of the wide acceptance of certain events, institutions, and traditions—the American Revolution in the United States, parliamentary government in Great Britain, for example—nearly everyone avows himself in support of them. But, of course, emphases and degrees of enthusiasm differ. Different meanings and nuances are attached to the same words and images. For the nationalist of a particular locale, the range of available institutions, traditions, precedents and, ultimately, symbols has its limits. The same is true, of course, of his democratic and socialist competitors.

With respect to concepts, much borrowing and intermingling has characterized all the ideological mainstreams. Nationalism has both "learned" and "appropriated" from the experiences and the successes of democracy and socialism alike. Above all, it has appropriated a regard for the importance of the masses and the value of equality.

Equality in the service of the nation—though not necessarily legal, political, or economic equality—has become its watchword. The ideal that members of the core group are all equally soldiers in the service of their country, from the king on down, has proved admirably well-suited to gaining a popular following without sacrificing hierarchic social structures and individual or group privileges.

Among other adaptations of nationalism have been those that balance the democratic aspirations toward individual diversity and self-expression on the one hand, and the characteristic socialist aspirations to general economic well being and equality in society, on the other.

In countries whose traditions have been evolved under colonial rule, under the exploitation of the poor by the rich, and where the indigenous middle class has been small or minuscule, the balance of socialist adaptations has been preponderant. In Africa, Asia, and Latin America, the two mainstreams have generally merged. Even in the developed, industrialized nations, not exposed to the colonial experience, nationalism has often borrowed from the teachings of socialism, in its emphasis on the need for social justice, firmly administered by the state, as a prerequisite of true national unity and power. Hitler and Mussolini, with their attacks on bourgeois liberal laissez-faire, exemplified these approaches. The great majority of nationalist movements in the twentieth century could be described as either "statist" or "socialist" in their approaches to core-group integration. But there is room in theory, logic, and the circumstances of particular nation-states, past and present, where nationalists could rally substantial middle class elements on a platform of "lasting unity only through freedom and diversity."

5. This brings us to the final problem: the practical applications of the ideology of nationalism. Political practice of any sort, requires adaptations to concrete circumstances and often compromises. The values of an ideology require balance in order to make them viable, or in other words to make them operational.

    A sense of national identity, its worth and uniqueness, may bring men together to form a nationalist movement. It may inspire them to seek cohesion and consciousness of that identity within their own society and also every possible aggrandizement of the "nation." Nevertheless, all societies are, in fact, divided into very different, sometimes antagonistic subunits and interests, and all societies have needs—economic, cultural, and political—that require aid or collaboration with communities outside the core group.

    An attempt to impose unity or to maintain unity must be realistic in terms of these constraints. Nationalists who are unwilling to recognize cultural, ethnic, tribal, or economic diversity within their communities may paradoxically precipitate civil war or other forms of overt conflict by being too unrealistically and inflexibly dedicated to only one value. Similarly, nationalists who wish to preserve their independence from all foreign influence must somehow balance that concern with the needs for trade and technical assistance. Economic independence at the cost of mass starvation, malnutrition, and bankruptcy is rarely a feasible alternative. Thus, all nationalist movements are forced to seek a balance of values in their programs. At best, they emphasize some things more than others. Their ultimate success or failure depends as much on the beliefs and goals pursued as on the practical skills and good fortune of the pursuers.

1. The prevalent beliefs of liberal democracy about the nature of man-in-society are universalistic and hopeful. People are seen as basically

sociable and benevolently disposed toward one another. Their aspirations and needs are seen as generally the same the world over. Men are believed to be rational creatures, desirous of self-preservation for themselves and, other things being equal, for society at large. All are believed to possess an equal innate worth as human beings. All are believed entitled to, and indeed in need of, freedom to develop their distinctive personalities, characters, and abilities. The fulfillment of individual lives is seen as the prime objective of government, the ultimate justification of political power. Whenever people do not achieve freedom and individual fulfillment, the causes are seen as largely external. Bad government and socially induced ignorance are generally held responsible. Freedom, as well as the diffusion of learning and information, are among the most characteristic democratic prescriptions for curing social ills. All branches of democracy subscribe to an underlying faith in the common man, and in people generally. Given freedom to discover what is "good" and "true," people will somehow find it, apply it, and make the necessary changes in their social environments.

2. Democracy's blueprint for change is overwhelmingly consensual. Starting with the belief that human needs and qualities are basically alike and that men are rational, democracy places great store by discussion, persuasion, negotiation, and reasoned compromise. If people are free to exchange ideas and information with one another, their combined efforts at finding solutions are likely to advance the welfare of each person in society and of the collectivity as a whole.

   Thus the characteristic biases and emphases of democratic ideology revolve first around the rights of individuals composing the community. What constitutes man's true freedom? How should this freedom be safeguarded? What are its limits? How may public opinion be properly ascertained and invoked? Such questions are among the most characteristic concerns of democracy.

3. Its complementary feature is concern with the institutions and processes by which individual and group preferences are voiced and by which they may be translated into the outputs of policy. Freedom of the press, the great prestige and mystique attaching to the so-called "Fourth Estate," and to other means of communication are characteristic of democracy. So is a preoccupation with the rights, powers, and attributes of legislative assemblies, the mechanics of elections, the roles and powers of elective officials, representation and negotiation by interest groups, and a host of closely related questions. Voluntarism and consent are characteristic aspects of democratic

social controls, their mechanisms invariably resting on widespread representation, bargaining or negotiation, and elaborate safeguards for the rights of the participants in all these processes.

4. Since its heyday in the eighteenth century, the democratic conception of what constitutes the just rights of each citizen—that is, those which render him a fully free and equal member of his community—has evolved in its socioeconomic dimension. More people who identify themselves as "democrats," "liberals," or both, believe that some minimal standard of material and social conditions is necessary to individual freedom and genuine political equality than ever before.

This evolution of democratic ideology in the direction of a welfare state has opened a gap between the "modern liberals" whose preferences are not much different from those of moderate socialists and the more conservative, "old liberals" who cling to economic notions of eighteenth- or nineteenth-century laissez-faire.

5. But democracy with all its emphasis on representing popular opinion *and* protecting idiosyncratic individuals faces a continuous problem. First, it must reconcile these values *against* one another; second, it must reconcile any possible combination of them against the overarching issue of communal integration and effective government. Individual freedom and the preferences of the majority may, at any given point, be on a collision course in a particular society. Occasionally, the wishes of the majority and more often of lesser groups within the society, may even conflict with the maintenance of peace and order in the streets. Free dissemination of information may sometimes jeopardize national security or undermine diplomatic negotiations. The resolution of such issues is a constant practical problem for any system that aspires to be a "democracy." The emphasis of some values over others in proposed or attempted solutions, may well "tilt" the particular form of democracy in a new direction. An out-and-out majoritarianism, could render the doctrine (or the system as the case may be) into a form of populist, possibly neo-Nazi or Fascist, dictatorship. If the people demand an end to individual freedom, presumably they must have it and with it goes also the suicide of democracy, for no mechanisms are left by which the people could *consider* changing their minds. On the other hand, if someone maintains an all-out commitment to specific individual rights and privileges, he too, may wind up with an autocratic government that will insure them beyond majority challenge. To some, the resultant autocracy will be meritorious and enlightened. To others, it will seem arbitrary and pernicious.

Both in theory and practice, democracy with its predominant sensitivity to popular aspirations, group and individual, must constantly borrow and adapt the integrative elements of law, order, and authority that are particularly characteristic of authoritarian nationalism; in modern times it has also adapted from the substantively oriented, economic-egalitarianism of socialism, so as to render individual rights more meaningful and to make its whole system of "belief-and-behavior" more popularly acceptable.

1. The ideologues of socialism generally share two assumptions with their democratic counterparts. They believe in the essential goodness of human nature, in man's fundamental sociability; they also believe in the crucial significance of environment in shaping the human potential. On these points, like democrats in general, they are universalistic and optimistic. They subscribe to the idea of human perfectability on a global scale. But beyond these assumptions, socialists differ among themselves.

   The radical Marxian wing of the socialist movement shares great hopes for the future with the moderate Christian Socialists. But its assessment of the realities of today and its forecast of how those realities may be changed are very different. The militant Leninist or Maoist believes that the masses of people are being exploited and duped by their imperialist masters in a system of ruthless class oppression. As long as such regimes persist, the masses of people are far from being the rational, sociable creatures that an end of exploitation and oppression and a vast expansion of means and opportunities of a classless society would make of them. As dupes of their masters, the people may not be trusted by revolutionists. To be sure, they must be used and appealed to against their capitalist masters. But correct knowledge of doctrine and tactics is beyond the ken of most of them. It is the business of expert and dedicated revolutionaries. They have a special obligation to serve the masses' true interest, an interest that the masses only sometimes, and only very imperfectly, comprehend. The agents of social change, the revolutionaries, are thus necessarily an elite of the best, most class-conscious, most experienced, ardent, knowledgable, and skillful people.

2. Until Khrushchev's "revisionism" of the 1950's and 1960's, it was a basic tenet of all the communist parties of the world that ultimately only force, only violent revolution, could bring about the overthrow of imperialism and the successful triumph of socialism and communism. Since the 1960's the Soviet communists and their allies have

become more ambivalent, or generally somewhat more open-minded on this issue.[1] The Chinese, however, and their allies throughout Europe, Asia, Africa, and the Americas, continue the commitment to revolution as the only way to meaningful change.

More moderate socialist movements, often styled Social Democratic or Christian Labor, do not accept the somber view of class oppression that the Marxian Left has of the capitalist (or imperialist) present. Concomitantly, they reject revolutionary violence for changing the status quo. In fact, most of moderate socialism shares the political methodology of democracy. The socialists of Britain and Scandinavia are much more like American Democrats or even Republicans, than they are Leninists or Maoists. They believe in change by electoral means, through constitutional, consensual procedures. They believe in persuasion, negotiation, and bargaining. They share a regard for individual rights and respect for majority rule. They do not vilify the bourgeoisie and call for a special elite to save the workingman from its clutches.

Marxian socialism in its Soviet and Chinese versions espouses a marvelous utopia of freedom and abundance. Its cost, however, is a dictatorship of the Party intellectuals over the rest of a society. Moderate socialism is incremental. It believes that a good society is indeed one where men do not exploit one another and where wealth and well-being are shared and each member of society is cared for by all others. But they see their ideal already substantially realized in many present-day societies and, above all, they believe that by significant single steps further progress can be made toward it.

3. The characteristic means of social manipulation for the communists is a monopolistic party—monopolistic not in the sense that other parties may not be occasionally permitted co-existence with it, but

---

[1] See the most recent CPSU 1961 Program adopted at the Twenty-Second Party Congress in Moscow, October 1961: "Communists have never held that the road to revolution lies *necessarily* through wars *between* countries. . . . although both world wars, which were started by the imperialists, culminated in socialist revolutions, revolutions are quite feasible without war. . . . Today the conditions for this are more favorable than ever. . . . (But) where the exploiting classes resort to violence against the people, the possibility of a non-peaceful transition to socialism should be borne in mind Leninism maintains, and historical experience confirms, that the ruling classes do not yield power of their own free will." See Jan F. Triska (ed.), *Soviet Communism: Program and Rules* (San Francisco: Chandler, 1962), pp. 50 and 51, respectively. The 1961 program simultaneously pledges the USSR to respect the sovereignty and integrity of all states and proclaims as the Party's cardinal duty "to assist the people who have set out to win and strengthen their national independence, all peoples who are fighting for the complete abolition of the colonial system". See *Program of the CPSU* (New York: International Publishers, 1963), p. 57.

rather in the sense of subordination of all Party programs and activities to the communists. Virtually all organized groups in society are seen as transmission belts for the realization of Party objectives in typical formulations of communist ideology. This is the meaning that practically attaches to the recurrent phrase about the leadership of the proletariat and its vanguard.

Another salient characteristic is state control of the economy. Under the Party's leadership, it is designed to and has historically exceeded, even in the cases of relatively "liberal" communist regimes such as the Yugoslav or the Polish since 1956, all known peacetime cases of direct economic controls in liberal-democratic or predominantly nationalist regimes. It has connoted virtually complete state ownership of industrial and commercial enterprises, in a few cases stopping short only of small service shops and retail outfits. It has also meant either collectivization of land under state or cooperative auspices, or at the very least, as in Poland and Yugoslavia, significant direct controls over agriculture in the wake of expropriation of large and middlesize landholders.

It has also involved an official intolerance of class enemies—those identified with the former ruling classes. Both by doctrine and practice, Marxism-Leninism has refused to accede equal rights, access, or equal legal protection to all persons and all views regardless of their political biases. Some classes—the bourgeoisie, the nobility, those officially classified as their allies and spokesmen—have been cast in the roles of corporate outlaws. Even "good behavior," obedience to laws, or protestations of loyalty do not lift the ban on their right to organize or propagate their ideas. Terror and force are seen as justifiable and necessary weapons against the "enemies of the people." Only those within the legitimate orbit of the "working people" may be accorded lesser or greater rights, freedoms, and privileges by the Party. In substance, all communist regimes—even in the wake of de-Stalinization—still subscribe to an *overtly* political/ subjective concept of justice. In this respect, they are most like nationalist dictatorships of the Nazi-Fascist variety. There, too, the uses of secret police, torture, concentration camps, and execution squads fluctuated from crisis to crisis. Here, too, the resort to such methods is implicitly justified by an ideology that painted the enemy as too evil to be tolerated. Merely the identity of the enemies has constituted the principal difference.

Finally, the Marxist-Leninist ideology has consistently emphasized the role of propaganda and indoctrination—the psychological and cultural as well as physical mobilization of the masses. In this respect, too, it has had common ground with nationalist regimes seeking to appropriately integrate their societies through the mobilizational devices of propaganda and organization.

On the other hand, socialist regimes and movements of the moderate, democratic-gradualist, variety have eschewed all of these mechanisms. In addition to employing the standard devices and institutions of electoral-parliamentary politics, they have often supported cooperative associations in trade, industry, and agriculture; the extension of democratic political controls to industry and service trades through such means as factory worker councils, union representation on management boards, accountability of nationalized enterprises to legislative bodies, and cooperative, voluntary planning agencies combining employers, employees, consumers, and government officials. They have also resorted to indirect means for controlling and levelling economic power in society. Where communists have relied on expropriation in land and industry, and on government bureaucracy to run directly every branch of the economy, moderate socialists have used capitalist-like devices to bring about social and economic change: taxation, statutory regulation, monetary policies, persuasion, and legally safeguarded reasonable compensation to dispossessed private owners.

4. The outlook and policies of many moderate socialist parties have made them barely distinguishable from those of various nonsocialist democratic political groups.

Communist movements share some of democracy's rationalism and faith in the perfectability of man but they radically diverge in the means to the ultimate end of human equality and freedom.

In the realm of the here-and-now, communism has much in common with nationalist dictatorships both of the right-wing, reactionary kind and of the socialist, progressive variety. With the former, its affinity lies in methods of mass mobilization and techniques of repression. A ruling elite, a monopolistic political movement, terror and propaganda are all familiar aspects of reactionary nationalist and Nazi and Fascist dictatorships, too.

Communism's special dedication to the destruction of the economic and political influence of Western nations that once ruled Asia and Africa gives it a significant community of outlook with the radical left-wing nationalists of the so-called Third World. Another link is communism's blueprint for development, calling for the liquidation of the old "compromised" ruling classes, and for an intensive, essentially autarkic effort, under the leadership of local intellectuals for the achievement of industrial power through enormous social discipline of consumers and producers. The vision of economic technological power, even grandeur; the ultimate eradication of poverty through ruthless policies of capital investment and "soaking the rich"; independence of former colonial masters, economically as well as politically—all these are common vistas of nationalists and communists in the Third World. These are their ideological common denominators.

Since we must remember that people make idiosyncratic choices among various values, it is perfectly plausible for someone to change his allegiance from, say, conservative nationalism to Maoist communism rather than to, say, liberal democracy. One could object, of course, that communism would jeopardize the conservative's property far more drastically than democracy. On the other hand, the common denominator of communism's intolerance toward opposition, its uncompromising striving for an integrated community against all external and internal "foes", might appeal much more readily to, for example, a Nazi than the openness, the groping, and the perpetual uncertainty of a consensus-seeking democracy.[2]

5. The application of communist ideology to concrete social situations has been beset by certain characteristic problems and dilemmas. Among these have been the disparity between what the proletarians and members of other allegedly oppressed classes see as desirable and what the Party believes is "really good" for them. The distant goals of utopian plenty and freedom are not readily supported by people who, naturally enough, think in terms of adequate food, clothing, shelter, and other consumable amenities here and now.[3] Communist regimes have had to sacrifice economic efficiency to the pursuit of ideological goals, one of their recurring problems being the lack of incentive and excessive bureaucratic control of economic life—all resulting in low labor productivity, high real costs of production,

---

[2] See Zevedei Barbu, *Democracy and Dictatorship* (London: Routledge and Kegan Paul, 1956), pp. 256–266, on how personality needs may establish an "interchangeability" for some people between political memberships in politically polarized but ruthlessly authoritarian movements.

[3] That the spontaneously voiced wishes of the workers and the leadership of the Party have been at variance is the theme of virtually all past "unrest" in Eastern Europe. See, e.g., Paul E. Zinner, *Revolution in Hungary* (New York: Columbia University Press, 1962), pp. 201, 262, 293; this was also true in Poland in 1956 and in 1970. See, e.g., M. K. Dziewanowski, *The Communist Party of Poland* (Cambridge: Harvard University Press, 1959), pp. 270, 283–285, and only somewhat less in 1968—before the Soviet invasion—in Czechoslovakia; see Harry Schwartz, *Prague's 200 Days* (New York: Praeger 1969), pp. 89–90.

and undersupply of consumer goods, foodstuffs, and services to society.[4] Communist attempts to integrate society on the basis of class solidarity have frequently proved unrealistic and brittle in the face of stronger national solidarities and links. Since Lenin's disappointments of World War I "proletarian internationalism" has rarely matched the force of old-fashioned class-cutting national loyalties in the world arena as well as domestic politics.

Marxism-Leninism has been congruent with the anti-capitalist, anti-Western nationalism of the Third World. It has been remarkably incongruent with the several anti-Russian nationalisms of Eastern Europe and the USSR itself.[5] Another problem has been failure to develop stable means of ensuring peaceful succession in the mechanisms of Party power. Thus far, communist regimes appear generally unable to assure the transition from one leadership to another without resort to force, duress, and violently upsetting conditions throughout the "system."[6]

There are various dangerously contradictory elements in the Marxist-Leninist doctrine which—to borrow its own language—could convert the Party into its own gravedigger. Among such aspects are the Party's dedication to the intellectual-cultural uplift of the masses: emphasis on literacy, education, vocational training, diffusion of popular theatre, library, museum facilities and the like. The consequences of such intellectual mobilization are not only to produce technically competent scientific cadres, which the communists want,

[4] On the historic inefficiency and waste of Soviet planning, see Harry Schwartz, *Russia's Soviet Economy*, 2nd ed. (Englewood Cliffs, N.J.: Prentice-Hall, 1954), pp. 179–180; Alec Nove, *Economic Rationality and Soviet Politics* (New York: Praeger, 1964) pp. 83–98, and his earlier *The Soviet Economy* (New York: Praeger, 1961), pp. 200–201.

[5] On the strength of anti-Russian nationalisms in the USSR, see Richard Pipes, *The Formation of the Soviet Union* (Cambridge: Harvard University Press, 1954); J. F. Brown, *The New Eastern Europe* (New York: Praeger, 1966); Andrei Amalrik, *Will the Soviet Union Survive Until 1984?* (New York: Harper and Row, 1970); see also John A. Armstrong, *Ukrainian Nationalism, 1939–1945* (New York: Columbia University Press, 1955).

[6] Succession has been one of the major problems of the Soviet system. As Zbigniew Brzezinski and Samuel P. Huntington observe: "(In the United States) the state is always led by a legitimate leader accepted as such by the political system and society as a whole. (In the USSR) legitimacy follows the seizure and consolidation of power by a leader. Until he emerges from the succession struggle, legitimacy rests vaguely in the ruling Communist Party, precluding the claim to power of anyone outside it but not preventing bitter and destructive conflict within." *Political Power: USA/USSR* (New York: Viking Press, 1966), p. 412. See also Myron Rush, *Political Succession in the USSR* (New York: Columbia University Press, 1965).

but also to stimulate inquiry and criticism, which are difficult for them to contain.[7]

As with nationalism, the communist philosophy of integrating the community against corrosive influences from within and without frequently leads to a drastic inflexibility and unresponsiveness at home. The regime does not accommodate a sufficient number of demands and grievances from the surrounding community to give it the necessary popular support both for the execution of specific policies, and for legitimizing its power in a more general sense. It separates itself from the mass of the people and is apt to be regarded as a hostile oppressor.[8]

Its emphasis on maintaining an equivalent cohesion against "enemies without" frequently leads to economic and cultural deprivations at home. Militant adherence to communist ideology has frequently predisposed its practitioners to shun or curtail contacts with the world outside their own politically pure domain. Desirable and even necessary trade relationships have been disrupted causing all sorts of hardships to consumers and producers dependent upon foreign markets and sources of supplies, such as was the case, classically, with Eastern Europe during the height of Stalinist domination of that area in the 1940's and early 1950's. The enforced autarky promoted general discontent.

For socialists of democratic persuasion, the dilemmas of governing have been not much different from those of other exponents of liberal democracy. One persistent problem, however, is linked to the working-class identification and background of many of the socialist parties. Historically, the socialists in Britain, France and Germany have always faced the challenge of "authenticity" from among the more radical, militant elements. They have had to defend themselves against charges of being "no different from all the bourgeois parties." At the same time, the parties' efforts to win electoral support from

[7] On communist intellectuals and their difficulties with the Party, see Harold Swayze, *Political Control of Literature in the USSR, 1946–1959* (Cambridge, Mass.: Harvard University Press, 1962); Max Eastman, *Artists in Uniform: A Study of Literature and Bureaucratism* (London: Allen and Unwin, 1934); Stuart R. Tompkins, *The Russian Intelligentsia: Makers of the Revolutionary State* (Norman, Okla.; University of Oklahoma Press, 1957); Richard Pipes (ed.), *The Russian Intelligentsia* (New York: Columbia University Press, 1961).

[8] See Khrushchev's account of how Stalin insulated himself from the reality of Russian life ("he was not aware of the real state of affairs in the provinces . . . never travelled anywhere, did not meet city and Kolkhoz workers . . ."). *The Anatomy of Terror, Krushchev's Revelations About Stalin's Regime*, introd. by N. Weyl (Washington, D.C.,: Public Affairs Press, 1956), p. 65.

elements outside the working class have often met with distrust accorded dangerous radicals.

All three ideologies had their beginings in Europe as a result of the processes of social mobilization. The ideology of liberal democracy was *not* first in the sense that its constituent ideals reach farther back into the past than those of socialism or nationalism. But it became a socially more significant idea, commanding a larger, more coherent and articulate body of supporters earlier in history than the others. The representational-individualistic qualities of liberal democracy made it well-suited to the requirements of an age in which man was becoming increasingly emancipated from communal, religious, and secular links and traditions.

The ideologies of socialism and nationalism arose largely in response *both* to the disruptiveness of the social, economic, and cultural processes ("mobilization") which gave rise to democracy, *and* also to the "perniciously atomizing" emphases of democratic-liberal ideology itself.

To the extent that socialism and nationalism may be regarded as reintegrative because of their communalism, it is also clear that in each case reintegration has had its price. In the case of socialism, it has frequently meant drastic conflict first—to purify society of its "parasitic elements." In the case of nationalism, it has often denoted the extermination or removal of hostile aliens with whose presence or influence reintegration allegedly would not be possible.

Beyond these differences of origin and outlook, we find that all ideologies have much in common. Ultimately, this is because the process of politics, the nature of human conflicts and aspirations have many common denominators.

Each of these orientations can have its "conservative" and "liberal" tendencies, depending primarily on the rigidity with which democrats, nationalists, or socialists adhere to particular institutional forms of their creed.

Another much-used term of political science, "totalitarianism," may be regarded, strictly speaking, as a form of nationalist or socialist communalism carried to its extreme. It is the very antithesis of liberal democracy although, like socialism and nationalism, it may develop out of liberal democratic politics.

Every ideological program or platform must somehow address itself to a whole range of human problems—even if somewhat differently or with different emphases—if it is to have any substantial impact or appeal. Democrats cannot rest content with representational devices and the protection of individual rights; nationalists cannot wholly disregard the management of conflicting claims emanating from their core community; communists can subordinate the actual needs of people living now to the Party's blueprint of the future only up to a point. Disintegration, revolt, and failure lurk beyond each possible imbalance.

This brings us to our final consideration. The worth of a political ideology may be appreciated either in a normative or an empirical sense.

Viewed as a set of normative propositions about what people *ought* to do or believe, the ideals of any given political faith may be regarded as timeless and as "metarational." They constitute the idiosyncratic, absolute "givens" of an ideology. And each person may believe that human equality or freedom of speech, for example, are principles equally valid and sacred for all times. Everyone is entitled to a preference here. Perhaps "blue" is as good as "red" and "red" is as good as "black."

We can also look at ideologies in terms of their empirical consequences. This would involve making tests and comparisons. Given a set of preferences embodied in ideology X, what evidence have we on the implementation of these ideals by any and all systems that profess allegiance to it? How do these systems compare with those professing allegiance to other schemes of values?

Without entering upon all of the great difficulties in making such comparisons, we should note that "failure" and "success," either in terms of what the ideology itself seeks, or in terms of criteria that we ourselves may pose for it, is contingent on many variables of each time and place.

A program of seemingly absurd propositions may be sometimes widely accepted; a more seemingly reasonable one may be rejected. Without recourse to the knowledge of specific places and times, we cannot tell whether democracy "will fail because it is too permissive and will yield to anarchy" or "fascism will falter because it is too repressive." The resolution of such problems depends, among other factors, on the political culture of the people upon whom the whole system rests, the nature of the crises confronting it, the effectiveness of control exercised by the proponents of the ideology, their skills and adaptability, and the nature of the alternatives open to all the participants in the system.[9]

---

[9] If ideology is seen as a "recipe" for dealing with society, and the world at large, what factors determine the success or failures of such recipes? Among recent books that offer clues are Chalmers Johnson, *Revolutionary Change* (Boston: Little, Brown, 1966); Gabriel A. Almond and Sidney Verba, *The Civic Culture* (Princeton, N.J.: Princeton University Press, 1963); Gabriel A. Almond and G. Bingham Powell *Comparative Politics: A Developmental Approach* (Boston: Little, Brown, 1966); Lucian Pye, *Aspects of Political Development* (Boston: Little, Brown, 1966).

Index

Adams, John C., 177n
Adenauer, Konrad, 174
Adoratski, V. V., 67n
Adorno, T. W., 1n
Afghanistan, 215
Africa, 108, 115, 129, 139-141, 143, 163, 197-200, 209, 215, 217-218, 220, 225
Agard, Walter R., 22n
Age of Reason, 20, 32
Albania, 151, 153, 162, 170
Alexandria, 131
Algeria, 140, 211, 215
Allen, J. W., 39n
Almond, Gabriel A., 22n, 198n, 232n
Alperovitz, Gar, 192n
Amalrik, Andrei, 229n
America, 93, 144, 176
Anarchism, 64-66, 79-80, 82-83
Anderson, Ronald E., 10n
Angola, 206, 212
Antisemitism, 7, 94-95, 99-102

Appleman, Philip, 186n
Apter, David E., 86n, 177n, 210n
Arabs, 16
Argentina, 108, 215
Armstrong, John A., 229n
Asia, 108, 115, 129, 136, 140-143, 147, 156, 163, 182, 190, 197-200, 215, 217-218, 220, 225
Athens, 22
Attlee, Clement, 174
Australia, 170-171
Austria, 14, 84, 86, 130, 151, 153, 170
Austro-Hungary, 77, 119, 130
Avignon, 25
Avineri, Shlomo, 67n

Babeuf, Francois, (Gracchus), 66
Babylon, 71
Bachrach, Peter, 186n, 189n
Bakunin, Mikhail, 64-65n, 68, 83
Balboa, Vasco Nuñez de, 23, 25

Balfour, Michael L., 177n
Balkans, 100, 131, 135
Bao Dai, 192
Barbu, Zevedei, 228
Barile, Paolo, 177n
Barker, Ernest, 41n
Barry, Eldon, 181n
Bastille, 53
Bate, W. J., 92n
Bauer, Raymond A., 12n
Beard, Charles, 33n, 179n
Becker, Carl, 41n
Beer, Max, 47n
Beethoven, Ludwig van, 100
Belgium, 55, 84, 130, 139, 152, 170-171
Bell, Daniel, 2n, 177n
Bella, Ben, 215
Bennett, H. S., 22n-23n
Benson, Mary, 108n
Bentham, Jeremy, 49, 191
Bere, L. H., 31n
Beria, Lavrenti, 124, 145-146
Berkman, Alexander, 64n
Berle, A. A., Jr., 180
Berlin, Isaiah, 28n, 67n
Bernstein, Eduard, 61n, 175-176n
Bevin, Ernest, 174
Beza, T., 40
Biafra, 212
Bismarck, Otto von, 131, 207
Black, Cyril E., 212n
Blanqui, Louis, 66
Bloch, Marc, 22n
Blum, Leon, 127, 174
Bodin, Jean, 25n, 27, 40n
Bolivia, 142
Bondurant, A., 202n
Borkenau, Franz, 127n
Boulanger, General, 94
Bourgeoisie, see Middle class
Bourgiba, Habib, 210
Brailsford, H. N., 30
Brandt, Willy, 193
Braunthal, Julius, 127n
Brazil, 25, 142
Brecher, Michael, 203n
Brezhnev, Leonid, 3, 10, 150, 156, 163, 170
Brezhnev Doctrine, 156, 170n
Brisbane, Albert, 63n
Britain, 3, 12-13, 24, 29-31, 41-43, 49,
51-55, 57-58, 61-62, 64, 77, 81, 84,
102, 106, 115, 118, 127, 130-132,
137, 139-140, 144, 170-172, 174,
176, 178-179, 202, 220, 225, 230
British Commonwealth, 172
Brockway, Fenner, 199n
Brogan, D. W., 31n
Bromke, Adam, 155n, 156n
Brown, J. F., 229n
Brzezinski, Zbigniew, 229n
Bukharin, Nikolai, 123, 125
Bulganin, Nikolai, 147, 149
Bulgaria, 131, 151, 153-154, 170
Bullock, Alan, 12n, 174n
Burckhardt, Jacob, 143n
Burke, Edmund, 5n, 91-93
Burks, R. V., 164n
Burma, 140, 142, 169
Burns, Emile, 67n
Butler, R. A., 176n

Cabot, John, 25
Cabot, Sebastian, 25
Cabral, Pedro A., 25
Calvin, Jean, 38
Calvocoressi, Peter, 108n
Cambodia, 169
Campanella, Tomasso, 61
Canada, 138, 171
Capitalism, as interpreted by, Lenin, 114-119
  Marx, 73-76
  Smith, Adam, 47
Carnot, Lazar, 86
Carr, E. H., 59n, 65n
Carter, Gwendolen, 209n
Cartier, Jacques, 25
Cartwright, Edmund, 29
Cassirer, Ernst, 28n
Castro, Fidel, 168-169
Castroism, 168-169
Ceausescu, N., 166
Cefkin, J. Leo, 159n, 204n
Cervenka, Zdenek, 207n
Ceylon, 142, 198
Chamberlain, Neville, 14, 15n
Chandler, A. R., 100n
Chapman, Colin, 165n
Chapman, Guy, 95n
Charles I, 29, 46, 53

Charles II, 30
Charles V, 24
Chiang Kai-Shek, 157, 160, 161
China (Communist), 15-17, 81, 132, 139,
    141-144, 147-148, 153, 157-163, 169-
    170, 182, 204, 206, 214-215
Chou En-Lai, 197
Churchill, Winston, 131-135, 140-141, 174
Ciechanowski, Jan, 136n
Clark, Colin, 186n
Clayton, James E., 179n
Clemenceau, Georges, 94
Clough, Shephard B., 98n, 179n
Cogley, John, 23n
Cold War, 15-16, 129, 133-139, 144, 183-
    184
Cole, G. D. H., 49n, 67n, 91n
Coleman, James S., 141n, 198n
Colin, Legum, 108n
Colin, Margaret, 108n
Collectivization in USSR, 124
Colombia, 142
Colonialism, after World War I, 141
    after World War II, 139-143
Columbus, Christopher, 23-24
Commercial Revolution, 61
Commons, John R., 54n, 178n
Communism, 15-18, 66-84, 109-128,
    144-171, 224-229
  higher phase, 76-77, 119-120
  lower phase, 120-121
  resource allocations, 151-153, 170-171,
    227-229
Condorcet, Marquis de, 28n
Congo, 208, 212
Conquest, Robert, 125n
Conservatism, 3-4, 8, 10n, 87-88, 231
Contract Theories of Government, 40, 41-
    42, 46-47
Convergence of socialist and liberal-demo-
    cratic opinion, 172-176
Copernicus, Nicholas, 27
Cortez, H., 25
Council of Mutual Economic Assistance
    (COMECON), 170
Cowan, L. Gray, 209n
Cripps, Sir Stafford, 140
Crocker, Lester G., 51n
Crompton, Samuel, 29
Cromwell, Oliver, 29

Crook, John, 22n
Crusades, 23, 24, 33
Cuba, 17, 142, 150, 168, 170
Curtis, Michael, 93n
Cushman, Robert E., 60n
Czechoslovakia, 14, 130, 137, 151-153,
    156, 159, 165-166, 168, 170, 182-
    183, 228n

Dahm, Bernhard, 203n
Dallin, David J., 125n
Das, M. N., 203n
Dasent, Arthur I., 53n
Dawson, Richard E., 11n
Declaration of Independence, 59
DeGaulle, Charles, 130
Democracy, 8-10, 20-33, 37-60, 173-188,
    216-217, 221-224
  characteristic ideas, 43-51, 173-175
  institutions and symbols, 51-56, 177-179
  origins, 20-32, 37-41
  problems and criticisms, 32, 44, 56-60
  sources of support, 29-31, 32-33, 42-43
  summary, 216-217, 221-224
  and welfare state, 174-175, 179-182
Democratic man, 45-46
Democrats, 8-10
Denmark, 84, 130, 170, 171
Dennis Case, 60
DeSola Pool, Ithiel, 164n
De-Stalinization, 145-149
Deutsch, Karl W., 21, 86n
Deutscher, Isaac, 122n
Dewey, Thomas, 7, 174
DeWitt, Nicholas, 125n
Dia, Mamadou, 207n
Dicey, A. V., 43n
Diderot, Denis, 28, 50-51n
Dienbienphu, 140
Discoveries, 23, 24-25
Divine Right, 29; see also Royal Absolution
Djilas, Milovan, 154n
Dmowski, Roman, 93
Dogmatism, in Communist Schism, 157-163
Dolbeare, Kenneth M., 189n
Dommanget, M., 66n
Doob, Leonard W., 86n
Draper, Theodore, 169n
Dreyfus, Captain Alfred, 94-95
Dubcek, Alexander, 166

Dugdale, E. T. S., 14n, 97n
Dulles, John Foster, 16
Dumbarton Oaks, 135
Duplessis-Mornay, 40
Dziewanowski, M. K., 228n

Eade, Charles, 134n
Eastern Europe, 101, 137-138, 149-151,
    153-155, 164, 165, 170, 180, 200,
    228n-230
East Germany, 154-155, 157, 170, 183
Eastman, Max, 230n
Easton, David, 2, 21
Ebenstein, William, 41n, 83m, 173
Eden, Anthony, 134
Egalitarianism, and democracy, 37-38, 44-
    45, 47-48, 186-188
  and nationalism, 86, 94-95, 97, 101, 103-
    104, 108
  and socialism, 63, 65-66, 186-187
Egypt, 71
Eichmann, Adolf, 102
Eisenhower, Dwight David, 10n, 138
Elliot, W. Y., 39n, 47n
El Salvador, 142
Emerson, Rupert, 197n
End of Ideology Phenomenon, 176-181
Engels, Frederick, 10, 68, 74n, 76, 77, 84,
    110, 115, 120, 156
Ergang, Robert, 25, 29n
Erhard, Ludwig, 174
Ethiopia, 139, 215
Europe, 7, 20, 21, 25, 26, 28, 35, 39, 43,
    52, 62, 72, 77, 83, 86, 87, 89, 90, 93,
    101, 106, 108, 110, 114, 118, 127,
    129, 130, 131, 132, 133, 136, 138,
    139, 142, 143, 144, 156, 167, 170,
    172, 173, 174, 176, 177, 179, 181,
    182, 183, 190, 192, 193, 197, 199,
    200, 201, 210, 212, 213, 216, 225,
    231
Evans, Trevor, 174n

Fabius, 79
Fabreques, Jean de, 93n
Far East, 170
Fascism and Nazism, 95-108
  and imperialism, 97-98, 101-102
  and leadership, 97, 103-104
  sources of support, 104-107

Feiling, Keith, 15
Fenno, Richard F., Jr., 56n
Ferdinand and Isabella, 24
Feudalism, 24
Feuer, Lewis S., 70n, 74n
Feurbach, Ludwig, 69
Field, John Osgood, 10n
Final Solution, 101-102
Finer, Herman, 96n
Finland, 171
Fisher, Louis, 202n
Fischer-Galati, Stephen A., 167n
Fleming, Denna F., 192n
Florence, 72
Follett, Mary P., 53n
Fourier, Charles, 63-64, 67
France, 6, 12, 13, 14, 24, 31, 35, 39, 51,
    52, 53, 55, 57, 62, 64, 65n, 74, 77,
    84, 90, 93, 94, 95, 100, 102, 115,
    118, 127, 130, 138, 139, 167, 170,
    171, 172, 174, 178, 179, 192, 211,
    230
Franco, Francisco, 127
Franklin, Julia, 63n
Franklin, Julian H., 40n
Freedom, and democracy, 41-43, 46-47,
    174-175, 221-224
  and nationalism, 93-94, 209, 220-221
  and socialism, 76-78, 119-120, 188
Friedland, William H., 199n
Friedman, Robert, 67n
Friedrich, Carl J., 92n
Frobisher, Chancellor, 25
Fuller, Basil, 108n
Fussell, G. E., 22n

Gaitskell, Hugh, 176n
Galbraith, John Kenneth, 180
Galileo, 27
Galloway, George B., 56n
Gandhi, Mahatma, 200-202
Gangulee, N., 93n
Garibaldi, Giuseppe, 93
Garrison, William L., 93n
Gay, Peter, 50n, 176
Geertz, Clifford, 177n, 198n
General Will, 48-49
Gentile, Giovanni, 96
Germany, 7, 10, 12-14, 40, 55, 57, 61, 84,
    93-95, 101, 105, 107, 115, 119, 122,

126, 130-131, 136, 138, 151, 165,
166, 167, 171, 172, 174, 177, 178,
192, 199, 207, 230
Gettysburg Address, 53
Getzler, Israel, 111n
Ghana, 210, 215
Gheorzhiu-Dej, 166
Gierek, Edward, 156
Gierke, Otto, 41n
Gignoux, Claude J., 90n
Goa, 211
Godwin, William, 64, 68
Goebbels, Joseph, 97n
Goering, Hermann, 102
Goldsmith, M. M., 25n
Goldwater, Barry, 4, 10n
Gomulka, Wladyslaw, 153, 155, 156, 166
Goodman, Elliot R., 127n
Gordon, David C., 205n
Gorgolini, Pietro, 97
Graham, Malbone W., 89n
Grant, Lee Michael, 22n
Gray, Alexander, 63n
Greece, 20, 71, 131, 138, 139, 153
Green, Thomas Hill, 47, 174, 175
Gregor, A. James, 96n
Griffith, William E., 148n, 168n
Groth, Alexander J., 7n, 94n, 107n, 135n,
146n, 165n, 170n
Grotius, Hugo, 27
Guatemala, 142
Guevara, Che, 168-169, 196
Guinea, 208-210
Gutenberg, Johann, 27

Haines, Charles G., 41n
Haiti, 142, 215
Halasz, Nicholas, 95n
Halpern, Ben, 207n
Hamilton, Richard F., 185n
Hammond, Barbara, 33n, 62n
Hammond, J. L., 33n, 62n
Hare, Thomas, 178n
Hargreaves, James, 29
Harrison, John F. C., 64n
Harrison, Martin, 6n
Hartman, Robert S., 69
Hausner, Gideon, 102n
Hayden, Thomas, 184n, 189n
Hayek, Frederick A., 180

Hayes, Carlton J. H., 85
Hazard, John N., 112n
Hearst, William Randolph, Jr., 16n
Heckscher, Eli F., 179n
Hegel, Georg Wilhelm Friedrich, 69, 71, 91,
92, 96, 175
Hermens, F. A., 54n, 178n
Hibben, John G., 28n
Higgs, Henry, 47n
Hilberg, Raul, 102n
Hilferding, Rudolf, 114n
Himmler, Heinrich, 102, 193
Hindenburg, Paul von, 178
Hiroshima, 182, 185
Hiscocks, Richard, 155n
Hitler, Adolf, 10, 12, 13-15, 93, 94n, 95-
102, 104-108, 126-128, 130, 131,
133, 178, 193, 194, 201, 204, 221
Hobbes, Thomas, 25n, 27, 43n, 46
Hobson, J. A., 114n
Ho Chi Minh, 140, 197
Hoffman, Paul J., 8n
Holborn, Hajo, 130
Holland, 139
Holsti, K. J., 15n
Hook, Sidney, 167
Honduras, 142
Horowitz, Irving L., 64n
Hotman, 40
Hottinger, Arnold, 207n
Houphouet-Boigny, Felix, 209
House of Commons, 52-53
Hoxha, Enver, 153
Hughes, H. Stuart, 184n
Hungary, 122, 131, 137, 150, 151, 153,
155, 164, 165, 166, 170, 183
Huntington, Samuel P., 229n
Hus, John, 38
Hyman, Herbert H., 11n

Iceland, 171
Ideology, applications, 5-18
definitions, 1-4
evaluation of, 232
genesis, 19-36
overlapping, 231-232
India, 25, 139-142, 159, 200-201, 203-204,
211-212, 215
Individualism, and democracy, 42-43
and nationalism, 85, 91-92, 96

and socialism, 64-66, 71, 76-77, 188
Indochina, 16, 139, 140, 182, 184, 192
Indonesia, 139, 141, 142, 159, 169, 198,
    211, 212, 215
Industrial Revolution, 29, 33, 61
Inkeles, Alex, 12n
Iraq, 215
Ireland, 142
Irvine, Helen D., 22n
Israel, 16, 207, 211, 212; see also Palestine
Italy, 10, 13, 55, 65n, 66, 77, 84, 93, 97,
    98, 100, 107, 115, 130, 131, 138,
    139, 153, 167, 170, 172, 177, 178,
    199
Ivory Coast, 209

Jackson, Barbara (Ward), 86n
Jackson, John H., 67n
Jamaica, 198
James I, 29, 102
James II, 30
Jansen, G. H., 212n
Japan, 130, 131, 132, 169
Jasny, Naum, 145N
Jefferson, Thomas, 41, 44, 84
Jennings, Sir W. Ivor, 43n, 53n
Jerusalem, 220
Jews and Nazi race theories, 99-103; see also
    Antisemitism; Zionism
John I, 52
Johnson, Chalmers, 22n, 232n
Johnson, Douglas W., 95n
Johnson, Lyndon B., 10n
Joll, James, 64n
Judeo-Christian tradition, 37-38
Judiciary, 59-60

Kadar, Janos, 166
Kaganovich, Lazar, 146, 149
Kamenev, Lev, B., 125
Kao, Ky, 192
Kase, Francis J., 151n
Kautsky, John H., 161n, 170n, 199n, 213n,
    214n
Kautsky, Karl, 175, 176n
Kay, John, 29
Kecskemeti, Paul, 155n
Kedoure, Elie, 85
Kelf-Cohn, Reuben, 181n
Kenafick, K. J., 65n

Kendall, Willmore, 181
Kennedy, John F., 150
Kenya, 205, 206n, 211, 215
Kepler, Johannes, 27
Khrushchev, N. S., 10, 65n, 146, 147-150,
    156-159, 165, 167, 224, 230n
Kirk, Russell, 5n, 181n
Knapp, Wilfrid, 86
Knox, John, 38
Koestler, Arthur, 125n
Kohn, Hans, 85, 87
Kolko, Gabriel, 181n
Korsch, Karl, 67n
Kosciuszko, Tadeusz, 93
Kosminsky, E. A., 22n
Kostov, Traicho, 153
Kosygin, Aleksei, 150, 160
Kropotkin, Prince Peter, 64, 68
Kulski, W. W., 144n

Labedz, Leopold, 156n
Lafayette, Count de, 93
Laissez-faire, 47-48, 51
Lakeman, Enid, 54n, 178n
Lambert, James D., 54n, 178n
Lamprecht, Sterling P., 43n
Lane, Robert, 2n
Laos, 169
La Palombara, Joseph, 2n, 3n
Laqueur, Walter Z., 149n, 156n, 207n
Laski, Harold J., 39n-40n
Latin America, 108, 129, 139, 141, 142,
    143, 156, 169, 190, 197, 198, 199,
    215, 220
"Leftist", 6
Legislation, 56
    delegated, 58-59
Lenin, Vladimir I., 10, 11, 65n, 78, 80, 81,
    109, 110, 111, 113-124, 136, 144,
    147, 148, 156, 160, 163, 187, 188,
    196, 213, 229
Leningrad, 53
Leninism, 109-122
    and colonialism, 114-117
    and democratic centralism, 111-113
    and dictatorship of the proletariat, 120-
        122
    and imperialism, 114-120
    and intellectuals, 117
    and role of party, 111-113

strategy and tactics, 119-121
  and workers, 114-118
Levin, Deana, 125n
Liberia, 139, 215
Liberalism, 4, 7, 8, 10n, 50, 87-88, 232
Lichtheim, George, 67n, 149n
Lincoln, Abraham, 53, 59, 191
Linebarger, Paul M., 143n
Lipset, Seymour Martin, 7n, 105n
Litvinoff, Maxim, 117n
Liu, William T., 161n
Locke, John, 5n, 27, 41, 42, 46, 47n, 48,
    51, 69, 90, 91, 194
Loucks, William N., 173n
Louis XIV, 103
Louis XVI, 53
Lowi, Theodore J., 56n, 59n
Luther, Martin, 40
Luxembourg, 130, 171
Lynd, Staughton, 184n
Lyon, Peter H., 212n

Machiavelli, Niccolo, 27
Mackinnon, James, 40n
Macpherson, Crawford B., 43n
Magellan, Ferdinand, 23, 25
Maistre, Joseph de, 90n
Majority Rule, 44-45, 52
Malaya, 139, 140, 182
Malaysia, 169, 211, 212
Malenkov, G., 10, 146, 149
Malthus, Robert, 69
Manchuria, 132
Mannheim, Karl, 1n, 2n
Mao Tse-Tung, 10, 132, 147, 148n, 153,
    154, 157-163, 166, 169, 188, 194,
    196
Marcuse, Herbert, 181n, 184n, 188n
Marlowe, John, 207n
Marsiglio, 25, 38
Martin, James J., 64n
Martin, Laurence W., 212n
Marx, Karl, 2, 10, 11, 33, 62, 65-72, 74-78,
    80, 81, 83, 84, 109, 110, 114, 115,
    117-120, 156, 160, 161, 175, 187,
    188, 203
Marxism, 66-84
  and the classless society, 76-77
  and class struggle, 70-76
  and the dialectic, 69-71

  and the dictatorship of the proletariat, 76
  and revolution, 77n
  and science, 84
Marxism-Leninism, 10-12
Maurras, Charles, 93
Mayer, Peter, 127, 156n
Mazrui, Ali A., 205n, 207n
Mazzini, Giuseppe, 93n, 108
Mbeki, Goran A. M., 108n
McClosky, Herbert, 8n, 125n
McDonald, Neil A., 39n, 47n
McKay, Robert B., 179n
McNeilly, F. S., 25n
McPherson, Thomas, 42n
McVicker, Charles P., 154n, 164n
Meek, Ronald L., 47n
Mehring, Franz, 67n
Mein Kampf, 12-14
Mendelssohn, Felix, 100
Middle Ages, 21, 26, 29, 43
Middle class, 30, 43, 73-74, 105-106
Middle East, 24, 139, 141
Mikolajczyk, S., 136fn
Milbrath, Lester W., 11fn, 56fn
Militarism, 94-95, 103-104, 105, 107-108
Miliukov, Paul N., 117fn
Mill, James, 50
Mill, John Stuart, 47, 49, 50, 88n, 174, 175,
    194
Miller, J. D. B., 156n
Mills, C. Wright, 180
Milosz, Czeslaw, 155n
Minority Rights, 44
Mitchell, John, 193
Moch, Jules, 174
Modernization, and development, 141-143
Molesworth, William, 43n
Mollett, Guy, 174
Molotov, V. M., 146, 149
Moltke, Count Helmuth von, 94n
Monnard, Jacques, 125
Montagu, Ashley, 100n
Montesquieu, Baron de, 27, 51n
Moore, Barrington, Jr., 184n, 188n
More, Sir Thomas, 61, 67
Morris-Jones, W. H., 203n
Mozambique, 206, 212
Mozart, Wolfgang, 100
Muller, Steven, 177n
Munich, 14, 127-128, 133

Murray, R. M., 25n
Mussolini, Benito, 10, 93, 95-98, 101, 104, 107-108, 127, 131, 201, 221

Nagasaki, 182, 185
Nagy, Imre, 155, 166
Nanda, B. R., 202n
Napoleon I, 86
Nasser, Gamal Abdul, 207, 211
Nationalism, 20-36, 85-108, 197-215, 216-221
  characteristic ideas, 86-87, 90-94, 95-101
  definitions, 36, 86
  and democracy, 86-90
  and fascism and nazism, 96-98, 103-105
  institutions and symbols, 94-95, 101-104, 107-108
  integral, 93-95
  origins, 20-36, 85-90, 93
  problems and criticisms, 99-100, 102-103, 108
  and racism, 96, 98-103, 108
  and Rousseau's General Will, 91
  socialism and communism, 199, 202, 208-210, 211-212, 213-215
  sources of support, 35-36, 87-90, 104-107
  summary, 217-221
  Third World (non-European), 197-215
    and community integration, 42, 199-202, 204, 207-210
    and democracy, 197-198, 200-203, 210
    and international attitudes, 204-205, 206-207, 211-213, 214-215
    institutions, 207-210
    policies, 211-215
    racism, 204-207
    and socio-economic development, 205-207, 213-215
Natural Law, 27
Nazism, 12-15; see also Fascism and Nazism
Neal, F. W., 154
Nehru, Jawaharlal, 200, 201, 202, 203, 204
Nepal, 215
Netherlands, 84, 130, 171
Nettleship, R. L., 175fn
Neumann, Franz, 51fn, 97fn, 107fn
New Lanark, 64
New Left, 184-196
  and antinationalism, 190-193
  and criticism of liberal democracy, 186-189
  goals, 195-196
  criticisms of, 193-195
  and elitism, 186-187, 195-196
  and imperialism, 192-193
  and the masses, 195-196
  and participatory democracy, 188-190
  and tolerance, 188fn
  and violence, 195-196
Newton, Sir Isaac, 27
New Zealand, 169, 171
Ngo Dingh Diem, 192
Nicolaevsky, Boris I., 125fn
Nicolson, Harold, 28
Nigeria, 208
Nkrumah, Kwame, 197, 202, 210
Nollau, Gunther, 127fn
North America, 83, 118, 142, 172, 182
North Korea, 17, 162, 169
North Vietnam, 170; see also Indochina
Norway, 84, 130, 170
Nove, Alec, 229fn
Nutter, G. Warren, 123fn, 124fn

O'Hara, Rosemary, 8fn
Ortega Y Gasset, Jose, 88
Osgood, Samuel M., 93
Owen, Robert, 64, 67
Owens, J. R., 8fn

Padua, 25
Pakistan, 140, 141, 142, 204, 212
Palestine, 16; see also Israel
Palme, Olof, 3
Papacy, 25, 42-43
Parker, S. E., 65fn
Parliamentarism, 52
Parsons, Robert, 40
Parties, 6-10
Payne, Pierre, S. R., 67fn
Payne, Robert, 109fn, 122fn
Pearl Harbor, 131
Peiping, 158, 169, 205, 215
People's Democracy, 136-138, 150-156
Peronism, 108
Perry, John, 186fn
Petain, Marshal, 130
Philip II, 24
Philippines, 139, 140, 120, 182
Philosophers, 5-6, 20, 28

Piao, Lin, 162
Pipes, Richard, 229fn, 230fn
Pizzaro, Francisco, 25
Plamenatz, John P., 50fn
Plekhanov, G., 109, 111fn
Poland, 7, 18, 52, 93, 122, 125, 130, 135,
    137, 150, 151, 153, 155, 164, 165,
    166, 170, 228
Polycentrism, 164-168
Ponce de Leon, Juan, 25
Popovic, N. D., 154fn
Portugal, 208
Pospelov, P. N., 109fn
Possony, Stefan, 109fn
Post, Charles G., 179fn
Postgate, Raymond W., 66fn
Potsdam, 133, 135
Poujade, Pierre, 220
Powell, G. Bingham, 22fn, 232fn
Power, Paul F., 201fn
Pressure groups, 55-58
Prewitt, Kenneth, 11fn
Proudhon, Pierre Joseph, 64
Pulaski, Kazimierz, 93
Purges, in USSR, 124-125
  in People's Democracies, 153
Pye, Lucian, 232fn

Racism, and nationalism, 94-103, 204-207
Radicalism, 4, 48-49, 89
Radice, Giles, 111fn
Rajk, Laszlo, 153
Rakosi, Matyas, 155
Randall, Francis B., 144fn
Ratner, Lorman, 191fn
Reed, John, 117fn
Reformation, 38-41
Rejai, M., 148fn
Religion, 25-26, 37-41
Renaissance, 23, 61
Renan, Ernest, 86
Representation, legislative, 51-53, 88
  organized groups, 56-58
  proportional, 54-55
Republic, Plato's, 61
Republicans, 6-7, 8-10
Revisionism, in communist schism, 146-149,
    153-154, 163-164
Revolution, American, 28
  English (1642), 29-30

(1689), 30
French (1789), 20, 28, 31-32, 35, 53, 86,
    87
Russian (1917), 109, (1905), 110, (1917),
    120-121
Rhineland, 14, 130
Rhodesia, 206
Riasanovsky, N. V., 63fn
Ribbentropp, Joachim von, 133
Ricardo, David, 69, 76
Rigby, T. H., 156fn
"Rightist", 6
Rights, under liberal democracy, 44-45, 52
  under Marxian socialism, 73-74, 121-122
  under nationalism, 93-94
Rocco, Alfredo, 96
Rodman, John R., 175n
Roehm, Ernst, 97n
Roesch, Eugene J., 43n
Rogger, Hans, 89n
Rommel, Fieldmarshal Erwin, 131
Roosevelt, Franklin D., 132, 133, 135, 141
Rosberg, Carl G., 199n
Rose, John, 186n
Rosenberg, Alfred, 99, 102
Rossiter, Clinton, 181n
Rothchild, Donald S., 141n, 205, 205n,
    206n, 210n
Rothstein, Andrew, 124n
Rousseau, Jean Jacques, 48, 49, 90, 91, 92,
    186, 188, 194
Rowe, C., 50n
Royal absolutism, 103
Rozek, Edward, 136n
Rudolph, Lloyd I., 202n
Ruhle, Otto, 67n
Rumania, 131, 134, 151, 153, 164, 165,
    166, 167, 170
Rush, Myron, 146n, 229n
Russell, Bertrand, 5n, 66, 69
Russia, 3, 7, 10, 16, 64, 65, 77, 78, 101,
    109, 110, 113, 114, 118, 119, 120,
    121, 122, 124, 125, 126, 128, 130,
    131, 132, 134, 135, 137, 139, 142,
    144, 145, 146, 150, 156, 158, 160,
    162, 163, 167, 182, 183, 192n, 193,
    206, 208, 214; see also Soviet Union
    and USSR
Rykov, Aleksei, 123, 125

Sabine, George H., 31n, 38, 61n, 84
Saint Simon, Henri de, 67
Salvemini, Gaetano, 97n, 107n
Scandinavia, 52, 55, 77, 83, 172, 225
Schneider, Herbert W., 98n
Schoenbaum, David, 107n
Schram, Stuart R., 148n
Schubert, Glendon A., 179n
Schwartz, Benjamin I., 158n
Schwartz, Harry, 124n, 165n, 228n, 229n
Science, 26-27
Sedan, 53, 94
Senghor, Leopold, 199n
Seton-Watson, Hugh, 199n
Shaw, Bernard, 79
Shub, David, 110n
Sigmund, Paul E., 198n
Simon, Yves, R. M., 42n
Singapore, 170
Sino-Soviet Schism, 157-163
Sithole, N., 207n
Skilling, H. Gordon, 138
Slansky, Rudolf, 153
Smart, Nimian, 23n
Smith, Adam, 47, 61, 69, 91
Smith, Ian, 206
Smith, Munroe, 94n
Snyder, Louis L., 28n, 86n, 100n
Sobolev, A. I., 151n
Social mobilization, 21, 129-130
Socialism, 62-84, 109-128, 144-171, 217,
    224-231
  characteristic ideas, 62-77, 109-122
  democratic, 77-79
  institutions and symbols, 77-83, 111-113
  origins, 20-35, 61-62
  problems and criticisms, 83-85
  sources of support, 33, 61-62, 83
  summary, 217, 224-231
  syndicalist, 79-80, 82-83
  "Utopian", 67-68
  and democracy since World War II,
    172-182
  and nationalism in the Third World,
    197-215
  and New Left, 182-196
Southeast Asia, 16, 140
South Vietnam, 16, 170, 184
Soviet Union, 6, 11, 13, 112, 120, 123, 124,
    127, 131, 132, 135, 143, 144, 148,

    151, 152, 157, 164
  and power struggle after Lenin's death,
    122-129
  and power struggle after Stalin's death,
    145-146, 149-150
USSR, 12n, 17, 65n, 122, 124, 125, 126,
    128, 129, 136, 138, 140, 147, 149,
    155, 165, 166, 168, 170, 180, 229
Spain, 24, 52, 66, 77, 100, 170
Spencer, Herbert, 51
Spulber, Nicholas, 165n
Stalin, Joseph, 10, 11, 65n, 81, 122, 123,
    124, 125, 126, 127, 128, 131, 132,
    133, 134, 135, 136, 138, 139, 144,
    145, 146, 147, 149, 150, 153, 154,
    155, 156, 157, 163, 164, 167, 170,
    173, 182, 183, 188, 213, 230n
Stalinism, 122-128, 145
Staudenraus, P. J., 8n
Stehle, Hansjakob, 155n
Stephen, Leslie, 50n
Stevenson, Adlai E., 10n
Strasser, brothers, 97n
Strauss, Leo, 42n
Strausz-Hupe, Robert, 123n, 160n
Stumpf, Samuel E., 66n
Sudetenland, 14
Suez Canal, 131
Sukarno, 202, 203
Swayze, Harold, 230n
Sweden, 3, 170, 171
Swisher, Carl B., 179n
Switzerland, 170, 171
Symmons-Symonolewicz, K., 86n
Syria, 215
Syrop, Konrad, 155n

Taborsky, Edward, 153n
Talmon, J. L., 194n
Tanner, Joseph R., 52
Tawney, R. H., 79
Taylor, A. J. P., 15
Taylor, Telford, 56n
Technology, 29
Teheran, 133, 135
Thailand, 170
Third World, definition, 198n
Thompson, Virginia, 209
Tito, Marshal J., 65n, 137, 146, 150, 153,
    154, 156, 158, 163, 164, 166, 215

Tocqueville, Alexis de, 50, 88
Togliatti, Palmiro, 167, 168
Tojo, H., 107, 131
Tompkins, Stuart R., 230n
Tomsky, M. P., 123, 125
Totalitarianism, 231
Toure, Sekou, 208, 209
Towster, Julian, 145n
Toynbee, Arnold, 33n
Treadgold, Donald W., 148n
Triomphe, Robert, 90
Triska, Jan F., 225n
Trotsky, Leon D., 10, 109n, 122, 125
Truman, Harry, 7, 16, 139, 174
Tuchachevsky, Marshal M., 125
Tunisia, 210
Turkey, 139
Turner, John E., 125n
Tutsch, Hans E., 207n

Ukraine, 13
Ulbricht, Walter, 157
Union of South Africa, 108, 206, 208,
    212, 214
United Arab Republic, 212, 215
United front policies, 127
United Nations, 138, 143
United States, 7, 10n, 17, 51, 52, 55, 58,
    64, 89, 106, 129, 130, 131, 132,
    137, 138, 139, 141, 142, 143, 154,
    158, 159, 162, 163, 168, 169, 171,
    172, 174, 178, 179, 182, 184, 189,
    191, 192, 211, 220
Unterman, E., 74n
Utilitarianism, 49-50

Vali, Ferenc A., 155n
Valley Forge, 53
Valmy, 53, 86
Van den Berghe, Pierre L., 108n
Van Thieu, 192
Vasco de Gama, 23, 24
Venice, 72
Verba, Sidney, 232n
Versailles, 12
Viereck, Peter, 5n, 181
Vishinsky, Andrei, 124
Voltaire, 50, 51, 90
Voroshilov, Klimenti, 146
Vucinich, W. S., 154n

Wade, L. L., 170n
Wagner, Richard, 100
Waldringer, Renee, 50n
Wallace, Henry, 7
Wallas, Graham, 79
Waltz, Kenneth, 16n
Waring, L. M., 40n
Warrender, Howard, 43n
Wars of Religion, 24
Warsaw Pact, 170
Washington, George, 93
Waterloo, 86
Webb, Beatrice, 79
Webb, Sidney, 79
Weber, Eugen J., 89n, 94n
Welfare state, 172-174
Weyl, N., 230n
Whitney, Eli, 29
William and Mary of Orange, 30
Williams, Albert R., 117n
Williams, Francis, 174n
Williams, William A., 192n
Willkie, Wendell, 174
Willoughby, 25
Wilson, Harold, 3
Wilson, Woodrow, 141
Winstanley, Gerrard, 31n, 61n
Wolfe, Bertram D., 110n
Wolfe, Robert P., 184n, 188n
Woodcock, George, 65n
World Communist Congress, 169-170
World War II, 130-132
    and the Grand Alliance, 131-136
    and post-war problems, 182-186
    and post-war reforms, 177-182
Wright, Gordon, 89n, 178n

Yalta, 135
Yemen, 211, 212
Yevgrafov, V. Y., 109n
Yezhov, N., 124
Young, James P., 2n, 173n, 177n
Yugoslavia, 18, 65n, 131, 137, 144, 146,
    151, 153, 154, 162, 163, 170
Yugoslav-Soviet Schism, 146, 153-154,
    163-164
Yung Ping Chen, 148n

Zeigler, Harmon, 56n
Zetterbaum, Marvin, 50n

Zhdanov, Andrei, 145
Zhukov, Marshal G., 149
Zilversmit, Arthur, 191n
Zinner, Paul E., 155n, 228n

Zinoviev, G., 125
Zionism, 16
Zola, Emile, 94
Zurcher, Arnold J., 89n, 177n, 178n

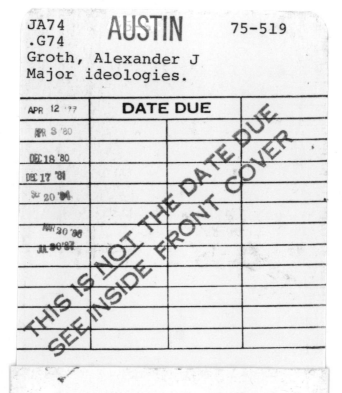